BELIEVE ME

BELIEVE ME

My Battle with the Invisible
Disability of Lyme Disease

....

YOLANDA HADID

with Michele Bender

St. Martin's Press
New York

www.stmartins.com

The Instagram logo is a trademark of Instagram.

The Library of Congress Cataloging-in-Publication Data is available upon request.

ISBN 978-1-250-12165-3 (hardcover)
ISBN 978-1-250-12166-0 (ebook)

Our books may be purchased in bulk for promotional, educational, or business use. Please contact your local bookseller or the Macmillan Corporate and Premium Sales Department at 1-800-221-7945, extension 5442, or by email at MacmillanSpecialMarkets@macmillan.com.

First Edition: September 2017

10 9 8 7 6 5 4 3 2 1

To Gigi, Bella, and Anwar,
thank you for teaching me the meaning of
unconditional love and for making my life complete.

Thank you for loving me the way that you do and
for standing by me every step of the way
during this challenging journey.

You are my shining stars and guiding lights
and I am so proud of all that you do
and all that you are.

To all my fellow Lyme warriors and those
whose voices can't be heard, this is book is
dedicated to your strength, courage, and
your ability to fight every day. You are not alone.

Disclaimer

••••••••••••••••••••••

The information in this book is not intended to replace the advice of each reader's own physician or other licensed medical professional. You should consult a medical professional in all matters relating to your health, especially if you have existing or chronic medical conditions, and before starting, stopping, or changing the doses of any medications you are taking, or any medical or health regimen you are following, under the supervision of a physician or licensed medical professional.

The intention of this book is to recount Yolanda's own personal experiences with various chronic medical conditions, in order to raise awareness. It is not intended to give medical advice. Please be aware, and keep clearly in mind, that individual readers are solely responsible for their own health-care decisions. The author and the publisher therefore cannot accept responsibility for any adverse effects individuals may claim to experience, whether directly or indirectly, from the information contained in this book.

The fact that a physician, medical professional, organization, or Web site is mentioned in this book, as a potential source of information or treatments, does not mean that the author or the publisher endorse any particular physician or medical professional, the information they may provide, or the medications, devices or other products, or the courses of treatment they may have recommend in Yolanda's case.

Again, individual readers are solely responsible for their own health-care decisions.

Foreword

....

GIGI, BELLA, AND ANWAR HADID

Gigi

For a whole year when I was sixteen years old, I watched my mom struggle to understand the pain, confusion, and symptoms that she was experiencing, but that no doctors seemed to have answers for. At one point, she became so ill that she couldn't attend my horse shows or volleyball games anymore, she couldn't watch TV, and in our home where Luther Vandross used to blare through the speakers, things became quiet. My mom used to be a super mom with endless super powers so watching her lose her brain capacity and physical energy was heartbreaking and confusing for me. Finally, after being misdiagnosed with many things such as chronic fatigue syndrome, migraines, and depression, she was diagnosed with chronic neurological Lyme disease in Belgium. We were so excited and thought the ninety-day course of IV antibiotics would cure her. However, I quickly learned that this was not the case for my mom and so many people who suffer from late-stage chronic Lyme. The many years that followed were tough. I watched my mom have endless treatments and work with many doctors all over the world, but without much progress. She never gave up and never stopped fighting although her quality of life continued to diminish drastically. I tried to help and be a source of support but the hardest part for me was not being able to fix her or my siblings.

My mom was diagnosed with Lyme disease after her first season on *The Real Housewives of Beverly Hills*. I remember when she was going into that season of filming, she said to me, "I don't know why my life has led me to this show, but for some reason I think it will lead to something bigger." My mom is usually right. But this time she was *really, really* right. She knew there was a higher purpose for her journey and all of a sudden the show's platform became her vehicle to bring awareness to Lyme. She was honest, unapologetic, and raw in how she shared her journey on the show and through social media. I saw her turn a mess into a message and in no time after she announced her diagnosis to the world, she got thousands of e-mails and letters from families who were suffering and felt lost, misunderstood, and scared. No matter how sick my mom was she would always call some of them, give advice, and lend support.

Unfortunately, there were so many people who were uninformed and quick to shame her, something I've learned many Lyme patients experience. Yet, my mom rose above it and stayed strong through it all. "I have nothing to prove to anyone," she would say. "I only want to support and educate people about the mystery of chronic disease." I saw her fight for her life, work relentlessly, and heal strategically one day at a time. More than anything, my mom wanted to give people a road map of her journey so that they will be able to find answers faster with more clarity and in a less stressful way than she had to.

Before my mom got sick, I never really understood the meaning of the word "hope," yet today I know my mom is hope for Lyme disease. I am so proud that she is making her journey one that will help so many and that she continues to fight so passionately for a Lyme-free world. I think if someone is going to find a cure, she will probably be the one because her persistent and righteous heart is unbeatable and she won't stop until she finds the answers for my siblings and all children with Lyme so that they can live the pain-free lives they deserve.

Bella

Mommy, I'm so proud of you for opening up about a very important and sensitive part of our lives. You didn't choose this path for yourself, nor did you choose to victimize yourself. Instead you continued to raise me, my brother, and sister in the best way possible—you wrote a book to help all of those suffering around the world whether that be with the invisible disability of chronic Lyme disease, mental wellness, immune diseases, or just being understood in general. You slowly but surely found your happiness again.

I know how hard it was for me to see how much you struggled in the past few years and vice-versa, but to see others constantly judge you and doubt your integrity while you were down was even worse. Hundreds of doctors' appointments around the world, countless medications, IVs and remedies, the blood, the pain, and the tears to find healing and help people around the world find their own voice. I admire your relentless search to find a cure and a proper diagnostic affordable for all. Throughout my whole life, I never saw you as anything less than tough as nails so every time you would look at me with tears in your eyes, pain in your bones, bruises on your body from all the needles, in the fetal position, and ask me when this would all be over, I would always say, "It will be over soon, Mommy" without ever really knowing the answer. Now I can finally say you are coming out of this stronger than ever. Thank you for being so strong and speaking up about our journey. I am so proud and I love you.

Anwar

My mom was a busy single mom who dedicated her life to us and everything that we did until her health declined drastically and she was diagnosed with neurological Lyme disease in 2012, right after we moved to Malibu from our home in Santa Barbara. It was confusing and hard to understand why doctors could not fix her so I spent many nights online educating myself about Lyme disease to sadly learn that there is no cure. But instead of sharing that bad news with my mom, I wanted to give her hope so I only told her about the success stories I read.

Still, my mom didn't accept that there was no cure. She was tough and never took "no" for an answer, which is also the reason she eventually got my sister Bella and me properly diagnosed. I struggled with chronic sinus issues, joint pain, and severe fatigue for many years and because of my mom's journey she was able to understand and identify that my symptoms were not allergies or growing pains like many doctors told us.

So, although it has been a very challenging road at times, I like to look at the positive part of the experience and the way it has brought us closer as a family and strengthened our bond. We learned that together we can get through anything. I saw my mom navigate through many obstacles these past five years, but she never stopped putting us first. She grounds us and is the anchor that keeps our family together. I have learned a lot about the power of holistic medicine and spiritual healing and I believe that our family was given this experience in order to bring awareness to Lyme disease and raise the collective consciousness around this global epidemic.

My mom helps many people find healing every day and her determination to find a cure for Bella, me, and all the children in the world is inspiring. I admire her everyday fight for a Lyme-free world.

BELIEVE ME

Introduction

....

SOME OF LIFE'S LESSONS ARE LEARNED AT THE MOST CHALLENGING TIMES.

In my more than five-year battle with Lyme disease, I've struggled with a seemingly endless list of debilitating symptoms. Too many nights, I found myself lying naked on the bathroom floor, the only relief being the cold tiles on my bare skin, wondering how much more pain I could take and how many more days, months, and years I could suffer. This journey has been long, arduous, and devastating on various levels. There were plenty of times when I thought that I wouldn't make it through the night alive, and others where I *wished* and *prayed* that I would die.

In the first months and years of my illness, I'd feel so guilty and inadequate for not being who I thought I was supposed to be. The old me was a multitasking superwoman with endless energy. I didn't want to surrender to my illness, because I saw that as a sign of weakness, which I fought for years. But once I evolved in this humbling experience, I learned to surrender. I prayed more. I asked for guidance, and somehow things started falling into place. It didn't bring me a cure, but it brought me a lot of clarity. As the years passed, I realized that the higher purpose of my journey was to bring awareness to a global epidemic that was growing in the shadows. How could I not share what I have learned? It's a miracle that I am here to tell my story. Trust me, I would much rather share a new clothing line, face creams, or beautiful housewares, because there's nothing glamorous about Lyme disease. But I wouldn't be able to sleep at night knowing that I had gone through all of this and didn't give back to educate and help others.

It took so much time, heartache, research, money, and effort for me to get properly diagnosed. This made it even *more* infuriating to then find out that there was no cure for what I had! Once I started to uncover the mystery of chronic Lyme and saw the stigma around it, I felt a strong obligation to the millions of people suffering from this and other chronic illnesses. I have met so many debilitated and financially devastated people who have sold their homes, spent their life's savings, or gone bankrupt in order to pay for their Lyme treatments or those for a family member—and *still* they're not getting better. They're fighting to stay alive with no cure in sight.

Even though I learned to adjust to my new normal, the rebel inside of me is not able to accept this silent disability that can be cured only at early detection. Once it becomes chronic, the Lyme bacteria can go from living in your bloodstream to living in one of your organs, making it hard to detect and almost impossible to eradicate. Not only is this harder to diagnose and treat, it also can ruin your life. I know this firsthand because I've never suffered as deeply as I have with Lyme. Even though it brought me to my knees at times, I believe that there are no coincidences, as I learned that I am a lot stronger, braver, and determined than I ever imagined.

What follows is my journey, and I want to share it in the hope that I can help you and others navigate through the dark maze of chronic disease, in times that you might feel scared or alone. Often, we are misunderstood by even our closest friends and family because they don't get it until they get it. Many times while I was sick, I thought that if God granted me life after this journey, I was going to use my wisdom to help others. If I can shed light on and educate even a handful of people about this invisible disability that hijacks your life, I will gladly open my medical records. That is the point of this book. So let me start at the beginning. The very beginning.

gorgeous blond with the prettiest cherry-red lips. She was nineteen years old and working as a hairdresser when she met my father, who was twenty, at a dance in Sliedrecht, a neighboring town. They got married in 1961. A year and a half later, they had my brother, Leo, and eighteen months after that they had me. Leo and I were, and still are, the best of friends. No one makes me laugh harder or feel as connected to my roots than he does. As kids, we'd walk to school hand in hand as my mother watched from our apartment window and waved to us until we crossed the main road.

My father and I were very close. I was definitely a daddy's girl, and he always gave me the sense that I could do anything that I set my mind to. On Saturday mornings, he would take me to the shirt factory with him to look at fabrics and check his production. There was no safer feeling than sitting on my father's lap in the car and him letting me think that I was driving us home from work. My mother was an extraordinary homemaker. Our sweet little apartment was humble, but it was always meticulously kept, with fresh flowers on the table and the comforting smell of home-cooked meals wafting through it. In fact, my mother was such a good cook that her sandwiches were always a hot commodity at the sandwich trade with the kids at school. She sewed our clothes and always created that secure feeling of home, even after the worst of tragedies occurred.

In the middle of a cold winter's night when I was seven years old, I woke to the sound of my mother crying. I got out of bed and listened through the crack of the living room door. My mother was talking to her parents, my Opa and Oma. I heard the words "car accident," "hospital," and "Gerard." I was confused.

"They don't think he's going to make it," my mother said to Oma. A lot of their conversation was muffled and difficult to understand. This was when I figured out that my father was in intensive care. *How could that be? He was just in Hong Kong buying fabric for his next collection. He was coming home soon.* My Opa, who saw me standing at the living room door, put me back in bed and tucked me in, promising that everything was going to be okay.

DON'T EVER FORGET YOUR ROOTS, SINCE THEY ARE THE TRUE FOUNDATION AND ESSENCE OF WHO YOU ARE TODAY.

Before I take you on my health journey, I would like to tell you a little bit about me, my childhood, where I came from, and how a little farm girl went from Holland to Hollywood . . .

In 1964, I was born in Papendrecht, a small village nestled against the dike that holds the Noord River. It was a lush, beautiful place with seemingly endless farmland, gorgeous fields of flowers, and apple and pear orchards. With a population of just five thousand people, our town was a warm community where everyone knew each other. It was a place where you actually *would* knock on your neighbor's door if you needed sugar, flour, or anything else. You never had to ask for a helping hand because one was always ready and within reach. Life was very simple and modest, and if I'm making it sound idyllic, that's because it was always glorious in my mind. Although buses and water taxis could take you to neighboring villages, bicycles were our main source of transportation, and there was nothing better than the independence I felt biking around town with the wind blowing through my hair.

My father, Gerard van Den Herik, was a tall, handsome man with dark hair and blue eyes. He was a men's shirt designer and ran his own business, Van Den Herik Shirtmakers. My mother, Ans Groenenberg, was a

The next morning, my father died in the hospital. Our whole world fell apart. I felt sick to my stomach with a big, giant knot that didn't leave me for years. *How was this possible?*

"Why did you let my daddy die?" I asked God over and over again. *What did he do wrong?* It was so hard to understand. At the funeral, I sat on the bench in church feeling heartbroken. I was so small that my legs didn't even reach the ground, and as I swung them nervously back and forth, I looked over at my mother and brother. They were both so distraught that I felt a deep sadness that I had never experienced before. In that fraction of a second, I made the strangely mature decision not to cry, but rather to be strong for the family that my father left behind. *I have to take care of them.* I'm not sure why I had the higher consciousness to think this way at the age of seven, but I did.

My mother picked up the pieces of our lives and showed great strength in this very difficult time. She was a kick-ass single mom who led by example with a strong set of morals and values. Maybe she shared her grief with Opa and Oma, but she never shared it with Leo or me. Even though *I* felt the need to talk about my father's death, my mother never spoke about her loss. In time, I learned to soothe myself and manage my emotions by drawing, writing, riding my horse, and spending time in nature. But one thing was for sure: my momma wasn't going to let this experience be a crutch for failure. She pushed Leo and me even harder to strive for success in every aspect of our lives. Although she loved us with everything she had and dedicated her life to us, she was also strict, and we were raised to be very disciplined. For example, I had to iron for my mom every Friday after school and dust, clean the bathroom, and vacuum my bedroom. She also had a huge heart and sense of charity. No matter how little *we* had, my mother always helped those less fortunate than us, pushing my brother and me to go door to door to raise money for the Red Cross so they could feed starving children in Africa. She volunteered at the old peoples' home and was extremely generous with our friends and neighbors, cooking a meal for someone who was sick or watching their kids in times of need. When my best friend Gina's mom died, Gina often stayed with us and my mom also cared for my other girlfriend, whose parents were battling through a divorce. My mom has the biggest heart and taught me to always have great compassion for others.

Soon after my dad died, we moved to D. Nieuwenhuis straat 22. Thank God my Opa and Oma lived within walking distance, so we saw them often. My Opa was a retired lieutenant from the army and he was super strict, and Oma was the most proper woman I've ever met. Her home, which was her sanctuary, was spotless at all times. She took great pride in her vases of beautiful fresh flowers and potted azaleas in the window-sills. We didn't have a lot of money, a big house, or fancy things, but we had what was most important: love, commitment, and togetherness as a family. Every Sunday night, we had dinner and enjoyed debates as we sat around the table. We played Monopoly and card games for real coins that we collected in old jelly jars with our names on them. Opa always said he played competitively so he could use his winnings to pay for that week's cigarettes and bread. After dinner, the adults drank coffee and Leo and I nibbled on homemade cookies and hot chocolate milk. Then the girls would do the dishes while the boys watched soccer games on our black-and-white TV. At around eight o'clock, my mom would serve cognac to Opa and coffee liqueur to Oma along with cocktail snacks of Dutch cheese, sausage, and crackers with her legendary tuna or chicken-curry salad.

When I started riding ponies at the age of five, at my aunt Lany's barn, my great love for animals, especially horses, was born. The summer after my father's death, my mother sent me to a three-week pony camp in North Holland. There, I met my first soul mate and spirit animal: a pony who came off a train from Russia where his front legs had been tightly shackled. His scars were symbols to me that the hardships we experience in life can heal with love and tender care. The pony's name was Bruno and my nickname was Gigi, so I romantically blended our names to create "Gino." For those three weeks, Gino and I were inseparable. He became my best friend. I spent all day long riding, grooming, and loving him. I even snuck out of my bunk bed to sleep with him in his stall at night. With just a few days left of camp, my time with Gino was coming to an end. Leaving him behind was unthinkable, so I called my mother from the pay phone and had a huge meltdown.

"Please, *please* let me bring Gino home," I begged. I wasn't sure what she would say because we lived a very modest life, but she made me a promise.

"Let me think about it," she said. *At least she didn't say no!* Something in my gut told me that my mother would make it possible. When she came to pick me up from camp, I waited anxiously for her answer.

"Yes, you can bring Gino home, but he's one hundred percent your responsibility and you must do everything to care for him," she said. My heart skipped a beat. I'd never felt that happy. Clearly, my mother realized that Gino was a crucial healing tool to help me overcome the loss of my father. She found a milk farm near our house where boarding was cheap. Every day, no matter if it was raining, snowing, or hailing, I rode my bike to the farm before and after school to clean stalls and feed, ride, and brush Gino. I worked hard in school so that the hours would pass quickly and I could return to him. The owners of the farm, Mr. and Mrs. Van Wijngaarden, treated me just like a daughter. I worked alongside their sons, who taught me to milk cows, deliver baby calves, and harvest the straw and hay that would feed our animals through the cold winter. I had blisters on my hands from the hard, physical labor, but I thrived in my role as a working farm girl. It made me feel complete. Once a week, I rode my horse on the dark country road to take lessons at the Papendrechtse Riding Club. My mom drove behind me in her car, shining its headlights on the road ahead of me so I could see where I was going.

Unlike many girls my age, I was not into boys. The only thing that got my heart racing was horses. I didn't care about fashionable clothes; I longed for riding gear and the ability to one day buy my own show horse. I knew that I wanted more in life and rode every day with the goal of becoming an Olympic equestrian in dressage and a professional rider. I had been dreaming about a new saddle and bridle so I told my mother this one day when I was twelve years old.

"You'll need money for that," she said. So I got my first job, working in my favorite Chinese restaurant in town. There, on Saturdays and Sundays, I washed the endless stacks of dirty dishes and buckets of used silverware. Luckily, I had plenty of training in cleaning thanks to the super-neat homes that my mom and Oma both kept. I made one bucket with just knives, another with forks, and a third with spoons, and organized the dishes by size. After hours and hours of washing, I rode my bike home. I was exhausted and smelled like a fried noodle, but I also had a great sense of accomplishment and independence. My hair and clothes were so greasy that my mom made me get undressed before I even entered our home and sent me straight to the shower. Otherwise, the aroma of fried food would linger throughout the whole house.

I finally saved enough money to purchase that brand-new saddle and felt like I had died and gone to heaven. At this point, I was winning a lot of riding competitions. My horse wasn't fancy like those I competed against, but I was definitely the most driven girl there. I was also serious about gymnastics and actually got to the junior Olympic tryouts. Around the time I turned thirteen, I started feeling severely fatigued and had trouble falling asleep at night no matter how tired I was. My mother thought that I was just doing too much, but then she realized that this was more than a case of spreading myself too thin. She took me to the doctor, who diagnosed me with a severe case of the Epstein-Barr virus and put me on bed rest for six weeks. I had to take a break from riding and gymnastics, which was devastating to me. A few months later, I had an appendicitis and was hospitalized. Looking back now, I truly believe that this virus was probably the culprit of my health journey.

"You can't be the best at riding *and* gymnastics at the same time," my mother said one day. "Pick one." Although I was passionate about both sports, I chose the barn over the balance beam. I needed money to help support my love of horses and riding, so at fourteen years old, I got a part-time job selling cheese and sandwich meats at the local grocery store, HEMA. I was quickly promoted to cashier. Although it was hectic to juggle school, riding, barn work, and my job, that monthly check made it all worth it. I was so motivated that nothing was ever too much, and my energy was endless.

"Can you come to Amsterdam with me in a few weeks?" my girlfriend Dorothy, a hairstylist, asked one day when I was sixteen years old. "I need a model for a hair show I'm doing."

"Uh . . . I'm not really into the hair and makeup thing," I said, hesitating.

"Please?"

"Let me think about it."

"I can't find anyone else with long enough hair for the braids that I'm doing," she said when she called me a week later to ask again. "Can you come?" I still wasn't sure, but I wanted to help a friend, so I agreed to go. The show was a week later on a freezing-cold and snowy winter's day. When we got there, a woman who worked for the top Dutch designer Frans Molenaar approached me.

"One of our models is sick with the flu and canceled. Can you take her place and walk in Frans's show?" she asked.

"Okay," I said, even though I had never worn a stitch of makeup or a pair of high heels. In fact, I hadn't done anything that feminine or seen anything as fancy as the clothes I wore in the fashion show. I was straight from the barn to the catwalk with no idea what to do, so I just looked at the other models and imitated the way they walked and held themselves. I'm still not sure if I was a natural or just a convincing copycat, but after the show, I was approached by Pieter van der Schaft, owner of Intermodels who was also a scout for Eileen Ford. He asked me to do a test photo shoot a few days later. When those pictures were sent to various clients and advertising agencies, I immediately got offers to shoot at different locations all over Europe.

"Give it a shot and try it for a little while and then we'll see," my mother said when we discussed these opportunities, even though she knew nothing about the modeling industry. She promised to take care of my horse while I was gone and I knew she would.

I was signed by Eileen Ford in New York who got me a working visa to come to America and before I knew it I was immersed in fashion and traveling the world. I was on runways all over Europe and traveled to an array of exotic locations for modeling jobs, making more money than I had ever dreamed of. My income helped me support my family and it sure beat my jobs at the Chinese restaurant and grocery store. Amazingly, when I was only a teenager, I fulfilled the promise to my seven-year-old self to provide for my family. Of course, this opportunity to become financially independent was a dream come true, but in the blink of an eye, it was also the end of my teenage years. Although I never returned to live in Holland, which I love so much, I took every piece of the moral and emotional foundation that my mother gave me and used it while traveling the world for work. I was extremely disciplined, focused, and motivated. Nothing was going to stop me from succeeding in this industry and I wanted to make my momma proud.

At nineteen, I signed a three-month modeling contract in Tokyo and got to experience the amazing Japanese culture. It was an inspiring time and I loved working long days. I exercised as much as I could to stay in top shape. One day, I pulled a muscle in my back, so my agent, Himari, took me to her acupuncturist. I was fascinated because it helped immediately so I had treatments every day after work for a couple of weeks until my pain was completely gone. From Japan, I went back to New York, where I was based, and booked my first *Cosmopolitan* magazine cover with Francesco Scavullo, the well-known fashion photographer. I felt extremely exhausted the day of the shoot, but I blamed it on jet lag and the different lifestyle I'd experienced in Tokyo. During hair and makeup, I felt very strange and faint, but pushed through.

"Are you okay?" one of the *Cosmopolitan* editors asked me.

"Not really," I said.

"Your eyes are kind of yellow. I think you need to go to a doctor," she told me. Someone on set called Eileen Ford to get me an appointment with a doctor immediately. Dr. White did an array of blood tests and sent me home to rest. Two days later, I returned and when the nurse interrogated me about any potential drug use, I was not only confused but offended.

"You tested positive for hepatitis B," she explained. "Which is a liver infection that you can get from a blood transfusion or dirty needles."

"I must have gotten it from acupuncture needles, because I've never used drugs," I said. Today, acupuncturists use only disposable needles, but back then they would simply sterilize the needles by cooking them in a huge pot of boiling water and reuse them. I had already learned I had a weak liver because out in the modeling world, when I tried to go out at night to party with the other girls and drink, I couldn't keep up. The same thing happened in high school on a class trip to the Heineken factory, when I got violently ill from the beer tasting at the end of the tour.

The hepatitis B diagnosis was scary. I was only nineteen years old and in an English-speaking country where I had no family or support system at all besides my agency. We canceled all my upcoming modeling bookings and I flew back to Holland to be with my mom and get a second opinion from my hometown doctor. Unfortunately, he confirmed this frightening diagnosis. But after a month of my momma's TLC and Dutch cooking, I made a good enough recovery to get back in action. I was extremely driven and well aware my lucky draw wasn't going to last forever. Momentum was incredibly important, as was being in the right place at the right time, and being sick in Papendrecht wasn't any good for my business. So I got back on the road and back to work.

Over the next fifteen years, my life was very hectic and busy. I lived like a gypsy, constantly on airplanes, flying all over the world without much time off. I was a workhorse who always kept going no matter how I felt. Coming from humble beginnings was my greatest gift because the motivation and hunger to be successful was ingrained in me. I lived in Paris, Milan, Hamburg, Sydney, Cape Town, Tokyo, New York, and Los Angeles. Being able to experience all these different cultures so early on in my life gives me great respect and admiration for the diversity in the world. Besides feeling extremely grateful for the blessing of this life, I earned an incredible amount of money and successfully invested it. The financial independence felt powerful and gave me a lot of self-confidence. I was proud of how far I had come and how much I had accomplished since I was that little girl on the farm.

One day during a photo shoot in Marbella, Spain, a woman from the hotel's front desk came to find me on the set.

"Your brother called with an emergency. He needs to talk to you immediately," she said. I rushed back to the hotel as quickly as possible and called Leo from the lobby.

"Mamma has breast cancer and needs a double mastectomy," he said. My world felt like it had collapsed. *OMG. Not my momma! Cancer? Is she going to die?*

I raced to my room, packed my luggage, and jumped into a cab to the airport, where I waited six hours to get on a flight to Amsterdam. I stayed in Holland while my mother, who was forty-six years old, recovered from surgery. This motivated me to become extremely health conscious and live a very clean life. I was tired and started to feel extremely lonely having lived out of a suitcase for over a decade. Never in one place long enough to connect with people or build meaningful relationships. I started to long for a family, my own family, and a place to call home.

Chapter One

. . . .

YOU ARE NOT WHAT HAS HAPPENED TO YOU. YOU ARE WHAT YOU CHOOSE TO BECOME FROM THAT EXPERIENCE.

Fast-forward to 1993, when I'm in Aspen, Colorado, for a photo shoot. I meet Mohamed Hadid on the gondola going up Ajax Mountain. We start talking. He is kind and very handsome. Soon we fall in love, get engaged, marry, and settle in Los Angeles. With his first wife, Mary, Mohamed has two girls, Marielle and Alana, who live in McLean, Virginia. On April 23, 1995, we welcome the first of our three angels, Jelena Noura Hadid (Gigi). Just a year and a half later, on October 9, 1996, Isabella Khair Hadid (Bella) is born. Then my son, Anwar Mohamed Gerard Hadid, arrives on June 22, 1999. I stop modeling after giving birth to Bella because traveling with two babies is not doable so I start working with Mohamed, who is a real estate developer and extremely smart, creative, and a genius in design. After losing most of his fortune in the early nineties' real estate crash, he is determined to turn things around. Like me, Mohamed came from very humble beginnings and was raised by a strong and loving mom, Khair Hadid. I have no doubt he will make it back on top. I have always had a passion for design and he teaches me about things like antiquing and wholesale furnishings. We are a great team; he creates the big picture and I am the detail person who follows right behind to put on the final touches. I enjoy working on his projects and designing interiors.

I also love being a mother of three and am immersed in my life as a mommy and wife. It's a dream come true. I've finally found a place where I belong, my own special family in beautiful America.

Sadly, our marriage is short-lived, and in 2000 Mohamed and I separate. He's a good human being and provider for his children and always has been an amazing son to his mother. But unfortunately for me, he's not a faithful husband. It's a sad experience and hard for me to accept. It's also a big blow to my ego. I thought I was a pretty good catch: financially independent, on the covers of magazines, and absolutely loving my home life and roles as wife and mother. It takes a long time for me to truly understand that the breakdown of our marriage has nothing to do with who I am, but nevertheless it feels like a failure, even though there is nothing I could have done differently. Growing up without a father, this is the last thing I want for my children but I adapt.

As soon as Gigi finishes her pre-K year, the kids and I are off to Casa Amore, in Punta Mita, Mexico, a beautiful place that Mohamed and I built together and I decorated in authentic Mexican style. It's a colorful and happy home that I created with the vision of a lifetime with Mohamed and our family, but life isn't always what you think it will be. So I keep telling myself to pull up the bootstraps, a saying from my riding days that I've used throughout my life, meaning that I've got to push through and move forward, no matter the circumstances, and deal with the cards life has dealt me. After all, I have three beautiful babies, I am healthy, and I have a whole life ahead of me. The kids and I spend a quiet summer with my mom, my brother, his wife, Liseth, and their two daughters, Joann and Lizzy, barefoot on the beach, building sand castles, catching crabs, bodysurfing, watching birds, going on jungle rides in the pickup truck, and discovering all kinds of amazingness right in our backyard connected to Mother Nature. The kids learn about lizards, armadillos, and snakes. Sometimes we sleep on the beach to watch momma turtles lay their eggs. I take long walks to think and process. Leo, Liseth, and I enjoy margaritas at the local beach bar while we pick up the fresh catch of the day. Life is beautiful and meaningful in this magical little town. I loved the people from the minute I arrived for the first time, just two years earlier.

While detoxing from my Beverly Hills life on my daily long sunset walks, I start to slowly digest my experience and find clarity. I realize that I don't want to go back there. Even though I always loved the palm trees and sunshine, I never really felt at home in Beverly Hills, and it is not an environment where I want to raise my children. *But where am I going?* That question consumes me the whole summer. I'm so grateful to have my mom and family here from Holland. They are so rational and always put things in perspective for me. It turns out to be the most difficult summer of my life so far, but I make it a magical one for my children. They have no idea what is really going on and don't need to know anything that is happening between their father and me. I tell them he is very busy working. They don't have a clue that this is the beginning of our new life.

I am reluctant to go back to L.A. I am humiliated and distrust the life I built there and most of the people in it. I'm actually toying with the idea of staying in Punta Mita for a year. I have grown to love this town and its people—I feel connected to the simplicity and honesty of life here. It will make me happy and give me hope. It's far away from Gucci and Chanel on Rodeo Drive and the fast, superficial world that now feels even emptier than ever before. As in every defining moment in my life thus far, however, I wake up one morning with a clear vision. I see us moving to Montecito, a small town close to Santa Barbara. *That* was the California I fell in love with some fifteen years earlier when I was modeling on the Santa Barbara pier with Kathy Ireland, a native of the area.

"If I can ever live in America full-time, this is where I want to be," I told her back then as we were looking at the breathtaking coastline in front of us. The town was so charming, the architecture magnificent, and it felt as if you could be anywhere in Europe. I always remembered the safe and familiar feeling it gave me, and now it suddenly makes sense that Montecito is where I need to go and raise Gigi, age six; Bella, five; and Anwar, just eighteen months old. I call a broker and start inquiring about rental properties and find out that I have only a week to get the kids enrolled in school. I ask my mom to stay with the little ones for two days so I can fly to Santa Barbara with Gigi to visit the Montecito Union School. It's the cutest little school, with beautiful green trees, a track field, and outdoor spaces. Gigi immediately loves the art studio and the assembly room, which has a stage where they do musicals. We visit the local barns and this gets her very excited about a new home and the opportunity to bring her pony, Prince Philip.

I guess when things are meant to be, everything just falls into place. It's like God waving his magic wand. I find a furnished house we love on a little street right off Middle Road, which is a two-minute walk to Scoop, the ice cream store, and Rusty's Pizza. I am sure Bella is going to be very happy about that.

Although my life feels upside down, I can sense we are going to feel at home in this charming little town. It's important to me that my children can attend public school and enjoy a simpler existence with horses and the benefits of a close-knit community. A week later, I pack up my three children and move to Montecito, where Gigi starts kindergarten and Bella enters pre-K.

Although the children and I move two hours away, Mohamed stays in Beverly Hills, and of course my goal is to keep him close and involved in their lives. Establishing a friendship after our separation takes great effort and a lot of swallowing my pride, but I believe it's essential in order to raise confident and stable children, and that's really all that matters to me at this point. Regardless of our past, I'm not going to allow my bruised ego to destroy the commitment I made when we brought our children into this world together. The love of both parents is important, and it's valuable for the children to see us get along. I work on forgiving him and choose to focus not on the pain he caused me but rather on what it's teaching me. Mohamed and I come from such different cultures that sometimes we clash on parenting issues, but we always come back around the table.

At the end of the day, this journey is about the happiness and well-being of my children and how they feel about their daddy. What *I* feel is not important. Around seven forty every morning, I phone Mohamed as we drive to school so they can say good morning and connect with his voice. I remember missing my daddy as a child so my heart hurts for them and I try to compromise in many different ways. Even though separation is a hardship for any family, the children and I manage to plant strong roots in Montecito.

We create a beautiful and happy life filled with joy and a fantastic group of friends at school and at our barn, who become our extended family. One of these family members is Paige, whom I met almost seven years earlier at the Santa Monica car wash. Back then, as we were sitting next to each other on a bench waiting for our cars to come out, she asked, "Okay, I know why *I'm* at the car wash, but why the hell are *you* here?" she said, nodding toward my engagement ring. "Because if I had a ring like that, someone *else* would be taking my car to be washed!" Her tone was sweet, and I couldn't help but laugh at her comment.

"I just got engaged last night," I said. "So I'm still feeling very uncomfortable with this big bauble on my finger. I've never even seen anything as big as this." We laughed and made small talk for a few more minutes until Paige's car was ready. She got up to go and we said good-bye.

That night, Mohamed and I attended a dinner party, and there was Paige! It turns out that she was hosting the dinner with her boyfriend, Sylvio, and they were both Mohamed's friends. *Small world, isn't it?* We were instant friends after that.

In Montecito, I start horseback riding again and spend endless hours at the barn teaching my children to ride. They learn to work in the barn, clean tack, and ride six days a week. I find solace in the same quiet place where I've always found comfort since I was a little girl: in nature. It's a rough first couple of years, and I'm lonely at times. My life is nonstop crazy busy raising my three rascals, but I'm proud of myself for coping and learning to run this family single-handedly, especially living so far from my mother and brother in Holland. I feel strongly about investing this crucial time into creating a foundation for the children. They're thriving, and our life is absorbed with horses. Although Anwar is not crazy about riding, he loves being at the barn and is always digging in the dirt looking for crystals. I try to get him into different sports, but none of them really interest him. He is always just content to be with his girls. Once all the emotions around this chapter are settled, I feel like I am entering the happiest time of my life. I just love being a classroom mom in charge of photography at my kids' school.

After the first two years, I buy a little farmhouse on East Valley Road. It overlooks horse pastures with a beautiful barn. I decorate it in a Ralph Lauren equestrian theme, and we're in heaven as we are woken by the roosters each morning at sunrise.

Toward the end of 2006, Mohamed calls me on a Monday night.

"Yo, I'm having a dinner party next Thursday and you should come," he says, using my nickname. "It's at seven thirty at my house."

"Okay, that sounds like fun," I say. But a week later on that Thursday, the kids and I don't get back from the barn until six o'clock. I'm still wearing my riding clothes, helping with homework, and have spaghetti Bolognese cooking on the stove. I am juggling a lot and by seven I'm definitely not ready to shower, get dressed up, and go to a dinner party all the way in Los Angeles, so I call Mohamed.

"I'm sorry, but I can't make it tonight," I say.

He sounds pretty annoyed. "Yo, if you don't start making an effort to go out and meet people, you'll be single for the rest of your life," he says. "Nobody's going to ring the doorbell on East Valley Road and ask you out." It's sweet that he worries, and I know he is right, but I honestly am happy immersed in the lives of my children. I'm used to being on their schedule, going to sleep at eight o'clock and waking up at six, and like it that way.

The next morning, Mohamed calls me. "There was this really great guy at my party, David Foster. He saw your pictures with the kids and asked who the beautiful woman was," Mohamed says. "I told him you were my ex-wife and that you were available." We both laugh at how silly this sounds, but it is endearing.

"Maybe I'll meet him some other time," I say. We carry on our conversation about kid stuff. When I hang up, I think it's interesting that, after all these years, Mohamed finally wants me to date and get a life. A couple of months later, it's Paige's fortieth birthday party, which Mohamed hosts at his home. When David Foster walks in, Paige elbows me.

"That's the guy who asked Mohamed about you," she says. "Let's go say hi." We walk over to him and Paige introduces us.

"It's nice to meet you," I say. Then I step back and take a head-to-toe look at David because I'm curious what type of guy Mohamed thinks is good enough for me. Our eyes lock and we make small talk. After a few minutes, I excuse myself from the conversation because David is with a date and it feels inappropriate to talk to a man who is with another woman. Several days later, David, who gets my number from a mutual friend, calls to ask me out. We meet at Lucky's in Montecito for dinner and then head to the bar at the Biltmore hotel. We have an instant connection and talk until three in the morning. We fall in love, and because David lives in Malibu, we start to date long-distance. This actually works out really well: I'm running my own household, and my main priority is raising my children, and he is the hardest-working man in the music business and spends most of his time recording in the studio.

In 2007, after I've been coughing on and off for months and experiencing sinus issues, I go see Dr. Joseph Sugerman, an ear, nose, and throat doctor in Beverly Hills. When he checks my thyroid, he feels a mass and immediately sends me for an ultrasound downstairs. Results reveal a pretty large tumor. Because of my mother's battle with breast cancer, I freak out when I hear the word "tumor" and don't think twice when the endrocrinologist tells me that I should have my thyroid removed. After the surgery, the mass is sent for a biopsy. It is discovered that three of my four parathyroid glands were encapsulated with my thyroid so, unbeknownst to the surgeon, they were removed as well. These little endocrine glands sit behind the thyroid and regulate the body's calcium level. This is crucial to keep your nervous system and muscles, like your heart, working properly. To help my body manage without my thyroid and these glands, I am prescribed Synthroid, a synthetic thyroid medication. Although I recover quickly from the surgery, I do experience a number of side effects from the medicine, including hair loss, exhaustion, and insomnia. I see a different specialist to get educated because blood tests show that my body's thyroid-stimulating hormone is not working properly.

In 2008, I start thinking about moving to Malibu. Mohamed likes the idea of having the kids closer so he can see them more often, especially because Gigi and Bella will be off to college before we know it. I find a beautiful piece of property on Carbon Canyon Road. It's on a hilltop with a spectacular view of the ocean, and I am excited by the thought of building one last special family home for my children. Every morning, I drop my kids off at school, drive sixty miles to Malibu, work at the job site with dozens of construction workers, and then drive back to Santa Barbara for school pickup at three o'clock. It's a crazy schedule. My afternoons and evenings are like those of many busy parents carpooling kids to and from volleyball, basketball, horseback riding, and tutors; cooking dinner; and helping with school projects and homework.

I do this five times a week for two years, which is why I don't think much when I begin feeling more fatigued than usual and having migraines. After all, braving Los Angeles traffic, not once but *twice* a day, is enough to give anyone a headache. However, soon the occasional migraine comes a few times a week.

This project is a lot more than I had imagined. It's double the budget and the financial burden is starting to crack me and I'm starting to feel exhausted most of the time.

Of course, I'm tired. I had a glass of wine last night.

It's the stress. I'm doing too much.

Maybe I need to adjust my thyroid medication.

These are just some of the twenty excuses I have running through my head while I stubbornly ignore these symptoms and keep going. After all, when you're strong-headed with a type A personality like me, you're determined to do it all. Nothing—no headache, severe fatigue, or other symptom—is going to stop me. I'm on a mission to finish my house in Malibu. Occasionally, I go to my holistic doctor, Michael Galitzer, in Montecito, for things to boost my immune system and give me energy, such as vitamin C drips and B$_{12}$ shots. Unfortunately, they give me only temporary relief and don't resolve my problems. Despite this, I refuse to acknowledge that something is wrong. My body is giving me warning signs and screaming at me to pay attention, but I am in ignore mode. Getting sick isn't on *this* busy woman's to-do list.

One afternoon, I'm on the construction site in Malibu and my phone rings. It's my best friend, Ellie, one of the first friends I made in Montecito when our children were little. For four years straight, we had coffee Monday through Friday at Starbucks in Santa Barbara after we dropped our children off at elementary school. She recently moved to New York because of her job with 1stdibs.

"Hi, honey bunny," I say, but hear only crying on the other end of the phone. "Ellie? What's wrong?"

"You know the back pains I've been having?" she asks, trying to get the words out between sobs. "It's not my back. They say it's ALS."

"Are you sure?" I say. "Should we get a second opinion?" My heart is beating rapidly, but I am trying not to reveal how shocked and scared I am. I don't know much about ALS, but I know it's bad.

"What do I do? What about Gracie?" she says, referring to her daughter.

"I love you and we will find someone to fix this problem. Okay?" I say.

As soon as I get home that afternoon, I google "ALS" and I am devastated to find out what a horrible disease this is, one without a cure. ALS affects nerve cells in the brain and spine, and eventually people with the disease lose the ability to speak, eat, move, and breathe. Apparently, the mind stays sharp while one's body becomes paralyzed. I'm sick to my stomach when I read that life expectancy of someone with ALS is just two to five years from when it's diagnosed. *Two to five years? This is crazy. Ellie has a daughter to raise and a life to live!* There are no words to describe how I feel, and this added stress gives me another excuse for my symptoms. *Of course, I feel sick. My best friend has ALS!*

I call a powerful friend in New York and ask him to find me the best ALS specialist. He gets Ellie in to see the doctor the next day, but unfortunately he confirms her diagnosis. *Shit. Why is life so unfair at times?* I feel sad and helpless from this devastating news.

By December 2010, the new house is finished, and I convince myself that I will feel much better once we move in. Unfortunately, things get worse. I am starting to have really strange moments of brain fog. My kids tease me about tripping over my words and how I ask them the same question two or three times. Of course, this is all in good fun, but I know deep in my heart that it's no laughing matter. Also, my migraines become much more severe, lasting three to four days, accompanied by strange puffy half circles under my eyes. I experience severe hair loss, which is disconcerting, but I fix that with hair extensions. I don't share these crazy and serious symptoms with anyone—not my mother, not my close girlfriends, not David. I do mention them to my friend Tom Hahn, who is helping me unpack boxes in the new house. He was my agent at L.A. Models almost twenty-five years earlier and has become somewhat of a father figure to me. We are upstairs in my bedroom when I stop in my tracks and lean against the bed.

"I feel like something's eating my brain," I tell Tom.

"Eating your brain?" he asks, confused.

"I can't explain it, but that's what it feels like."

"To be honest, I've noticed that you're not yourself lately," he says. "But I thought it was the move and all the balls you're juggling. I know it's hard for you but you need to slow down and take time to regenerate."

It's mid-2011 and about a year since my symptoms first appeared. They come and go regularly. It's as if I have the flu for a week, then have a little bit of a reprieve and think I'm over it. But then the next week it's back, and I feel awful again. When I used to get the flu once or twice a year, I climbed into bed with a cup of chicken soup and rested it out for a couple of days. But when what seems like the flu comes and goes every other week, I have to learn to cope and push through. I keep going. Still, despite some good days here and there, I feel like things are really going downhill. I make an appointment with David's internist, Dr. Lawrence Piro, one of the best doctors in Los Angeles.

"You have too much on your plate," he says. "Take it down a notch and give your body and brain a chance to rest." I'm not surprised to hear this. Of course, any doctor who sees a strong woman doing a hundred things will tell her that she needs to slow down. And because Dr. Piro is not just my doctor but also a close family friend with whom we socialize, he has a front-row seat to my juggling act. Dr. Piro sees me managing a million things, including my children, helping David with his brand, organizing seating at his shows, taking care of my family in Holland, and running a big new house with a music studio. David and I are now engaged, so I'm also planning a wedding, working my job on the series *Dutch Hollywood Women*, a show about four women who have made successful lives for themselves in America after leaving Holland. The cast consists of a photographer, a writer, and a socialite. Although the four of us occasionally meet for coffee, the show isn't about us interacting or creating drama; it's more about sharing a lifestyle and positive message.

Yes, I *am* juggling a lot, but juggling is my forte and something I've been doing my whole life. Many people get overwhelmed when they have too many balls in the air, but I thrive on it. It's stimulating and exciting. I never go to sleep without a to-do list on my nightstand. So, although Dr. Piro's diagnosis is a seemingly obvious one, it doesn't resonate with me. Yet it gives me another excuse to avoid the truth that is staring me in the face: my body is trying to tell me something. I'm struggling, but I keep pulling up the bootstraps.

One day while shooting an episode of *Dutch Hollywood Women,* I look in the mirror and notice that the right side of my face is drooping very slightly combined with a strange numbness and pressure in the area. I google these symptoms, and they seem like Bell's palsy, a condition that causes facial paralysis, but I brush it off. *Could this be from Botox? I should be fine in a couple of days.* I massage my cheek trying to get blood flow to the area. This is just another example of my turning a blind eye to reality and trying to be a hard ass. Although "hardheaded" is more like it!

Beginning in October, I notice that my once very strong and distinct handwriting looks like scribble, and anything I read no longer sticks in my

formerly photographic memory. This is starting to upset me, because reading and writing are two things I've loved doing my whole life. Spiritual
guidance and health books are always stacked on my bedside table and
in my library, and writing has been a source of comfort and a way of ex-
pressing myself—especially through difficult times in my life.

It is starting to be really hard to stay on task and focus on the smallest details for our upcoming November wedding, like the guest list and
table settings, things that the old me could do in my sleep. I also notice
that watching TV is getting harder because somehow the light bothers
me and little things like soft music or noise at a restaurant become irritating. Yet I keep Piro's words in the back of my mind. *Maybe he is
right. Maybe I burnt out my fuse.* I am not sure how to deal with it, so I do
my best to go to bed early and eat healthy. Sometimes, when I try to talk,
I have difficulty with word retrieval. I can't find the proper words to express what I feel. It's subtle, but it's starting to alarm me, so I call Dr. Piro
again.

"I know we discussed this, but I'm telling you, my brain isn't working
properly. I feel like I have an infection in it," I say.

"Hmmm. What do you mean?"

"When I try to talk, the words are floating out there somewhere, but I
can't nail them," I say. "It's like I'm a computer and my browser is defec-
tive."

"Can you elaborate?" Dr. Piro asks. *Of course, I can't elaborate. My
problem is trying to find the right words!* A wave of frustration washes over
me as I feel lost.

"I'm scared that I'm losing my mind," I say. *Something is growing in my
brain. I can feel it.* "Plus, I have so many crazy symptoms, like joint pain,
cramps in my toes and fingers, exhaustion, insomnia, and anxiety—all of
it is overwhelming my entire system."

"You're probably just pushing yourself too much," says Dr. Piro. "But
let's get you in to see a top neurologist. I'll make an appointment."

"I don't see anything wrong with your brain," the neurologist says kindly after doing an array of tests. Then she scribbles a prescription for Adderall, medicine for attention deficit hyperactivity disorder (ADHD).

"But you just said you don't see anything," I reply, feeling confused. *Why give me medicine when nothing is wrong?*

"Well, maybe we just need to activate the part of the brain associated with focus. The medicine can help. Give it a try," she urges.

"I'm also giving you a prescription for antidepressants," she says. *Antidepressants?*

"I'm definitely not depressed," I tell her.

"Why do you say that?" she asks.

"Because I'm happy and I *know* what depression feels like. I experienced it when I broke my back giving birth to my son twelve years ago. I had a double-fusion and the pain medication really affected my mood," I say. "Back then I was *definitely* depressed. This doesn't feel the same at all."

Still, I fill both prescriptions. Although they seem like one-size-fits-all solutions for my unique problem, I'm so desperate for an answer that I *want* to believe the neurologist. I don't love the idea of taking medication, but I love that there is a solution. I was also raised to believe that doctors are like gods, all-knowing and brilliant, so you listen to what they say rather than question it. But taking the Adderall just makes me feel like I'm having a panic attack. My nervous system feels completely overwhelmed and overstimulated. For a typically Zen and balanced person like myself, this is horrible, so I stop taking it after two days. I stay on the antidepressants for several weeks, but they don't help either.

"Give them a little longer," Dr. Piro says when I ask his advice. "They can take time to kick in." *I don't know what is wrong with me, but Adderall and antidepressants aren't the answer.* I wean off the antidepressants and continue to see different doctors.

Besides some food allergies and heavy metal toxicity, there is no concrete explanation for how and what I'm feeling. Every doctor I see seems to focus on my symptoms instead of their underlying cause. I have one hundred reasons to be grateful, so I motivate myself through the motions of my life and fake my well-being. I put a smile on my face for my children and make sure David has his coffee in the morning and the candles are burning in our home by evening. I always have food on the table for our six o'clock family dinners, a ritual that I was raised with and am determined to maintain. It's a sacred time to talk and connect with my children after everyone's busy days out in the world. *My life feels uncertain, but I want to make sure that my kids' and David's lives keep humming along perfectly.*

I do this with the help of Alberto and Blanca, an amazing couple who worked with me in Santa Barbara for five years before they moved with us to Malibu. Because they originally worked for our good friends, the Davis family, and our children played together, Alberto and Blanca have known Gigi, Bella, and Anwar since they were born. They saw me in action as a single mom and know how I run my children's lives like clockwork. Alberto and Blanca are part of our family, and there is a great trust between us. I am so grateful to have them by my side.

With our wedding coming up, David and I are training hard to get into top shape. We work out with a personal trainer, Dale, who comes to the house and cracks the whip three days a week. I have always loved living a healthy and sporty lifestyle and really enjoy inspiring David to get fit, too. Not long ago, intense workouts of burpees, jumping jacks, stair running, treadmill sprints, and push-ups made me feel invigorated, but lately my energy to exercise has seriously declined. A couple of weeks before the wedding, we're in the gym, and as I am mid-push-up a profound and paralyzing wave of exhaustion comes over me and I drop to the floor.

Not sure what happened to me, but I can't do this one more minute. Not even one more second.

"I'm done," I say.

Dale and David exchange puzzled looks. "What happened to our ball-buster athlete?" they joke.

"I don't know. I just can't do it anymore. I'm exhausted." At that moment, I stop working out. *I cannot ignore my body one minute longer.*

Although this is the first memorable moment of realization, the one that breaks my heart involves my son, Anwar, who is now twelve years old. Ever since he was a little boy, we've had a nightly ritual of lying on his bed before he goes to sleep to talk about his day while I scratch his back. But before that, we play a game where I sit on top of him, lock his arms under my knees, and tickle him endlessly while he squeals with delight.

"Who do you love the most in the world? Who? Who?" I say while Anwar laughs those deep, wonderful belly laughs that are only reserved for children. If he says anyone else's name than mine, which he does on purpose, I tickle harder. Then finally, breathless from all the laughing and wrestling around, he says, "My *mommy*. My *mommy*. I love my *mommy* the most." This is the sign for me to stop tickling, and we both collapse on the bed laughing with joy. But one night that laughter abruptly ends. Bedtime starts like always, with Anwar brushing his teeth, putting on his pajamas, and calling me into his room. I shuffle slowly down the hall to him.

"Let's play our game, Mommy," Anwar says excitedly. "Let's play!" But my exhaustion is so severe that I don't have an ounce of energy. Something as simple as the effort required to sit and tickle my sweet boy overwhelms me. *This silly game that requires so little of me is too much.* I'm devastated.

"Tomorrow night we'll play. Okay, my love? Tomorrow," I say, trying to hide the knot in my throat. I walk out of his room so he won't see the tears filling my eyes, then get into bed and pull the covers over my head. The next night, Anwar asks to play again, but I still can't muster the energy. The same thing happens the next night and the next and all the nights after that until eventually Anwar stops asking. *These childhood games and special moments with our children fly by so fast. And now this one is over.* The thought breaks my heart.

It's the night before our wedding, and I'm supposed to finalize the seating chart. All I need to do is put cards with the guests' names around drawings of the tables. Organizing has always been my strength, and previously I'd just do it in my head, type it out, and be done. But in this moment, this simple task is impossible. I am overwhelmed. *It feels like the lightbulb in my brain has turned off.*

"Please help me," I ask my sister-in-law, Liseth. She calmly sits me down and tells me I need to take a deep breath and leave it in her hands, which I do. My brother, Leo, opens a bottle of wine and we sit in front of the fireplace with the whole Dutch crew and laugh as we share childhood memories.

On the day of the wedding, 11-11-11, the adrenaline of getting married and having my entire family here from Holland gets me through. I do a good job of holding it together and enjoying it the best that I can. After all, it's an extraordinary day filled with love and many special moments shared with ninety of the most important people in our lives.

That night, when we finally get back to our room, I'm thoroughly exhausted and every inch of my body hurts. I tell myself it's from carrying my beautiful hundred-pound beaded wedding gown around all night, but as the days pass after the wedding, my body feels worse, not better.

Chapter Two

....

SOME PEOPLE ARE MADE
WHEN THEY ARE BROKEN.

As the year ends and 2012 begins, my condition has declined gradually and life becomes a roller coaster of good and bad days. Determined to figure out what is wrong with me, I continue to go to different doctors but their basic diagnostic testing shows absolutely nothing. No answers. It's mind-boggling because I *know* something is really wrong as I have experienced declining brain function and am now starting to lose the ability to be social. I used to like being at parties and could speak to dozens of people at the same time, but even the smallest gatherings feel like too much. The moments of brain fog continue to catch me off guard. Like at an event for one of the many charities that David supports when a petite, dark-haired woman walks over to me. She smiles warmly and gives me a double kiss.

"Yolanda, darling. How are you?" she says with a clear sense of familiarity.

"Good. Good," I say, faking a smile. *I know her face, but for the life of me I can't remember her name.*

"And the kids?" she asks.

"Busy, but great," I respond, unclear what else to say or what to ask *her.* I don't want to give away the fact that all details about her totally escape me. I know that we have socialized with her and other people here many times. This happens throughout the night and it becomes more frequent at other social events we attend. *I used to have the memory of an elephant. What happened?* I also can't even remember the telephone numbers that have been ingrained in my brain for years. It's worrisome but I don't really know who to turn to.

Even though I still wake up for my kids every morning and see them off to school, it becomes harder and harder to participate in their after-school lives the way I used to. Both Gigi, age seventeen, and Bella, sixteen, are competitive horseback riders with jam-packed show schedules that keep them busy every day after school and on weekends. Gigi's horse is still at Sunny Brook in Montecito so she drives back there after school to practice and Bella has moved her horse to Far West in Calabassas. We've been at horse shows for fourteen years and I've never missed one in their lives, but now, sadly, I rarely have the energy to attend. Luckily, we have built a big horse show family over the years and the girls are well supported. Still, I carry great guilt for not being able to be there. I still drag myself to Anwar's basketball games because his school is only ten minutes away from the house. I am starting to feel inadequate and struggle with the inability to do me.

Until this time, I have been the anchor and the sole engine of our family, always a strong force juggling my children's lives and planning their futures. I used to love doing art projects with them and helping with homework, but this is getting difficult, not only because of my brain issues but also because, when it comes to school stuff, my kids are much smarter than I am. Gigi is a high school junior and very driven, but she needs help with college applications and test prep. A friend introduces her to Nicholas Lindsey from Malibu Tutors. This prestigious young man is a godsend for me and saves the academic side of my family. I honestly don't know what I would do without his help and guidance during this college prep stage.

That same year, Bella goes from being a vibrant, funny, energetic, and outgoing child to a quiet, anxiety-driven teenager with intense symptoms such as severe pain along her spine, extreme fatigue, and difficulty focusing on school work. She is often really sad because she doesn't have the energy to join her friends in activities. At first, I blame all of this on puberty and hormonal changes. *Don't all teenagers have some of these symptoms at one point?* Well, maybe not, so I take her to the doctor for checkups and her basic blood tests show that she is healthy. Something doesn't sit right with me so a couple of weeks later, I take her to the doctor again. This time we discover that she has mononucleosis, which has been going around her high school. Rest and a healthy diet is about all you can do to treat this but she continues to have other symptoms that can't be attributed to mono, and it's harder and harder for her to focus in class. This is upsetting and frustrating to Bella, and, as her mother, it's heartbreaking to see my baby girl struggle. Even though I don't know exactly what the issue is or how to fix it, in my heart I know she needs my support. I think that taking away the physical and academic pressure of eight-hour school days will help so I decide to have her homeschooled for the rest of the year. It's a big decision that definitely feels right to me, but Mohamed and David are totally against the idea. They think Bella is just being lazy and looking for an easy way out. But neither one of them is raising her day to day so they don't truly understand what she is experiencing. It's in these moments of motherhood that I learn to trust my own instincts about my child and not let outside noise influence me. I believe that taking Bella out of a traditional and high-pressure learning environment will not only be less stressful for her failing health but also will give her more time to spend with her horses. She loves being at the barn. It's her happy place and she has always wanted to become a professional rider. It's very normal for kids with this goal to be homeschooled and focus the majority of their time on training. I hire Nicholas to guide her, and she works hard to impress her dad with straight As.

During this time, I finish filming *Dutch Hollywood Women* after season two and am approached about being on *The Real Housewives of Beverly Hills.*

"I'm not sure that it's right for me," I tell David when we discuss the opportunity.

"First get the job and *then* decide if you want it or not," he says. He's right, so I go through a long casting process.

"Congratulations," says Alex Baskin, one of the producers, when he calls to offer me the job.

"I'm thinking about it," I respond. "When do you need to know?"

"Look at joining the cast from a business perspective," he says, aware that I'm creating a product line based on love and romance that includes candles, greeting cards, and a unique flower service. Somehow I've always been fascinated by love and romance and how it can ebb and flow in a long-term relationship. *Why is the divorce rate so high?* I think these products can help rekindle the falling-in-love stages if both parties make the effort. "Many of the housewives have used their platforms to launch successful businesses and succeeded because of the show."

"What do you think?" I ask David that night at dinner.

"I'm hesitant, but it's a great way for you to promote your line and remain financially independent," he says. I married David for love and not to be taken care of. He's been married three times, so I understand his sensitivity around finances. Of course, he doesn't want to provide for my children. That's Mohamed's job and my job and exactly the reason why I am very driven to keep working.

"Gigi, Bella, and Anwar," I say. "Please come down to the breakfast table." We gather around and discuss this opportunity. It's important for me to ask the kids what they think. Although they're not thrilled about the thought of having cameras in our home, they understand my motive and say they'll support whatever choice I make. In the end, my decision to be on the show is a family-based one. I call Alex the next day and say yes to joining the *Housewives* and agree to sign a four-season contract.

When I begin filming around March, I have no clue about the vortex of drama I'm about to step into. I am asked to watch the previous seasons of the *Housewives* to get up to date on the story line but I choose not to. I want to meet each woman in an authentic way and form my own impressions, not come with preconceived ideas of who I think they might be from what I see on the screen. Looking back, this is a mistake, because it takes me a long time to catch up in real life. As Lisa Vanderpump said, "You wouldn't make a reservation at a hotel before you look at the pictures of it, would you?" Lesson learned! The dynamics in this group of women are challenging because they have a lot of history that doesn't include me. I've met Lisa two or three times at Mohamed's house, but I'm not actually friends with any of the women. Interestingly, none of them really care about interacting with me off camera. *This will change. We just need to get to know each other.* I'm stunned when I learn how argumentative they are and feel as if I've been thrown into the shark tank and forced to swim. Usually, I can hold my own, but I feel off balance and obviously am not functioning at full capacity.

Although the housewives and viewers can't tell, my brain continues to fail as the season progresses. I'm not feeling well when we start, and it gets worse. I push through it, thinking that I'm just having a temporary breakdown of my health. I keep thinking, *I'll feel better next week.* My mother instilled in me a very strong sense of obligation to commitments and the serious work ethic that I developed as a young girl is still with me. I guess nothing is going to change it. It's just who I am.

In the middle of the season, I am working my way through a lot of commitments. One of them is filming a meeting with my Web site designers in West Hollywood. As I make my way along Sunset Boulevard I suddenly crash into the car in front of me. It takes a second to realize what happened, but when I do I start crying. As I get out of the car, the driver from the other car walks toward me, yelling a string of profanities.

"I'm so sorry," I tell him through my tears.

"Are you fucking stupid? A moron?" he says. Usually, I would stand up for myself. After all, it's an accident. But I'm so distraught that I just keep crying.

"I'm sorry. I'm just not feeling good," I say. "Should we call the police?"

"Call the police? Don't you think they have better things to do?" he yells.

We exchange insurance information. Then I continue my drive to the meeting, shaken and stunned. *I feel like I'm losing myself. Clearly, my depth perception has changed. I shouldn't drive anymore.*

After the accident, I feel the need to spend more time at home close to my children, so I start a new project. On Sunday afternoons, I invite friends and family members to come over and paint at our kitchen island that I cover with arts and crafts paper. I put out eight-by-nine-inch canvases, acrylic paints, and brushes, so that we can all sit around and paint while we talk and connect with each other. It's the perfect day to eat my famous spaghetti Bolognese and drink our favorite wine. I'm honestly not a great cook, but my children think my Bolognese sauce is the best in the world. My plan is to create a big art wall in our house made by the people who are closest to me and my children. I am feeling a little disconnected from our new life in Malibu. I definitely miss 2347 East Valley Road and my vibrant life in Montecito, but I guess relocating your family is a big shift for anyone.

That summer, David and I are invited on a boat trip to Italy hosted by our friends, Haim and Cheryl Saban, something we do every year with pretty much the same four or five couples. Even something simple like packing is becoming daunting, so I throw a pair of shorts, a few shirts, and some bathing suits into a suitcase and leave behind the beautiful pants, tops, and dresses that I normally bring. In Naples, we board a beautiful yacht, which has six bedrooms and a crew of fifteen. The first night, when our friends come down to the dining room for dinner, they're all dressed perfectly while I'm in shorts and a T-shirt.

"What's wrong with you? Why aren't you dressed?" my friend Vicky asks when she sees me.

"I don't know. I didn't pack right," I say. Usually, we go for long walks and swims, but I'm so out of sorts that I can't participate in much. I can't even walk up the steps to the piazza in Capri where we used to love to have coffee in the morning. I feel completely shut down.

Since before my wedding, I've been on a very strict diet. I cut out gluten, sugar, and alcohol because I wanted to be in great shape for my big day. Eating this way has proven to decrease a lot of unexplainable inflammation throughout my body but despite this, I'm on vacation and feel trapped and annoyed with my limited diet and decide to cut loose. *For*

once, I'm going to eat and drink anything that my little heart desires. Some-
times you've just gotta let it fly. I am not feeling good anyway so who
cares? I have pasta for lunch and dinner, happily indulge in irresistible
white baguettes with delicious butter and olive oil, and enjoy the sweets
that are available all day, every day. I am loving it but sadly the joy only
lasts so long before I pay the price big-time. I wake up even more exhausted and bloated, and all my other symptoms are multiplied by ten. I
realize that my diet is a very important part of whatever is going on with
me. I go back to Malibu bloated and sick.

On the last night of filming for the *Housewives,* we're at a party to celebrate the opening of Kyle Richards's clothing store. All my castmates are
there. Apparently, Taylor Armstrong was talking behind my back, which
I am learning is normal in this group but it doesn't sit well with me. I'm a
very straightforward person. If you have a problem, just tell me and we'll
go talk it out over a cup of coffee at Starbucks. I guess that's the Dutch
way to go. So I confront Taylor. She gets very heated and verbally attacks
me. Normally, I'm outspoken, articulate, and very capable of standing up
for myself. I can usually see all sides of a story and give my honest point
of view. But to my surprise, I stand there with no opinion at all and am
unable to defend myself. I'm scrambling in my head in a way that is hard
to explain. I have no word retrieval and can't form sentences. My memory
is blank. It's as if the scanner in my brain is broken. Taylor continues to
ramble on and on without my response.

Out of desperation, I blurt out, "You are such an asshole." I'm not sure
of *her* reaction, but *I* stun myself. Because my first language isn't English,
I'm extremely conscious of the words I choose, and I don't even know if
we have a word similar to "asshole" in Dutch. After the party, I get in the
limo and burst into tears. I'm so overwhelmed and confused by the letdown
of my own brain. It's the moment that shakes and wakes me up. *Something*
is really wrong with me. All the rest, healthy food, and fun in the world isn't
going to get me well.

In the days that follow, I'm exhausted from traveling and letting go of
the stress from my first season on the show. I made it through but don't feel

confident about the way I expressed myself. Still, I have five months to get well and hopefully do and feel better next season. My fatigue is so severe that it's hard to walk from my bed to the bathroom. No matter how many hours I sleep, I'm totally wiped out. My migraines are unbearable, and I now have unexplainable night sweats and fever. My brain fog gets worse, so simple things like answering an e-mail become difficult tasks. I also have this strange feeling that my heart is always racing. It's as if my body is stuck in a gear and my engine is always running. I'm too worn down to even go out or see friends. I feel like I've fallen off Planet Earth.

In the early fall, I can barely get out of bed because I have a severe migraine. David rushes me to the emergency room at Cedars-Sinai, one of the largest academic medical centers and best hospitals in the country. Dr. Piro meets us there, and I'm admitted. During a twelve-day stay at Cedars-Sinai, I'm absolutely turned inside out. They do an endoscopy, colonoscopy, upper panendoscopy with biopsy, PET scan, EEG, MRI of my brain, spinal tap, and an array of blood tests. They analyze my stool for pathogens and do cultures for all sorts of things, including fungus and yeast. I see internists, infectious disease doctors, gastroenterologists, neurologists, gynecologists, hematologists, endocrinologists, nutritionists, and more. I'm completely debilitated and can barely sit up to be examined. I just want to curl up in a fetal position until the doctors come in to meet me. Unfortunately, despite this army of top health experts, no one can give me a proper diagnosis or a cause for my pain and symptoms. We have access to the best medical minds out there, but it doesn't mean anything if they don't have the right diagnostic tools or knowledge. I often feel guilty for being so privileged and having all these helping hands, but unfortunately that privilege doesn't mean anything when it comes to determining what is wrong with me.

My mental decline is of the most concern to me, and during another neurological exam, I meet with Dr. Harris Fisk, a neurologist.

"I'm going to list three objects that I'll ask you about later," Dr. Fisk tells me.

"Okay," I say. *This sounds easy enough.*

"Apple, nickel, and calculator," Dr. Fisk says. "Now, tell me a little bit about your symptoms."

"Brain fog, joint pain, severe exhaustion, migraines. Sometimes my eyesight is bad."

"How long have you felt this way?" he asks.

"Awhile. Probably two years now."

"Can you tell me the three objects?" Dr. Fisk asks. It's been mere minutes since he listed them for me.

"Apple," I say. *The other two are not even on the tip of my tongue.* Dr. Fisk gives me several hints, but my mind is blank. He can tell how frustrated I am, so he moves on with the exam.

"Who's our president?"

"Barack Obama."

"And our vice president?"

"Joe Biden."

"Who's the governor of California?" My mind is blank. I shake my head.

"How about the mayor of Los Angeles?" Again, I have no clue. I feel the tears rolling down my cheeks because I feel so dumb. *I've had DINNER with the mayor. How could I NOT remember his name?!*

"It's okay," Dr. Fisk says. "Let's try something else. Start at one hundred and subtract by sevens."

"Ninety-three," I say. Then I pause. Ordinarily, math comes easily to me, but this seems like an impossible task. Again, I shake my head.

"Spell 'world,'" he says.

"W-O-R-L-D," I reply. *Phew.*

"Now backward," he says, making notes in my file. I close my eyes and think, but I can't find the letters. *How could I be so stupid? Well, I know I am not stupid, but what am I? What IS this?*

"I just want my brain back," I say out loud, as much to myself as to Dr. Fisk, while tears gently roll down my cheeks, not with sadness but with utter desperation and a sense of grief for the loss of the brain I once loved and was proud of.

The next day, David reads Dr. Fisk's examination notes out loud from my file that's at the foot of my hospital bed: "There has been a major disruption in the patient's lifestyle and ability to function. Clearly, she was functioning previously at multiple levels, performing a multitude of tasks which would ordinarily overwhelm most individuals."

I have a revolving door of visitors during my hospital stay. David comes by anytime he's not in the studio, and my kids visit after school. Paige, Tom, Kelly, Paul, Mareva, Cheryl, and my sisters-in-law Jaymes and Mary-Lou come by so that I'm never alone. I'm not very good company, but they visit anyway, and I'm grateful for their love and concern. I can't do much to pass the time besides sleeping because the light from the TV bothers me and the smallest sound—even the whir of a ceiling fan—irritates my brain. It's like my hearing is heightened in an unexplainable way. One day when Tom visits, he moves his chair across the room as far as possible from my bed when I try to rest. He is listening to a Marianne Williamson lecture on his iPod. When I ask him to turn it down, he looks at me as if I am crazy because he has the volume as low as possible *and* is using his headphones, but my hearing is so acute that it sounds like a megaphone.

I try to remain calm and positive, but I'm not going to lie—deep inside I'm starting to feel frustrated and scared to have such an unexplainable decline in my health. The doctors seem to have an excuse for every symptom but no real answers. They do the enzyme-linked immunosorbent assay test, better known as the ELISA, and Western blot to test me for Lyme disease. These are the two Lyme tests that the Centers for Disease Control (CDC) recognizes. Both are considered "indirect" because they look for the antibodies that your body has made to fight the infection rather than the *actual* infection.

"Your symptoms *seem* like Lyme disease, but your test results are negative," says one of the infectious disease doctors at Cedars.

After being poked and prodded, all they find is swelling in the left frontal lobe of my brain. This sounds serious, but the doctors don't seem too concerned. Yet it makes me wonder if it has anything to do with the rings under my eyes that appear every three weeks and the severe migraines I have. Some say the swelling could be from all the flying and traveling I've been doing. *All the flying? I've traveled much more at other times in my life and never felt this way.* Other doctors say it's age appropriate. *But I'm only forty-eight.* They find some cells of encephalitis in the fluid from my spinal tap and give me a week's worth of antibiotics, but they feel this is from a past exposure. *Whatever that means.* Other tests reveal that I have positive IgG for Epstein-Barr and hepatitis B. IgG is an antibody that is a marker that shows you've had past exposures. However, I don't have a positive IgM, which means I don't have a current or active infection. Bottom line? The doctors don't know what's wrong with me, so they send me home with a diagnosis of chronic fatigue syndrome and no real protocol or any idea of how to regain my health. I return to our Malibu home feeling totally defeated.

I'm no doctor, but I put a lot of effort into being health-conscious and savvy. I know that chronic fatigue is not a disease but rather an umbrella of underlying causes, a term doctors use when they don't know what's wrong with you. *This is BS. How many times do I have to tell the doctors that there's an infection in my brain? I KNOW there is something living in there, but no one else does. Am I fucking crazy?* I feel hopeless and confused as I land back in my bed, staring at the same ceiling and the same lightbulbs as I did twelve days ago. I lose the ability to properly read, write, and retain information, and it's scary. My eyesight also starts to get worse. Although some days I can see normally, other days I have severe black floaters or everything looks blurry when I wake up in the morning.

I've become a shell of the vivacious and outgoing woman I used to be and can no longer participate in my life. There are times when I feel inadequate for not being able to shake this, but I'm stuck and nothing is shifting. I joke with my kids that I should get the word "loser" tattooed on my forehead. I'm kidding, but that's how it feels at times. I'm scared of the unknown. No matter how sick I am, I push David and the children to live their lives as usual. I want everyone to focus on themselves, not me. Of course, I like my husband's company, but I don't hold him back from his social life, charities, and events and would never ask him to cancel his frequent trips. I am supportive where I can be and continue to pick out his clothes for each day that he will be away, label them with the events he will wear them to, and put each outfit in a giant Ziploc bag. Blanca helps me put the bags in his suitcase. Even at my sickest, I try to be a good wife, because not doing anything makes me feel even more inadequate.

The brightest spot in my day is seeing my children's smiles at my bedside when they come home from school. It gets me through the long, monotonous hours of pain and waiting for a miracle to happen. Sometimes they crawl into bed with me and we snuggle and talk. They are my everything. If I can't summon the energy to go down and eat with them at the kitchen table, they bring me dinner in bed. I try as hard as possible to put on a brave face and not share my fear or pain, because I never want to scare my kids. I also don't want them to worry about me or feel guilty when they can't be home all the time. We are all adjusting to this new normal.

Chapter Three

....

THE GREATER YOUR STORM,
THE BRIGHTER YOUR RAINBOW.

Although *I* am frustrated with my diagnosis of chronic fatigue because it does not resonate with me, Tom sees it differently. He has been by my side through many ups and downs in my life. So naturally, he is there when I get home from the hospital and need someone to think for and with me. I hope everyone is lucky enough to have a Tom in their life because I certainly am. He is smart with researching and making sense of all the medical information we have accumulated.

"So if it's chronic fatigue, we have the road to recovery," Tom says with optimism in his voice. He is referring to the fact that, back when he was an agent, another one of his clients was the successful model and actress Maren Jensen. All of a sudden, she disappeared from the modeling scene because she got very sick with chronic fatigue. Years later Maren created a makeup company that she ended up selling for millions. She used her wealth for chronic fatigue research and has spent the last twenty-five years meeting with doctors all over the world to find a cure. Tom calls her immediately.

"The world's top chronic fatigue doctor is in Belgium. Dr. Kenny De Meirleir," Maren says. "Let me call and see if I can get you an appointment."

"I really think this is where we should go, and I will take you," Tom says. Before I can even respond, he's looking into flights.

David is busy and doesn't understand why I am not satisfied with this diagnosis, so I call my confidant, Paul Marciano, who always gives me the most practical advice whenever I can't see it for myself. He and I became instant friends the day we met twenty-three years ago. Although it's hard to explain, we had an immediate connection. He is like a big brother who took me under his wing and has never let go. We have celebrated marriages, supported one another through divorce, and raised our children together. His opinion means a lot to me.

"*Petite fleur,*" he says, using the endearing French phrase that means "little flower." "If it feels right to you, go for it. Let me help with the airline tickets. I have tons of miles."

Everything seems to be falling into place. Even though I can barely get out of bed, going to Belgium feels right in my gut. It's also on the border of Holland, so I'll be able to see my mom and brother. That thought alone is motivating. However, David thinks I'm crazy.

"America has the best doctors in the world," he says, when I tell him about Dr. De Meirleir. Of course, this is a totally normal reaction, and before this journey I felt the same exact way. I thought America had the best of the best. But none of them have been able to help me so far. I am hopeful that I'll find answers in Europe, close to my hometown. Tom and I book our trip to Belgium.

A few friends ask why David isn't going with me. I tell them, and myself, that he is too busy and can't take a week off from recording in the studio. I have a tremendous amount of respect for his work ethic and think this is a legitimate excuse. That said, if the shoe was on the other foot, I wouldn't leave his side. When we met five years ago, I called him my "diamond in the rough." He needed polishing, and I rolled up my sleeves and got to work. I put him on a healthy diet, helped him lose twenty-five pounds, redid his wardrobe, and never missed one of his doctors' appointments. I was obsessed, in a good way, with his health regimen and kept careful notes on my iPhone of all his medications, doctors, checkups, and test results. I realize now that what I did for David doesn't come naturally to him. Maybe it's because I'm a woman and I was born to nurture. I do believe that David cares for me to the best of his ability, and to be honest I am not really demanding of him. As a new bride, I am cautious about burdening him with too many of my issues. I feel very lucky to have Alberto and Blanca's help. They will keep the house running while I'm in Belgium. They have now gotten used to taking my children to their after-school activities and keeping their busy lives going as I fade out of mine. I know I shouldn't, but I feel a lot of guilt about not being able to perform my duties as a mom and wife. I take these responsibilities very seriously and often allow these thoughts to put too much pressure on me. I need my house and family to continue to hum along smoothly while I try to figure out my health crises. The more normalcy they have, the less pressure I feel.

I'm not sure how I have the balls to go to Europe, but I'm determined to find out what is growing in my brain and why I have lost so much of its function. I have a long list of symptoms like severe fatigue, which is made worse from physical exercise, an inability to focus, calculation difficulties, memory disturbance, difficulty with word retrieval, frequently saying the wrong word, anxiety at night, insomnia, migraines, changes in visual acuity, numbness in my right hand, light-headedness, ringing in my ears, muscle weakness, intolerance to bright lights, non-restorative sleep, recurrent flu-like symptoms, swollen lymph nodes, muscle aches, burning joint pain, dry eyes, a severe cough, hair loss, and slight Bell's palsy in my face. The rings under my eyes that accompany my severe migraines show up every three weeks like clockwork. Doesn't that sound like it's a cycle of something? I'm not a doctor, but this feels infection-related to me, and I'm not going to take no for an answer. I keep telling myself that doctors are humans, too; they do make mistakes. I need to keep trusting my own intuition.

When Tom and I arrive at LAX, he gets me a wheelchair and pushes me through the airport. Even though I feel horrible, I look normal, so it's a little bit embarrassing to use a wheelchair, but I honestly can't make it through the security line and to the gate on foot.

I'm happy once we make it to the plane. I get settled and take out my earplugs and eye mask, thinking I'm going to take some melatonin and sleep a big dent into this twelve-hour journey. However, forty-five minutes into the flight, I start feeling sweaty and unwell. The altitude and rising pressure in the cabin cause some sort of inflammatory reaction in my brain, and I can feel a bad migraine coming on. The pain quickly gets intense, and my eyesight gets very blurry.

"Can you please get me three Excedrin Migraine pills and some ice packs?" I ask Tom. The pain is stabbing and unbearable, numbed only by the multiple ice packs the flight attendants bring me.

My body feels freezing cold. I try hard not to shiver because that hurts my head even more. Two hours into the flight, I break out in a high fever. The flight attendants are kind and helpful, but they don't really know what to do, so they ask the other passengers if there is a doctor on board. They find one, a man with a sweet face who is asking me questions.

He suggests that the flight attendants hook me up to an oxygen tank and continue to put ice on my head. All I can think about is my children. When I get scared, thinking of them soothes me, and inhaling the oxygen calms my nerves. *What's going on with my body? Do chronic fatigue patients have fevers like this? Do their brains blow up like balloons?* I'm not sure, but I *do* know that this is the most unbearable plane ride I've ever been on, not just because of the pain but also because of the unknown that suffocates my mind. *I need clarity. I need to understand what is going on in my body that doesn't feel like mine any longer.*

My loud, chronic cough is embarrassing. I can feel the other passengers looking at me, but I can't control it. I curl up into a fetal position and try to meditate; the rhythm in my breathing somehow calms me as I drift in and out of sleep. Next thing I know, I wake to Tom's gentle hand on my shoulder and realize that we're already at the gate, but my seat is still reclined all the way back.

"What happened?" I ask him.

"After ten and a half hours, you finally fell asleep," he says. "The flight attendants said it was okay not to wake you and let you land with your chair flat down." Then Tom lets out a really deep sigh.

"Are you okay?" I ask.

"I was really nervous," he admits. "In twenty-five years, I've never heard you cry or complain like that. It was scary, and at one point I worried that they were going to run out of ice, the only thing that seemed to help you." I feel drained, and my clothes are moist from the fever. I'm afraid to lift my head from the pillow and ice packs, but we make our way off the plane.

After a brief taxi ride, we finally arrive and check into our hotel. In my room, I take off my smelly clothes and sit on the shower floor and let the hot water run over the top of my head. I just need to sit and defrost for a while before I go to sleep. Although I've been dreaming about getting french fries with mayo, I'm not hungry. So instead I order a cup of hot tea and a plate of cookies. I call my mom, who still worries when I fly, to let her know I arrived safely. I text David and my kids to tell them the same thing. I don't mention what happened on the flight because I don't want to worry them unnecessarily about something that doesn't make any sense at this time. I am physically exhausted but filled with excitement about meeting this new doctor tomorrow.

I really hope I can sleep through the night. Maybe I should take some more migraine medicine to prevent another attack. That pain was unbearable, and I'm afraid it will happen again. What would I do? Who would I call? I guess I can always have the concierge call a local doctor, but I'm too tired to worry about it now. I just need to sleep.

The next morning, I wake up very early. I open the window. It's still dark outside. Of course, I feel hungry because I haven't really eaten since I left Malibu, but the nurses from Dr. De Meirleir's office asked me to show up with an empty stomach for my early-morning blood draw. I watch the sunrise, but I feel so exhausted that I can barely focus on the beautiful golden light or imagine its healing power clearing my cells as it enters my body. I throw on some sweats and wait for Tom to come by my room and pick me up. We make our way to the Himmunitas Clinic and finally meet

Dr. De Meirleir. He is very soft-spoken and speaks to me in my mother language with a sweet Belgian accent. I instantly feel a sense of hope and take this as a sign that I might find an answer to my suffering. Although I have lost the old me, I haven't lost my type A personality, which I have applied to the goal of getting well. For example, since my brain function started failing, I often can't tell my own medical history in detail, Tom and I created a big, well-organized binder with each doctor's reports and lab results. Before we left Los Angeles, Tom scanned all these files and put them in a Dropbox file, something that I can't quite figure out yet, but it seemed a lot easier than sending the entire binder by FedEx to Dr. De Meirleir to review before today's appointment.

"In forty years, I've never seen a medical workup as extensive as yours," Dr. De Meirleir says. "But even with all these fancy test results, I *still* don't have the clarity of a diagnosis or a defined answer as to how to treat you."

"So it's not chronic fatigue?" I ask.

"There isn't enough evidence of that." He shakes his head. "It seems like that diagnosis was made based on symptoms, but not with a clear cause. I'll have to do my own tests with the labs that I work with here in Europe."

"Okay," I say. I'm frustrated, but I'm up for anything that will give me some clarity.

"It will take six weeks to get the results," Dr. De Meirleir adds. *Six weeks? Are you kidding? I don't have six weeks. I really need to get better yesterday!* I had imagined that I was coming to Belgium to meet this world-renowned chronic fatigue expert who would give me a magic pill to make me feel better. *I guess that was just a dream!* The idea that I have to wait *another* six weeks for a diagnosis is overwhelming and disappointing. *How many more tests can I do?* Dr. De Meirleir orders a variety of blood, saliva, and urine tests, and I make my way back to the hotel like a puppy with my tail between my legs.

The only good part of my day is seeing my mom and Leo, who drive two hours from Holland to be with me. My mom immediately pulls all my favorite foods from her grocery bag, then orders some hot coffee and tea from room service. I usually talk to my mom and Leo on FaceTime, so they know how sick I have been, but they haven't seen me in person since my wedding just a year earlier. To strangers, I look perfectly normal. However, my mom sees right through to the core of me and is trying to hide her reaction to my physical appearance. I can tell it's hard for her to see me this way. I'm so exhausted that I can't even take them out to lunch or dinner, but the greatest thing is that we don't need to do anything or go anywhere. Being together in my little hotel room is enough; this is the true love of family that I was raised with. We lie in bed and reminisce about our childhood stories. They make me laugh and I feel happy with a cup of coffee and my favorite Dutch cakes Momma brought me. On days like this, I realize how very much I miss my family and how very alone I have felt this past year. I don't have any blood relatives in America besides my children, and, no matter how old I am, there is something very calming and comforting about having my family by my side. Their presence is the only thing that makes me feel better in Belgium. All I really want to do is go to Momma's house in Holland, curl up on her couch, and eat my favorite cheese sandwiches and french fries until I feel normal again, but I can't leave my children one day longer than I have to, so Tom and I fly home to Los Angeles two days later.

The next six weeks feel like an eternity. During this time, I go through periods of feeling really bad for ten days, then feeling a little better and pushing hard for a couple of days, only to find myself back in bed for another five. There is absolutely no rhyme or reason to this madness. No matter how long I stay in bed and try to preserve my energy, I never wake up feeling refreshed, just tired and burnt out in the morning. When I meditate on exactly what it is that I'm experiencing, I feel like the energy is being pulled from the core of my body through my feet into the earth.

In the midst of this, there is the premiere party for my first season on the *Housewives*. I haven't gotten dressed up in months, but I have to show up to this mandatory event. Both David and Tom will join me, and I'm grateful for this because going to a party is not something I can do on my own right now. Dusty, my makeup artist, and a hairdresser come to my house to help me get ready. I can barely sit in the chair, but somehow their magic makes me look presentable. They help me get into my gorgeous, hot pink Roberto Cavalli dress, and out the door to the Roosevelt Hotel we go. The minute I step on the red carpet, fifty cameras start flashing at the same time, which immediately puts my brain in overdrive. I make it to the end of the carpet, but my body is sweating and I feel shaky. All of a sudden, I feel faint, so I quickly walk behind the step and repeat wall, where I can lie down. *Why am I so weak? Why did I push myself so hard to be here? What's wrong with me? Is this worth it? And whose body is this? It certainly doesn't feel like mine.*

Alex Baskin brings me a cool cloth and a glass of ginger ale. As soon as I catch my breath, I want to go home and David and I walk back to the limo. I'm barefoot. I climb into the backseat, remove my jewelry, rip off my false lashes, and take out the fifty bobby pins that are keeping my fake ponytail and fancy hairdo together. *Ugh. I hate my hair extensions. All this shit is just a mask of who I'm not. I hate my life in my body right now.* I lie down on my back, staring at the car ceiling in the dark and dead silence, trying to digest what just happened. When I get home, I make my way up the stairway to my bedroom and turn on the shower. The hot running water on the crown of my head cleanses me energetically. *How am I going to make my way out of this?* When I get out of the shower, I walk over to the sink to brush my teeth and suddenly catch a glimpse of my reflection. It's hysterical and I start laughing at how deadly scary I look with black mascara smeared down my cheeks to the top of my upper lip. I look like a ghost. The funny thing is that right now I look exactly the way that I feel, but, of course, the next day when the premiere party photos hit the press, they tell a very different story, one that is merely a perception and very far from the truth about what is actually going on in my life. I look perfect from the outside. My pink Cavalli gown brings color to my white pasty skin, and all the weight that I lost from being sick makes my body appear perfect in photographs. *But who cares?*

I retreat to the endless days of staring at the ceiling, counting the perfectly aligned light fixtures. I marked those fixtures precisely myself back when I was building my supposed dream home, a house that is starting to feel like a jail. It's crazy to think that I used to stress obsessively about the detail and placement of lightbulbs that I'm now forced to stare at day in and day out. I ask myself "Why?" and "How?" often, but I guess those answers will reveal themselves in time when they're supposed to, not when *I* decide I need them. I'm feeling impatient. I need to work on that, but I'm sure we're going to figure this out soon so I can get back in the saddle and back to my life—which is currently at a standstill. Thank God for my great and generous friends who continue to send me flowers. It makes me feel like I live in a flower store, and their beautiful little notes of love and support keep me going. They mean the world to me.

David is busy 24-7, but thankfully his studio is downstairs in our house, so he often comes up just to give me a kiss and check on me. He has started to keep a diary of my journey and takes great pride in writing a couple of lines in my aqua leather-bound book. We laugh often about the silly things that come out of my mouth.

One night, around two o'clock, I wake up to go to the bathroom. This is not unusual. My sleeping patterns are terrible, and it's normal for me to get up every two or three hours feeling a strange sense of anxiety. I know every inch of this house so I don't even turn on the light when I enter my little toilet room. Suddenly, I feel really sick and my head starts spinning. Before I can sit down on the toilet, my body collapses. My forehead hits the small table in the corner as I fall to the floor. The loud sound in the silence of the night wakes David and he comes running into the bathroom.

"Yo, are you okay? Yo?" I hear his voice in what seems like the far distance, but I feel paralyzed and can't respond. My head is throbbing and on fire. Something warm is running over my face and down to my neck. I'm not fully conscious and feeling very far away. Apparently, David can't open the toilet-room door because my body is pressed up against it from the inside. Minutes later, the door gently pushes my body over just enough for David to wiggle his way in.

"Baby, are you okay?" he asks. He turns on the light, and I can see in his face that something is wrong. Tom, who is staying with us, is right behind him.

"Get some ice packs and the first-aid kit," David says calmly to Tom. David gets a washcloth and starts compressing an open cut on top of my left eyebrow to stop the bleeding.

"Do you have pain anywhere else besides your head?" he asks. I feel paralyzed and start crying because I don't know what happened to me. I try to be a good sport, but I'm scared. *What is going on with me?* Because it's my face and the wound is deep, Tom calls our friend Brian Novack, a Beverly Hills plastic surgeon. Of course, he is sleeping, so it takes a little while for him to return the call, but as soon as we connect, Dr. Novack gets his friend Dr. Lancer to meet me at his office, where he puts twelve stitches in my forehead, official proof of my warrior status. Thankfully, it is right at the start of my six-month hiatus from the *Housewives,* and cameras aren't rolling.

October 23, 2012
Beverly Hills Housewife Down
Thank you @drnovack and @drlancer for stitching my head at 6 AM.
I guess no need to dress for Halloween.

Just a week later, I have to pull myself together to take part in a deposition for Paige's divorce. It's been a bitter, ugly one, and she needs me as a character witness and to recall a timeline of events. My close friends mean the world to me, and I'll do anything for them, especially Paige, who is going through hell. This is why I get up and dressed even though every part of my body hurts, my eyesight is blurry, and I can barely stand up. Paige picks me up, and we drive more than an hour to Ventura to her lawyer's office.

"The fact that I'm asking you to do this when you feel the way that you do is embarrassing," Paige says. "But you're the only witness I have."

"I know," I say. "It's okay. I love you." Once we get there, I spend six hours being drilled by her ex-husband's lawyers. I need to take a few breaks, but I work through it the best that I can.

"I wouldn't be able to survive this divorce if it weren't for you scraping me off the pavement," Paige says in the car on the way home. I know she would do the same for me.

As I wait the six weeks for Dr. De Meirleir's diagnosis, I decide to focus on my diet, even though I don't have much of an appetite. Laurie Stark, the mother of one of Bella's best friends, Jessie Jo, hears that I am sick. She suggests I see her nutritionist, David Allen, who finds alternative solutions for various health issues. From unique and very sensitive tests to uncover food allergies and intolerance, I learn that I'm allergic to many foods, including pears, oats, peas, lentils, mushrooms, lobster, brewer's yeast, soybeans, egg whites, peanuts, cola, cabbage, pistachios, and barley. David Allen also finds really high levels of heavy metals in my blood.

"In fact, they're off the charts," he says. He recommends I stop eating sushi for the next six months. Although it's my favorite food and Nobu Malibu is my favorite restaurant, this resonates with me. David Allen also makes me special vitamin packs based on my blood work and any deficiencies he saw while analyzing it. I follow strict directions and use his supplements religiously, but without very noticeable results.

A couple weeks later, exactly six weeks to the day of the testing I did in Belgium, on December 5, Dr. De Meirleir e-mails to say that he has the results of his medical detective work. He schedules a Skype appointment with me for eight tomorrow morning. I wake up early, excited about what Dr. De Meirleir has to say. Ready with pen, paper, and a tape recorder, Tom, David, and I anxiously gather around the kitchen table.

"The good news is that you don't have chronic fatigue," Dr. De Meirleir says. "The bad? You've probably been sick for a couple of years with severe, chronic neurological Lyme disease."

"Neurological?" I say out loud, more to myself than anyone else.

"Yes. It's called neuroborreliosis. The *Borrelia* spirochete IgM serology is positive, meaning that there is a current and active infection in your brain," Dr. De Meirleir says. I have goose bumps all over my body. *This resonates with every part of my being!*

"You also have several coinfections," he continues and then lists them: *Chlamydia pneumoniae, Chlamydia trachomatis, Versinia,* and *Coxiella burnetii,* but I barely hear any of it. The words fly by and time stops. All I hear is someone confirming that I actually have an infection in my brain. *This is exactly what I've been trying to tell everyone since before my wedding. I knew it!* I try to focus on the rest of the information. Thank God Tom is recording it, because they lost me for a minute.

"Because you've carried this for a long time, it's gotten deep into your tissues and cells," Dr. De Meirleir adds.

"Whoa. How did I get this?" I know Lyme is a tick-borne illness, but I've never seen a tick on me or a bite.

"This also explains your loss of brain function. Lyme in the brain is in the syphilis family, and the cells of encephalitis in your spinal fluid at Cedars-Sinai confirm that as well. It all makes perfect sense."

"But they *did* two Lyme tests at Cedars," I say. "And both were negative."

"Yes, they did. But the tests they do in the U.S.—the ELISA and the Western blot—aren't always sensitive enough to pick up on chronic Lyme." Dr. De Meirleir explains that the Western blot uses electricity to separate specific blood proteins into bands, which look sort of like a bar code. The lab compares your band pattern to what the CDC has deemed the typical one found with Lyme. According to the CDC, you need five of the ten bands for a Lyme diagnosis. However, some of the bands are more meaningful than others, so if you have one of these bands without the others you could *still* have Lyme. Another issue is that not all the labs use the same method to analyze the Western blot, so you can get a positive result if your blood is sent to one lab and a negative one if your blood is sent to another. With Lyme, your only chance for a cure is at early detection, because once you pass the stage of an acute diagnosis and it goes untreated, the Lyme spirochetes set up camp in other places and leave only little traces in your bloodstream.

"This is exactly what happened to you, Yolanda. The bacteria are in your brain and it was too late for either test to detect that," Dr. De Meirleir says.

"So now what?" I ask. *Even though I feel relieved to know that I'm not crazy, how are we going to fix this?*

"Let's begin with ninety days of IV antibiotics and go from there. Even though your chronic case will take a lot more than that, it's a good start." All I hear is ninety days.

"Ninety days?" I exclaim. Don't get me wrong, I am grateful for a diagnosis. *But ninety days? I have a life to live. I'm a mother, a daughter, a newlywed, a stepparent, and a reality show cast member. I have children and a husband to care for, horse shows to go to, basketball games to attend, a product line to launch, a big home to manage, friends to see, and work obligations to fulfill.* Forgoing three *more* months of my life seems insane. Initially, it's hard to wrap my head around, but the clarity of my diagnosis also gives me a new "fuck you" attitude.

"You need various oral antibiotics, but since most of these don't cross the blood-brain barrier, they won't do the job alone," Dr. De Meirleir says. "I suggest you get a port as soon as possible and start a combination of ninety days of IV antibiotics as well." He prescribes Ceftrixane, tindemax, telithromycin, and diflucan to start with.

We immediately consult Dr. Jeff Harris, a Malibu internist. Oddly enough, Dr. Harris diagnosed and treated David with Lyme two years earlier. Yet after a couple of months of doxycycline, David seemed fine. Dr. Harris and Dr. Piro are going to work closely with Dr. De Meirleir to help me get back on my feet, hopefully ASAP. The next day, I have the port surgically implanted on the right side of my chest. This will allow the nurse to administer a combination of IV antibiotics and other medications into my bloodstream several times a day and hopefully they will cross the blood brain barrier. I don't think twice about the protocol. I'm convinced that it's my only chance at ridding my body of this silent spiral-shaped killer that has so obviously confiscated my brain. He also prescribes steroids to help my chronic cough, something none of my doctors here in Los Angeles have been able to figure out. The *Chlamydia pneumoniae* finding explains it. The crazy thing is that I'm not alone in getting a negative test result or going undiagnosed when I actually *do* have Lyme. This happens to 56 percent of people when the CDC's two-tiered testing system fails us!

Given my rigid and determined personality, I believe that if I take my antibiotics perfectly, I will be cured in three months. Throughout my life, I've always viewed antibiotics as something you save for when you really need them, so I have always used mostly holistic medicine. I hope this will make my ninety-day course even more effective. I have a new spark of hope and what I truly believe is a cure. *If I get through the ninety days, I'm home free. I'll be back in the gym, eating my healthy diet, and returning to the game of life.*

At first, a nurse comes to my house twice a day to administer the IVs, but eventually David and Blanca learn how to do it. David also keeps a perfect daily log of each dose and my resulting symptoms in the aqua book on my nightstand. Tom is at my house often, researching this diagnosis and its treatments just to make sense of it and get educated. For now, he is the brain that I'm missing. He prints out lots of articles on chronic Lyme, and we soon learn about the controversy surrounding it because some people say chronic Lyme doesn't exist. It's hard for me to understand and comprehend, but I definitely feel for this misunderstood community and identify with them, since it took so long for me to get properly diagnosed.

Nobody in my inner circle has any close or personal experience with chronic Lyme disease. I'm eager to learn all that I can about it, but my brain can't retain too much information at this time, so I have to read things two or three times just to make them stick. That's why I prefer Tom to sit by my bedside and tell me about his research. Anwar is very curious about Lyme and wants to understand, so he does his own online research. But, in line with his sweet personality, he shines light only on the positive outcomes of treatments that he finds and the success stories and doesn't tell me about the dark and negative things he reads. *God, I love this boy.* His name means "light," and that's really what he is to me every day of my life. Everything might not be perfect right now, but I'm blessed.

Part of my contract and obligation to Bravo as a *Housewives* cast member is to watch the show when it airs and blog after each episode. Even though I am diagnosed and dealing with Lyme in the off-season when the cameras are not rolling, it's important to share what's going on with me *in real time.* In one of my first blogs, I write, "I feel a lot of comfort in finally having a diagnosis that I can fight head-on! It will require many months of intravenous antibiotics and immune therapy, but I'm very optimistic and ready to fight the good fight." I always try to find the positive in every situation, but the days that follow are brutal. I can't get out of bed, and I feel as if the life and energy are sucked out of me. Just going up and down the stairs for breakfast feels like Olympic training.

I never read the little white paper inserts that come with prescription drugs because they make me not want to take the medicine, and, to be honest, my doctors don't really explain the severe side effects that occur from treating chronic Lyme. My migraine is a pounding heartbeat in my head, and I have been throwing up for days, so much so that I become weak and dehydrated. David checks my blood pressure. It is unusually low. He is uncomfortable with this, so he calls Dr. Piro.

"Larry, I'm worried about Yo being on this much medication," David says. "It's making her really sick. She hasn't eaten for days and keeps vomiting."

"Bring her to the ER at St. John's. I'll meet you there," Dr. Piro replies. Upon arriving at the hospital, my room is ready and I'm admitted. When the hospital staff starts calling you by your first name, you know that you come here too often! They're all so nice and I have a whole new appreciation for the nurses who kindly dedicate their lives to caring for others. They immediately start running large bags of fluids. Dr. Piro knows how to treat my migraines by now, and he also prescribes Zofran for my nausea and orders labs to try to understand what is going on. I don't bounce back as fast as I usually do. It takes days for my migraine to dissipate.

"Can I have some chicken soup, please?" I ask Susan, my nurse. I'm starving, which is the first sign that the couple of days' break from my antibiotics is exactly what I needed.

I learn that when you start such an intense course of antibiotics, you get a severe reaction called a "Herxheimer" or "die-off" reaction. When enormous populations of bacteria are killed off with antibiotics, they release endotoxins and biotoxins into the blood and tissues faster than the body can handle it. The immune system responds with a range of awful symptoms: fever, chills, muscle stiffness, very low blood pressure, severe headache, hyperventilation, rapid heartbeat, flushing, muscle and joint pain, skin outbreaks, and anxiety. My body feels like a toxic waste dump with many of these severe side effects. But supposedly the bigger your reaction, the better. *Well, I must be doing the right thing because it's a rough ride and a rude awakening.* I can't even find the words to describe what "herxing" feels like except to say that it is like having the worst case of the flu times ten, being hit by a truck, being run over by a train, and ending up in the washing machine on spin cycle. As the days go by, my symptoms start to ease. Besides being dehydrated, my white blood cell count is severely low, which is nothing new. One afternoon I wake up from a long nap. I look out my hospital room window and notice it's a beautiful sunny day with bright blue sky but I feel sad and trapped until my kids arrive. They snuggle in my bed. They tell stories and even show me some new dance moves with their new favorite songs. It's funny how my children and I never run out of things to talk about.

"I was actually hoping someone would bring me a Starbucks and slice of banana bread," I tell them.

"Well, that means you're getting better, Mommy," Gigi says.

The next day, I get released from the hospital after a six-day stay. Many nights thereafter, I lie on my bathroom floor, shivering from head to toe as if demons have taken over my body. The biotoxins in my brain make me feel as if I'm going crazy, like I am lost in space and time. I desperately need to ground myself back on Mother Earth so sometimes at night, when I'm home alone, I go outside to my backyard in my underwear with my warm blanket to lie on the grass, where I can hear the waves crash on the shore and stare at the stars and the moon. People might think I'm insane, but I feel like I lost my connection to the earth, and this is the only way I experience some sort of grounding in my spirit. I am determined and 1,000 percent committed to this protocol. However, I'm not going to lie: this is probably the hardest thing I have ever done. I'm fighting not only Lyme but also myself. I impatiently count the days of my protocol. I want a faster way to heal. I want to get back to my life. Most of all, I want control over my body.

Antibiotics also kill the good bacteria in the gut, which causes severe yeast infections. I have yeast coming out of everywhere including my ears, my mouth, and my vag. In fact, my tongue is covered in a white film as well. I try to drink a lot of water but keep getting severely dehydrated from bouts of diarrhea and vomiting, which we now learn to treat with extra IV fluids and vitamin drips at home. It's a truly miserable time. *Interestingly, the antibiotics that I THOUGHT would be the answer to my prayers are actually making me so sick that I feel as if I am going to die.* Through all of this madness, I still struggle with sitting on the sidelines of my life and feeling bad for not being productive.

"David, do you think I'll ever be normal again?" I ask. Trying to make me feel optimistic, he gets the journal from my nightstand and reads parts of the daily log he's been keeping. I can't feel it, but he says that I'm making progress. Of course, I believe him because he is my lifeline right now.

"We're in this together, baby," he often says. That may be true and I'm so grateful, but I also know that I'm not *even close* to the strong Dutch girl David met seven years earlier.

Thank God for my core group of real friends, who never give up on me and never stop visiting, because a lot of other people do. The lack of consciousness in this town is something I have always felt but I am finally starting to see it clearly. In late December, I ask Paige to help me decorate my Christmas tree. I am miserable but the holidays are my children's favorite time of the year. I am the only one in charge of keeping our Christmas traditions alive so when Paige walks into the family room, I've got my IV running while I'm up on a ladder trying to hang ornaments in my pajamas and Uggs.

"Are you nuts?" she says, rushing over to hold my legs.

"I have to," I say.

"Let me do it," Paige insists. Then she starts laughing.

"What's so funny?" I ask. She points to the fuzzy robe and the infusion pump in my pocket connected to the port in my heart. *Yes, I'm a crazy sight, and it's taking three times longer than usual to decorate my tree but I am determined because it's for my kids.*

"Please get off that ladder and take a break," Paige says. "Just point to where you want each ornament and I'll do it."

"Fine," I say. I know she is right, and she's the only person I would let do this task. I sit in a chair by the fireplace while she rummages through the box of ornaments. A fire is burning and we're having hot apple cider to keep the holiday spirit going. I watch Paige trying over and over to attach one of the metal hooks to the top of an ornament, but she can't seem to get it in. *Something is strange.* I also realize that she's repeating herself multiple times while telling the same story.

"Paige, are you feeling okay? When was your last checkup?" I ask.

"I don't remember," she says, shrugging.

"Something's not right with you, cowboy," I say. "Have you noticed that?"

She nods. "I've been feeling off for a while but thought it was post-traumatic stress from my divorce," she says.

"Mmm, that could be but something doesn't feel right, so let me call Dr. Harris," I say. His office is right here in Malibu, and he's an important part of guiding me with my new protocol. This simple country doctor is very smart and probably more Lyme literate than any other doctor in Los Angeles. I get Paige an appointment to go in for a large panel of blood tests the next day. Paige, Blanca, and Alberto finish the Christmas decorations. I honestly couldn't relax until it was done. So much has changed in *my* life that I fight with all that I have against change in my children's lives.

When Paige's test results come back from Dr. Harris a couple of weeks later, we find out that she has Lyme disease and many co-infections, too! Dr. Harris immediately puts her on oral antibiotics and starts monitoring her closely. I'm glad there is a proper cause for her symptoms but it is a shocking revelation. *What are the chances that BOTH of us have Lyme? One in a billion? We were pregnant together, raised our children together, and now we have Lyme together?*

Chapter Four

....

FOCUS ON YOUR GOAL.
DON'T LOOK IN ANY DIRECTION BUT AHEAD.

The standard treatment for Lyme disease is twenty-eight days of antibiotics, and most insurance companies won't cover any more than that. After twenty-eight days on a cocktail of four different antibiotics, I don't feel any better. In the midst of this, I'm obligated to write my weekly *Housewives* blog. It's difficult for me to focus and even harder to form an opinion about the craziness that takes place. It all seems frivolous compared to what I'm going through at this moment. Most of the time, it takes me a whole week to type a couple paragraphs, which causes me a lot of stress because I feel blocked in my communication. In one of my blogs, I write, "On day 40 of my IV antibiotic treatments, almost halfway. I'm starting to see the light at the end of the tunnel and hoping to get back to my normal life sooner than later." I sound positive and like to talk myself into being more hopeful than I really am. At the sixty-day mark, I notice some improvement, but it is *really* minimal. With the little that I *do* have, I put a smile on my face and pull up my bootstraps. Gigi and I are heading to New York in a few days to visit the New School and meet with modeling agencies. We missed the college tours last year because I was too sick, so we are excited to finally go and check it all out.

I remember when the kids were little, I was obsessed with dressing and styling them in cute outfits just to photograph them at the barn, the beach, or wherever I could catch them. They got so used to the camera that it was part of life in our household. But Gigi was the only one who actually *liked* our photo shoots, and, from the time that she was a little girl, I knew that she was going to be a model. From the ages of four to ten, I let her do a few jobs for Guess because it was my friend Paul Marciano's company so it felt like a safe place for her to work and learn about life on set. My little social butterfly loved everything about it: the stylist, photographer, makeup artist, motor-home driver, food, and teacher. She was fascinated by it all and fit right in even though she was very young. However, I felt strongly that she wait until she turned eighteen to start a modeling career.

"Please, Mom," she'd reason with me when she was in her early teens. "There are lots of fourteen-year-olds who model. Why can't I?"

"Trust me, angel. I've lived in that business most of my life. I understand it on many different levels that you won't get right now. But one day, you will," I'd say. "Before I expose you to a world where people judge you on the way that you look, I need you to develop a strong sense of self-worth and understand exactly who it is that you are. It's the only way to survive. Let's focus on your sports and work on being the best you can be."

Now, Gigi is almost eighteen, so it's time to keep my promise. She is dead set on fulfilling her dream, and I'm dead set on holding up my end of the bargain. Last year, I organized several test photo shoots for her with different photographers so she could start building her portfolio. I also researched the top five agencies in New York and made appointments to meet with them. Before we leave L.A., I learn to run my own IVs, connect my antibiotics, and flush my port with saline and heparin so that I can travel.

We stay at a cute little hotel in downtown Manhattan. On our first day, we're scheduled to meet with the modeling agencies. While Gigi is getting ready in the bathroom, she looks over at me.

"Mommy, what if nobody likes me today?" she asks.

"Gigi, please don't worry about that, just be *you*," I say. "You've got all it takes to be whatever you choose to be, my love. And remember: you're not going to work for them; *they're* going to work for *you*." I want her to feel in charge of this exciting expedition we're going on. We're finally here and we're going to have an amazing day. It's intimidating to walk into a big agency like IMG where you don't know anyone, but we've prepared for this. Gigi is a shy and reserved version of herself, but engaging, charming, and talkative when she meets David Cunningham and Lisa DiRuocco from IMG's development. Afterward we have a nice lunch and meet with four smaller agencies that afternoon. By evening, we are walking arm in arm back to the hotel, exhausted but happy. It was a beautiful day and now the sun has set and a warm spring wind blows through my hair. Regardless of how I'm feeling physically, emotionally, I feel so fulfilled for keeping this promise to my little girl.

"That was so great, Mommy," Gigi says. "But what if I don't get offers from any of them?"

"Don't worry, my love. Just wait until tomorrow."

We go out for dinner with Tom and David's manager, Marc Johnston, at the Spice Market, a restaurant right across the street from our hotel, and Gigi excitedly shares her day with our family friends. We talk about the different agencies and the people we met, some of whom I used to work with at Eileen Ford's agency.

The next morning, we wake up to four offers in my e-mail in-box. Of course, we scream with excitement. We order room service and discuss her options.

"I'd rather be a big fish in a small pond than a small fish in a big pond," I say. I'm kind of leaning toward a smaller, boutique agency, where I think she will have more personal attention—especially since she'll be so far away from home that first year. I'm just trying to protect my baby from being lost in a big place. Then again, it doesn't really matter what I say. It's the beginning of *her* journey, not mine, and she needs to use her own intuition in this decision and feel the human connection she made at the agencies.

"I'm going with IMG. I knew that was my place from the second we walked into their office yesterday," she tells me, referring to the biggest modeling agency in the world. I'm not surprised that she ends up doing exactly the opposite of what I suggest, and I'm certainly not surprised by her ability to make this decision. That's just who Gigi is.

"I support you one hundred percent in your choice, my love," I say. "Now, let's focus on the serious business." Gigi is graduating high school in June and was accepted to the New School to study criminal psychology. From a very young age, maybe five or six, Gigi was completely intrigued by crime shows on TV. She didn't just watch dramas like *Law & Order* but also loved hard-core murder mysteries and felt the need to understand why one human being could kill another. I always thought it was fascinating that her little mind was intrigued by this so I nurtured it and as she became older it became clear to me that criminal psychology was really something that she wants to explore and learn about. Going to college in the fall and working as a model on her days off, holidays, and maybe weekends will be a perfect combination. Education is very important but I also want her to be completely financially independent by the time she is twenty-one. We tour the New School and I can see her excitement about the thought of a life on campus. It's a hectic week, and I get through it on pure adrenaline and my determination to keep the commitments I made to my child. I consciously put a smile on my face as I push through my physical symptoms. These are such important moments for Gigi, and I'm not going to let any disease take that away from her! Most mothers would do the same—a mother's love is so strong that it gives us magic powers that exceed anything.

It's around day sixty-five of my antibiotics when we get back from New York, yet I'm nowhere close to feeling normal. I want to believe that ninety days will do the job, but, as I approach the finish line, I start to worry that this might not be the case. *What am I going to do now?* Reality is starting to set in. Being in New York was a humbling reminder of what I am not.

I need to contemplate my next plan of attack. A couple of days later, out of the blue, I get an e-mail from my friend Suzanne Somers, who tells me that her fourteen-year-old granddaughter, Violet, was treated and cured of chronic Lyme at the Sponaugle Wellness Institute in Florida. Tom is visiting on his way back to his mom's house up north, and the word "cure" has us researching the clinic immediately. They treat Lyme and autoimmune conditions using both holistic and Western medicine. When Tom calls Sponaugle, they tell him that the program is six weeks long. *Six weeks? How can I take that much time out of my life? Then again, what life am I referring to? I really don't have a life. If it wasn't for my responsibilities, I would probably never leave my bed.* At this point David and the kids are getting used to me living in my room most of the time. They often jump in bed with me and discuss their days like it's normal. I guess it *is* our new normal, but I'm starting to feel isolated and detached from my world more and more each day. The kids must sense this because they surprise me with a new iPhone. They convince me that I need Twitter and Instagram accounts and patiently teach my slow brain how to use them. I learn to love this new phone because it becomes my only link to the outside world.

At times, I'm so frustrated by being trapped in my body that I have a meltdown and bawl my eyes out, of course when my kids aren't around. Yet eventually the Dutch warrior comes out and I get back to researching my options for killing these horrible spirochetes that are living in my brain and clearly show their three-week cycles in my face. I know Dr. De Meirleir said ninety days was only the beginning of this but his words are now becoming a reality.

This is unbelievable! Why isn't this a cure? Why isn't there a black-and-white answer? Why does everybody seem to have a different opinion about this mysterious disease? Why is this such a mystery? My mind is screaming with unanswered questions, but instead of getting angry, I grow more quiet and introverted as time passes.

One of the rare joys during this time is to see that I raised three children whose empathy for others runs deep and how quickly they learn to take control in even the worst situations. You don't really know what your children are made of until the mommy engine of the family shuts down and they're forced to help out. One night when David is out of town, I have one of these excruciating migraines that my medication can't fade. The pain is intolerable and I can't stop crying. At eleven o'clock, Gigi calls Dr. Piro.

"Bring her to the emergency room at St. John's and I'll meet you there," he tells her.

After Bella gets me dressed and Anwar helps me down the stairs, Gigi drives the four of us to the hospital. My kids wait patiently and don't leave my side. Dr. Piro treats my unexplainable and severe pain syndrome with morphine, which makes it dissipate, and steroids, which reduce the inflammation in my brain. I'm discharged the next morning. This is just one example of how truly amazing my kids are and how they step up in their own authentic ways, tapping into their resourcefulness while bringing such different strengths to the table. I feel so much gratitude for who they are. It's a crazy good feeling beyond anything I've ever felt. They truly are the sweet spot in my life, my sugar.

Soon I have to get back to work on the *Housewives* and I'm still not well, so going to Sponaugle in Florida is really my only chance of possibly putting myself back together. *After all, staring at the ceiling of my bedroom is not getting me anywhere.* I try hard to be practical and talk myself into doing what is right.

Still, the thought of leaving my children and David for six weeks weighs heavily on me. The longest I've been away from Gigi, Bella, and Anwar is a week or two when they went on their summer vacations with their dad. Leaving them is the last thing I want to do right now. I will feel so naked without them, but what other choice do I have at this point? I know that I should be counting my blessings for the options available to me. I call everyone down for a family meeting in the kitchen.

"I hate to leave you," I tell them, my voice shaking as I try not to cry. "But I'm not feeling better yet, and I need to keep searching until I find a cure."

"It's okay, Mommy. We have a lifetime together," Bella says sweetly as she puts her arms around me.

"Don't worry. We're going to be fine," Gigi adds. "We just need you to get better."

"Dr. Sponaugle has cured so many people with Lyme," says Anwar, my little researcher, who's already checked out the Web site. Together we decide that this is the right thing to do for now.

I try not to let the kids see me crack, because I don't want them to take on my stress or worry about this any more than they have to. I want to be tough and give them strength. But the truth is, they give *me* strength. At this moment, when I don't want to leave them, they're *my* driving force, because I can't imagine what their lives would look like without me. *So I better get my ass in gear and keep shooting for the stars until I hit one.*

The good news is that Paige decides to go with me, since several rounds of oral antibiotics have not cured her Lyme, either. My sister-in-law Jaymes, who also has chronic Lyme, is coming, too, but she'll arrive a week after we do. Jaymes was originally infected in 1990 and supposedly treated with a short course of antibiotics. So it's not clear whether her Lyme came back last summer or if she got bit again when she was in Canada. Either way, multiple rounds of antibiotics didn't do anything. At one point, her health failed so much that she could barely work.

Tom sends all my medical files to Dr. Rick Sponaugle, and, next thing I know, Paige and I are curbside at LAX. If it weren't for David's organization, I don't think I would have made it to the airport on time this morning. Traveling with all these medications is a huge undertaking. A lot of them need to stay refrigerated while others need to be frozen, so it's complicated, especially in my mind.

"I don't know how you do it," Paige says when she sees me.

"Do what?" I ask.

"You look like a breath of fresh air in your blue leather jacket, matching blue sunglasses, and royal blue scarf," she says. "No one would know that you have a port in your chest under that ensemble!" She is right. It's day seventy-eight of my antibiotics.

"You don't even look sick!" she adds. We laugh because we know that's the irony of Lyme: you look good on the outside while dying on the inside. That's why they call it an invisible disease. Paige is smiling, but I know her so well and can tell that she is struggling. Frustrated with her memory loss, she keeps repeating herself over and over again. My brain is so shut down that I can't process her story *once,* let alone *three* times.

Four hours into the flight, I'm in a lot of pain. I'm so uncomfortable with nausea, my eyes burn, and I feel as if something is crawling under my skin. My brain feels inflamed and off balance. My tongue is covered in a white layer of yeast, and my gut has become very unhappy with the seventy-eight-day rampage of antibiotics. It almost seems as if the side effects of the medicine are becoming worse than the disease itself. At least it feels like that right now. Flying is just not my friend. I can't wait to land and get to my hotel bed, stretch my aching body, and sleep for a thousand hours. Sleeping has become harder and harder, because even during the night I consciously experience pain. There is no escaping.

Finally, we arrive in Florida and Paige drives our rental car to the hotel, which is near the clinic. Neither of us sleeps well, but we wake up excited about the possibility of healing at Sponaugle. By now, I've tried so many different protocols without success. *I pray that this one is different.* When we arrive, the place is buzzing. The treatment room is filled with at least sixty patients, all with IV drips, and nurses, who are darting around, busily changing needles, drawing blood, and preparing concoctions. Then, I am whisked into an office where I meet my personal nurse, Dennis. Sweet Dennis. He asks me to fill out some paperwork and answer questions about any missing health information that is not in the medical records that Tom sent in advance. Next, I'm brought in to see Dr. Sponaugle. He appears to be a genius whose treatments and ideas are outside the box. During my appointment, I can sense not only his excitement about healing but also his underlying frustration with the world of traditional medicine. His brain goes a million miles an hour, and with my current mental comprehension it's hard for me to follow. Yet he has diagrams on his wall detailing the biochemical reactions of toxins in the gut and the brain. I find his knowledge fascinating and he makes me feel hopeful.

"When you hit most bacteria with antibiotics, they die. But chronic Lyme bacteria are so smart and strong that they create a biofilm around themselves that antibiotics cannot penetrate," he explains. "This is why many people have little improvement from them."

"So what do you do?" I ask.

"To successfully treat Lyme, you need to kill the bacteria *and* biofilm," he says. After eighty days of battling severe toxic reactions, twelve days in the hospital, three trips to the emergency room, and six months of staring at the ceiling, it kind of makes sense. *I'm dealing with a monster, and he is making me see that I'm not just fighting Lyme. There are many more pieces to this healing pie.*

Treatments at Sponaugle include very systematic IV drips, where they rotate "kill drips," which attack the bacteria, and "detox IVs," which pull out the debris of dead bugs. They also do ozone, colonics, and coffee enemas, among many other things, and all of them are carefully thought through and tracked with weekly blood tests. Paige has a severe reaction to one of her first IV kill drips, and I can see the fear in her eyes.

"So how are you liking your first date with Mr. Herxheimer?" I say.

"It's hell," she says.

"You're going to be okay. I promise."

"I trust you," she says.

"Pull up the bootstraps, cowboy!" She smiles back at me weakly. It's interesting that people are starting to look to me for answers and advice about a disease that I'm still trying to figure out: not only my friends, Paige and Jaymes, but also hundreds of people who contact me each week by e-mail, social media, and the Bravo Web site with questions.

Several of my treatments at Sponaugle make me feel worse. But nothing compares with the reactions I battled during the initial days and weeks of antibiotics at home. I'm starting to get educated about many things, and I can tell you that as much as I hate having a tube up my ass, I'm pretty sure that these colonics are one of my lifesavers. I can feel the toxins that have accumulated in my body but I never knew that the only way to detoxify is through sweat, pee, and poo. I never realized that when I stopped exercising, I stopped sweating. I've suffered from chronic constipation since early childhood, so I am just now learning that flushing out this toxic waste is crucial to my healing. I thank God for Bonnie Barrett, who gently teaches me the art of a good and peaceful colonic and the importance of coffee enemas for detoxification purposes to increase bile production and flow. I've never heard of anyone putting coffee up their butt, but I'm open to anything and everything at this point as I slowly learn to surrender. Chiropractic treatments are another important part of the Sponaugle protocol because they believe that a healthy spine helps your immune system.

The treatment days are a full-time job, and I approach them like one. After six- or seven-hour days at the clinic, I go back to the hotel, shower, and crash into bed feeling totally exhausted, only to wake up and start all over again the next day. Though my life might suck right now, I am not complaining. I still have a hundred reasons to be grateful. I talk to my best friend, Ellie, almost every day and her ALS is always a great reminder to count my lucky stars that I am still able to get out of bed.

Paige and I usually order Reuben sandwiches from the deli across the street from the clinic. Strangely, my body is craving sauerkraut. Most of the time, we skip dinner because we're too tired, and sleeping is the fastest way to pass time. It sounds silly but right now I just want time to go as fast as possible so I can get home where I belong.

Paige and I share a room with two queen beds. They give us so many supplements at Sponaugle that our room looks like a vitamin store. It's overwhelming, to say the least. Soon we realize that even though it's off-season, the hotel is getting too expensive for such a long stay and we need a kitchen so that we can cook simple things if we feel like it. Jaymes is also on her way to Sponaugle. Since there will be three of us, we decide to rent a three-bedroom condo. Dr. Sponaugle points out that I have high levels of mold in my body, as do Paige and Jaymes. This is a big problem for people with Lyme because it weakens the immune system. Therefore, any apartment we rent has to be tested for mold before we can move in. This is a challenge given the high humidity in Florida.

I love having Paige and Jaymes with me, but I also feel a great sense of responsibility because they're looking at me for answers that I don't have.

"You're our fearless leader," Paige says. "We've been able to ride on your coattails for the best resources and we will benefit from your strength and dedication. That's why we follow along like ducks in a row."

The most profound, life-altering part of being at Sponaugle has nothing to do with us or our journey. It is meeting other debilitated patients who have been fighting the battle against Lyme disease a lot longer than I have. Before I was diagnosed, I had no idea that this was an epidemic and that more than sixty-three hundred new cases are diagnosed each week: that's more than nine hundred each day and almost forty every hour. *And that's just in the United States. Imagine what this means on a global scale.* And this number includes only the Lyme cases registered by the CDC, not unrecorded, misdiagnosed, or undiagnosed cases, which are believed to be many.

When I first got to Sponaugle, they put me in a private treatment room which is nice and quiet. Although I certainly don't view myself as a celebrity, I start to notice that the *Housewives* show is popular in Florida because everywhere I go people recognize me. It's shocking. When we are at a stoplight, a woman knocks on the passenger window to ask if I'm Yolanda. When we go to the mall for underwear at Victoria's Secret, I somehow end up taking photos with fans. This is all very new to me and not something I am conscious about and I'm certainly not looking too cute today because I wasn't prepared.

"Um, you might start making a little more effort when you go out of the house," Paige says in her sassy voice. "Because looking like this isn't that great for your image, baby." We crack up laughing because I know she is right. We end up leaving the mall without the underwear because it is a little bit overwhelming after being isolated for so long but also kind of strange to be recognized so far away from Beverly Hills.

Monday morning, we're back at the clinic. As I try to make sense of this experience, I want to connect with other Lyme patients and talk, so I decide to wheel my IV pole though the treatment rooms. Name and status do not matter at this point. We're all in this together, away from our friends and families, just trying to survive one day at a time. I'm especially drawn to the teenagers and elderly. They help me put things in perspective: no matter how shitty you feel, there is always someone fighting a worse battle than yours. It gives me a great sense of gratitude.

One day, I walk around the treatment room and am energetically drawn to a teenage boy sitting in a wheelchair. He seems barely coherent and is drooling.

"Hello," I say, smiling as I sit down in the seat next to him. He just stares into my eyes, unable to use his words anymore. I put my hand on his hand for a long time because I want him to know that I understand what he is going through. He looks the way that I often feel. An older woman walks over to us and sits on the other side of the boy. As she gets closer, I see that she is not actually old, just tired.

"Our health insurance covered only thirty days of antibiotics, but my son has been sick for seven years," she tells me, her voice shaking.

"So what did you do?" I ask, touching her shoulder. She looks so fragile and worn down that my heart breaks for her.

"We sold our home and everything we owned to pay for Lyme treatments, and now we live in a motor home," she says. "We've been all over the country. Sponaugle is our last chance to get him well." By the time she is done speaking, I can't hold my emotions back any longer. I think about my own three teenagers and can't imagine what her life is like. My interaction with this family touches my soul deeply. It changes the way I see this journey. I lie awake many nights. *Why did God give me this experience? And what am I going to do with it?*

The next day is rough. I'm emotionally drained and my body feels cold and agitated from all the fluids being pushed through my veins. After several hours of treatment, I walk outdoors with my IV pole just to feel a ray of sunshine on my skin. Standing in the parking lot, I notice a very old-looking motor home in the corner, which stands out because it's really a small lot for cars only. The mother I met the day before comes out of the motor home and holds the door open for a man who's carrying her teenage son in his arms. *Something is wrong with this picture! No one deserves to live like that.*

This is just one example. In six weeks, I meet many patients and their families with similar stories, and almost all of them are financially devastated. They took out bank loans or used retirement savings to pay for treatments. *This is money they worked for their whole lives!* The CDC says that a bull's-eye rash is the sign of Lyme, but most people I met never saw one and *none* of them got cured with twenty-eight days of antibiotics. Some patients say that on their way to determining what was wrong with them, they were often told that their illness was "all in their heads." Because a lot of these patients have gone untreated for so long, many developed other chronic conditions, like arthritis, headaches, encephalitis, painful or tingling neuropathy in their legs or arms, and facial paralysis. This is not surprising since it happens to 60 percent of untreated patients. The number-one complaint of all the people I meet is that living with Lyme is like being lost in a maze of the unknown: once you get in, it's very difficult to get out because it's a silent killer that ruins every aspect of your life. Every time you turn a corner, there's another obstacle. Although organisms other than ticks are believed to cause Lyme, it's insane that, when it comes to ticks, something the size of a poppy seed can devastate one's life. The fact that we can't get the treatment we deserve is even more unbelievable. These thoughts keep me up at night. *I need to figure this out.*

Lyme is a disease without an end goal. It's like shooting blanks into the sky, praying that one will put you into remission. When my mom was diagnosed with breast cancer, it was frightening, and chemo and radiation had awful side effects. However, there was a clear diagnosis, treatment plan, and end goal, and luckily she got her life back. But there is no clear path with Lyme. I'm truly stunned when I learn that the first case was diagnosed in 1972. *It's been forty-five years! How is there still no proper testing available? How is there still no affordable cure?* It's hard to comprehend that we live in such a medically advanced country, yet people are left to struggle with this silent killer on their own. In 1982, the medical community honored Dr. Willy Burgdorfer's discovery of a specific spirochete by naming it after him. This is *Borrelia burgdorferi,* which is probably the same one that has been nibbling on my brain for years. Lyme is six times more prevalent than HIV/AIDS ever was in the early 1980s, but the public awareness about it is virtually nonexistent. *The world has come such a long way in uniting to help combat AIDS, so why haven't we come together for Lyme? Why do I have to go all the way to Florida to get treated for a disease that is so common? This is an absolute crime. People can die of this disease, but you don't hear about it unless you exist in the Lyme community, where people are desperately waiting for answers. And can we trust the information the government is giving us about Lyme? In the 1980s, we were made to believe that HIV/AIDS was a gay disease because that's what the government was telling us. People would cross the street when they saw a gay person because they were afraid they would "catch" HIV/AIDS. How wrong were they then?* The government promotes outdated testing and treatment guidelines and doesn't acknowledge that chronic Lyme exists. As I learn about the injustice of the government's lack of responsibility in this matter, I'm determined to get well and change this. If you dig really deep you can find different studies that prove different theories. We don't really know all the different ways you can contract Lyme. Some say you can only get it from tick bites, yet others say it can also be transferred by mosquitoes. You should definitely be cautious about sleeping with your dog, since they often have ticks. Some even suggest that Lyme can be sexually transmitted.

My body is starting to respond to treatment and Florida is starting to look better to me. After about three weeks here, I have a little bit more energy. I feel well enough to push myself to walk on the beach every night at sunset. This feels like a huge accomplishment. In fact, I become obsessed with it, squeezing out every last drop of my physical energy to stroll on the sand and clear my mind at the end of each day. Sometimes Paige and Jaymes walk with me depending on how they feel. One night, there is a huge thunderstorm, the kind where the rain comes down in sheets. The girls don't want to walk; they'd rather stay safe and dry in the apartment. But I don't care about the rain; in fact, I get a big, black garbage bag, cut a hole in the top, and slip it over my head. The beach is empty and I'm the only crazy person out here.

As I walk barefoot on the wet sand, the rain whips against my face. It's harsh, but I almost like the pain of it. *I'm alive.* I feel so close to God and connected to Mother Earth. I imagine that my soles on the seashore are filling my body with the ions and earth energy that I need so much and that the rain is washing away all the disease. *Maybe the higher purpose of my journey is to bring awareness. I can use my platform to speak for Lyme sufferers who are too debilitated to speak for themselves. I truly believe that God often uses our deepest pain as the launching pad of our greatest calling. Perhaps this is mine. The scope of this disease is enormous. So many people struggle as much as I do or even more than I do, often with far fewer resources and much less support. I have to create awareness that helps develop better diagnostics and treatment.*

Once I come to this very clear realization, I begin to share more and more of my journey on Instagram, Facebook, and Twitter. I post unretouched photographs of myself doing both mainstream and alternative treatments. These are pictures of my daily life and journey, the good and bad. I do this to bring attention not to myself but to a disease that desperately needs it. Some insensitive folks say that I'm sharing this information to get pity. If they only knew what my life was *really* like or walked in my shoes for one day, they would be ashamed of themselves. I know they respond out of ignorance; after all, how can I expect *them* to understand a disease that *I* don't fully understand? Yet I don't care what people think. My motivation is pure. I just want to figure out a way to make a change for the chronically ill. We may have lost our lives but we are still alive.

David isn't able to visit me during the six weeks I spend in Florida. However, he wants me to meet him at Celebrity Fight Night, a charity event in Phoenix with Muhammed Ali where David is the musical director. It is a regular on our annual calendar. Although I'm starting to feel better, I use the word "better" loosely, *very* loosely, and I'm not in any condition to travel or stroll down a red carpet. But it's important to David, and I see it as part of my duty as his wife. Truthfully, I'm starting to feel that David is becoming unhappy with the fact that I can't be by his side the way I used to be. I try to make light of it and joke with him that he married a lemon. It's sad but true. I went from being the funny girlfriend who was up for anything and had endless energy to the wife who is too sick to be by his side. He lost his wingman, his partner in crime, and I feel as if he's starting to get impatient with my recovery. I understand that even brief periods of illness can strain important relationships in your life. A chronic condition like mine, one that has consumed years of our lives, poses enormous challenges.

I always say, "You don't get it until you get it." So maybe I can't expect David to understand what I'm going through. Especially when, with a little makeup, I look normal. I know he does the best he can. Although the truth is this: he has a front-row seat to my everyday struggles. He was right by my side when I crashed to the floor in the gym in 2011, he knows I got in a car accident because I had lost all depth perception, and he saw me go from a social butterfly to a recluse. He was the one who took my blood pressure every day and recorded my unexplainably slow and speeding heartbeats. He witnessed the severe muscle cramps in my fingers and toes and picked me up off the bathroom floor when I fainted. He saw that I lost the ability to tolerate noisy places and that I could no longer write or speak eloquently on command. The list goes on and on, but all this doesn't matter in this moment. There is no need to even talk about the frustration that comes with it all because there is no right or wrong. The only thing that matters now is that I stay centered within myself, focused on my recovery one day at a time.

Dr. Sponaugle doesn't think flying to Phoenix is a good idea but I want to keep my commitment to David. I leave the clinic not feeling well, throwing up, and white as a ghost but somehow make my way to Arizona. Once I get to the hotel, I'm thrilled to see David as well as Gigi and Anwar, who surprise me. The kids and I stay in the hotel bed and snuggle all day while David is in rehearsals. Getting ready for the event is a challenge. My body feels weak, and I haven't dressed in anything except sweatpants and pajamas for months. Makeup is not part of my daily routine anymore. When we arrive on the red carpet, I *look* good but don't *feel* good. I put a smile on my face, yet I feel shaky and unwell. The crowds of people, the flashing cameras, the giant spotlights, and the noise are overwhelming, so I hold tightly to David as we move through the press line. *This is difficult and I'm not really sure why I'm here.* Yet there is one true highlight. At the end of the red carpet, I see a young girl waving to me, and I'm told that she's been waiting to meet me. When I approach her, I notice a port in her chest right above the neckline of her dress. I instantly know that she is a chronic Lyme sufferer, too. I open my arms, and she gives me the biggest, tightest hug as we both tear up. We have an unspoken understanding.

"My parents didn't know what was wrong with me, and doctors said I was fine and needed to see a shrink," she says, barely getting the words out.

"But because of your story on *The Real Housewives,* we figured it out," she adds. "Finally, I got the proper diagnosis. I'm on a new protocol and starting to feel better." Meeting this beautiful angel is a profound and powerful moment and makes my cross-country trip worthwhile. It confirms, once again, why my recent epiphany about sharing my story is strong and right on. Helping others—even just one person at a time—is the higher purpose of my journey.

Fight Night is a success by all accounts: David does a great job, and I love and admire Muhammad Ali and his wife, Lonnie, for their dedication to Parkinson's disease. But I'm in no state to be sitting at a very loud event. I'm so disconnected from the world around me that I honestly do not care who is performing or what is going on in this big ballroom. Sitting here feeling out of place just reminds me how inadequate I feel because I've lost my social skills. It's hard for me to make small talk and hold a conversation. Thank God I have Gigi and Anwar on either side of me to keep my energy grounded while I fake my way through the night, pretending I'm fine. I smile and am polite to all the people who know me socially but don't know me well enough to know what is *really* going on in my life.

On Sunday, I make my way back to Florida so I can wake up in time for my eight o'clock treatment at the clinic Monday morning. The trip definitely sets me back. Flying isn't my friend. It always causes inflammation in my brain, which diminishes my eyesight and gives me an overall feeling of being unwell that adds to my daily soup of symptoms. That said, I'm happy to return to an environment I've learned to accept and to be back with Jaymes, Paige, Dr. Sponaugle, and all the familiar faces at the clinic. My weekly labs show that I'm making progress which really motivates me to work hard. I continue my nightly routine of beach walks and I focus on building stamina.

The highlight of my week is knowing that Anwar, who is in middle school, is coming to visit me for his spring break. This boy is the sugar in my life, and I can't tell you how excited I am to have him by my side for seven days. Just watching him sleep makes me happy. Anwar has always been extremely mature for his age. He's an old soul who intuitively understands things on a whole different level. He doesn't love school, but if a subject—academic or otherwise—sparks his interest, he is incredibly adept and smart about researching every fact and detail you might ever need to know about it. Anwar is the youngest in my camp of friends and family supporting me, yet he probably knows the most.

For years, he's had chronic sinus infections, exhaustion, and joint pain so bad at times that he'd cry in the middle of the night. When I mentioned it to the pediatrician, he attributed Anwar's joint issues to growing pains and said that Anwar was going to be very tall. So I would massage his knees, ankles, and hips with Traumeel, a cream that contains arnica, a homeopathic remedy for inflammation, but nothing really helped or relieved his pain. When I told the doctor that Anwar was always tired, sometimes too tired to play sports, he said it was a normal part of adolescence. For his chronic sinus issues, we saw one of the best ENT doctors in L.A. But the answer, after thorough exams and testing, was always a prescription for antibiotics and medications that would treat Anwar's symptoms without finding the underlying cause. Some doctors would blame it on allergies even though the results of his tests came back all within normal range. What I didn't know back then was that the normal range for one person isn't necessarily the normal range for another. In the past, I blindly trusted and never doubted what the doctors said, especially if it sounded logical.

But in the past couple of years that has proven me wrong. I am also learning that I really appreciate when a doctor walks the middle line, meaning he or she is educated in Western medicine yet acknowledges and is respectful of the power of the holistic world and vice versa.

Before Anwar arrives, I discuss his health challenges with Dr. Sponaugle. I have this strange feeling that there might be more to his story. *Maybe Anwar's joint pain isn't growing pains, maybe the extreme exhaustion isn't teenage fatigue, and maybe his sinus problems aren't allergy related. My intuition led both my best friend and sister-in-law to their diagnoses, but I never thought about Anwar having Lyme. I guess because he's a young, growing child. Yet the more I think about it, the more sense it makes. Especially since 25 percent of Lyme cases are children.* Anwar is in the clinic with me every day keeping me company, so I ask Dr. Sponaugle to examine him and draw his blood to have it sent to labs all over the country for extensive testing. I am determined to get to the bottom of his health issues and find the real cause of his symptoms.

At the end of the week, I sadly have to drop him off at the airport for his flight back to Los Angeles. I'm grateful for our time together, and his spirit motivates me to get through the remaining weeks of treatment before I meet his sisters in New York. There, I'm to receive the Starlight Award, for bringing awareness to Lyme disease, at the Lyme Research Alliance gala. This event is quickly approaching, and I need to write an acceptance speech. The old me could do this in thirty minutes. But it takes the new brain-fogged Yolanda at least a whole week to write something substantial. Typing a line or two on Instagram is the most writing I can do—and even that can take me hours. But I'm honored to be given this award and so I am determined to put my story on paper, no matter how long it takes.

At the end of my six-week stay, they retest me for Lyme using the ELISA, the Western blot, and the Fry, which isn't commonly used in the United States. After all the treatments I have done, the Lyme spirochetes have come out of hiding and back into my bloodstream—because all my lab results are now positive for Lyme. This may sound obvious since I *know* that I have

Lyme, but I share this with you because five months earlier, when I was hospitalized at Cedars-Sinai, two of these *same tests* came back negative. This is common if you haven't had the infection long enough for your body to develop antibodies that will appear on the test or you've had the infection *too* long, as I had, so it's traveled from your bloodstream to an organ. The ELISA test detects only 50 to 65 percent of Lyme cases! You can also get a negative result if you were infected with a strain of Lyme or co-infections that the CDC-approved Lyme tests can't detect. This can easily happen, since there are more than one hundred strains of the Lyme spirochetes in the United States and over three hundred strains worldwide.

When I leave Sponaugle, I feel better. I am walking every night and a lot of my symptoms are less severe. I definitely have a lot more energy and am not in bed all day, every day. This small improvement feels like an enormous victory. Dr. Sponaugle opened my eyes to many different things. His seminars were helpful and educated me on the complexities of this multifaceted disease. It's more clear now that I am not only fighting Lyme but also the co-infections—parasites, viral and bacterial infections, mold exposure, and heavy metals—and most likely a long road of healing in front of me.

The Lyme Research Alliance gala is in Greenwich, Connecticut, and I fly from Florida to New York City. I meet Gigi and Bella at the hotel, and it is wonderful to catch up with my girls. David isn't able to attend this important event, but I'm super grateful to have my angels by my side as well as Tom and Marc. As an honoree, I'm invited to sit in on the Lyme conference that is held earlier in the day of the gala. I am very excited to hear a group of leading scientists discuss their latest discoveries about Lyme, and it's one of the most fascinating afternoons of my life. One top expert from Germany shares her research on neurological Lyme and its similarities to neurosyphilis, an infection of the brain or spinal cord. She shows images of her discovery on a big screen. One is the skull of a person who died from Lyme. During his autopsy, they found that spirochetes literally bored through the bone. *This proves my point! This is exactly what I've been saying for two years, and nobody believed me! I must have said* the following a hundred times: "I have an infection in my brain," "Something is growing in my brain," and "I feel like something is eating my brain." How else could I have said this? How? And still no one understood me. The images on the doctor's screen are clear evidence. The minute that the presentation is over, I run outside to call David.

"I just saw scientific proof of what I've been trying to say for years, about my brain," I tell him. "It validates that I was one hundred percent right." He's happy for me, but I don't think he really understands how powerful this moment is for me. I rush back to the hotel room to tell my girls. They think it's very interesting, but they can't truly comprehend its significance either. I can't blame them. It's all part of "You don't get it until you get it."

Despite my excitement about this discovery, it's time to get ready for the gala and focus on my acceptance speech. It will be on the teleprompter, yet I'm very nervous because my world has become so small and I haven't interacted with many people in a long time. When I step up to the podium, I feel shaky in my high heels and uncomfortable in my somewhat tight dress. I try to pull myself together and my speech goes well, but I realize that my emotions are raw from living this journey and I choke up a bit from sharing something so personal with a roomful of mostly strangers. I am happy to have my girls there to see me back on my feet as we are learning to make sense of the uncertainty we have faced as a family. At the end of this informative and heartfelt night, a teenage girl and her mother walk up to me. The girl has tears in her eyes and hugs me like she's never going to let go.

"My name is Lauren," she says. I keep my arm around her.

"The only reason that my daughter was finally diagnosed with Lyme is because you shared your story on the show," her mother says. "We flew our whole family in from Canada to hear you speak and learn more about the Lyme research."

"For years, my dad told me that my symptoms were all in my head, and so did my doctors," Lauren says. "Actually, it wasn't until my dad heard you speak that he believed me." Perhaps having a stranger describe the same exact symptoms and invisible disabilities his daughter complained about made him finally realize how wrong he had been.

"He was so emotional after your speech tonight that he went outside for a breath of fresh air," her mother says. "Thank you." By now, I've heard stories like this a hundred times and met so many children who say that the worst part of their Lyme battle is being doubted by their parents. This is really sad to me because what child *wants* to be sick? No child *chooses* to stay home for long periods of time and miss out on being with friends. Yes, once in a while a child might need a day to stay in bed and watch mindless TV, but the symptoms of Lyme are real and unfakeable, and I'm not sure if that's even a word!

Meetings of this kind are very meaningful as they remind me why I put myself out there to be judged and ridiculed by those who are uneducated. The next day, the girls and I fly back to L.A. I stare out the window at the beautiful clouds with a great sense of completion. I shared my story with the world in a way that was open and honest. I pray that it brought awareness to this disease and inspired others to take the baton to share their journeys so that the story stays alive until a cure is found. *Lyme deserves and needs awareness, but I did my part and now I need to get on with my life.*

Chapter Five

....

YOU MAY SEE ME STRUGGLE,
BUT YOU WILL NEVER SEE ME QUIT.

Coming home after so many weeks away, I have a totally new appreciation for my life. The beauty of our Malibu home is breathtaking, and seeing David, Anwar, and my puppy, Lucky, warms my heart. My attitude is positive, and I'm excited to get back to all the things I love doing. I have a life to live. I am planning on going to Bella's and Gigi's horse shows and Anwar's football game this week. Right away, I get into a walking routine and stick to the protocol I was sent home with. I am okay for a couple of weeks but as soon as I start getting back into the swing of my old life, my symptoms slowly kick back in. After spending the day at the girls' horse show one Saturday, I get home feeling achy and fatigued, and my chronic cough comes back. The next morning, I wake up with rings under my eyes again, which I have learned is a measure of inflammation in my brain. I'm so exhausted that even after nine hours of sleep, it still feels as if the earth is pulling me down by my feet. I don't really know how to describe this severe exhaustion in any other way.

Still, I try to go through the motions of a "normal" life. One night David tells me that we have dinner plans with some important businesspeople. Although it takes all I have to get dressed, I force myself to pull it together and look presentable. Within ten minutes of arriving at the restaurant, the sound of people talking, silverware clinking against plates, and background music immediately shuts down my brain. I can't focus. David and the other couples make small talk, but I can't follow the conversation or speak. David is confused and gives me a look that says, "What's wrong with you?" *I don't know!* But there is nothing I can do about it. The only thing I'm craving is complete silence. *I've gone from being a social butterfly to being trapped in a mentally paralyzing cocoon.* This is a totally devastating moment because I realize that the life I *thought* I gained back is still unattainable. I felt much better in Florida because I was in treatment six days a week with no TV, no music, no stress, no social calendar, no wife duties, and no mommy duties. I want nothing more than to get back into my life, but I just don't have the fuel to do so.

I also feel the yin and yang of my marriage starting to shift; the balance is off. I don't like it, but I can't change it. We used to love listening to music in our house and in the car, but now it's just irritating noise to me. Obviously, this is very difficult since David's job is *all about* music. I used to enjoy the flow of artists, musicians, and managers coming in and out of David's downstairs studio all day. I actually designed and built that studio myself. But now all this action is just chaos and noise that my brain can't handle. At night, I just want to snuggle up with David and talk to connect. But he likes to unwind from a long day of work by watching TV before he goes to sleep. That all used to work, but now the lights and sounds overstimulate me and make me anxious, sending my nervous system into overdrive. Still, I want to be a good wife and don't really believe in sleeping apart, so I cover my eyes with a sleep mask and use earplugs and David uses the wireless headphones that I got him. Some nights David doesn't come to bed until one or two because he's busy working in the studio. Yet my mom always told me that the sleep you get before midnight is the most important, especially when healing. It's hard to find balance right now.

At the end of March, the final episode of my first season on the *Housewives* airs. The last episode has a little write-up about each of the women. It explains where her life is or what has happened to her in the months since filming wrapped. My write-up says, "Yolanda is receiving treatment and getting stronger after being diagnosed with Lyme disease." I really wish the "getting stronger" part was true because I am not feeling it right now. Even after months of treatment, I'm definitely not cured. Instead, I'm just trying desperately to hang on. *I lost my life.* This reminds me of a day back in 2010 when David wasn't feeling well and I took him to see Dr. Harris. As we walked into the office, we bumped into a famous actor. I don't remember his name, but David knew him.

"Hi. How are you?" David asked.

"Miserable. Absolutely miserable," the actor said. "I have Lyme disease and lost my life." At that time, I did not understand the meaning of his words. Unfortunately, I do today.

Even more upsetting is this: I find out that Anwar tested positive for Lyme. When I see the pictures of the spirochetes on his Fry Labs results, my anxiety goes from one to a hundred in mere seconds. *My baby! How could this be possible?* A wave of helplessness washes over me. I am totally panic-stricken. *How can I cure Anwar if I can't cure myself?* Once I get over the initial shock, I settle my thoughts and take control of the situation in good Capricorn fashion.

"We finally found the reason for your symptoms," I tell Anwar. He doesn't seem to be shocked but is interested in how we're going to treat it. "I don't want to do antibiotics," he says. "Let's go the holistic route." I go from feeling scared to being enraged by the fact that there is no cure. Yet I feel strangely empowered not only for my son but also for the countless children and teenagers I've met on my journey. The fire roars inside me, and my momma-bear powers ignite. There have been times when I thought I couldn't handle another day of being sick, but this puts everything in a whole new perspective. *Shame on me for ever thinking that way! I need to keep blazing this trail until a cure is found, an affordable cure for ALL!*

In late April, I decide to get my port removed after having it for five months. Many people have ports for years, but it feels really unnatural to have this foreign object hanging out of my chest, and it feels like the site is a bit infected, as it has been red and itchy lately. Intuitively, I have to get it out. Maybe it will make me feel like I have accomplished *something*. I view it as the start of a new chapter. I've missed taking bubbly baths, which have always been a ritual for me, a way to relax and get centered after a long day, so I'm dying to have a long bubbly bath and soak until my fingers are wrinkled like prunes.

The morning of the procedure, Gigi is in the kitchen and I'm getting ready to leave for the hospital.

"You must be nervous, Mommy," she says.

"Why do you say that?" I ask.

"Because you always wear your clogs when you're nervous," she replies. I guess no matter how much you try to put on a brave face for your children, they know you inside and out. And she is right. I've had the same little Dutch clogs for twenty-five years and rarely wear them for fear of running into the fashion police, who seem to be everywhere in L.A. Somehow they give me a safe feeling and a sense of grounding, and to be honest they're comfortable like no other pair of shoes I own.

"Don't forget we're starting the master cleanse, okay?" Gigi says. "I'll squeeze the lemons." I can't really think about a cleanse at this moment, but I smile at her.

"Of course, my love," I respond, not so sure. Gigi has seen me do this cleanse many times in her life, and recently it started to spark her interest. The master cleanse entails eating no solid food and drinking a tonic made of lemon juice, cayenne pepper, maple syrup, and spring water in order to cleanse. It reboots your metabolism and energizes your body, mind, and spirit. For me, it's like practicing discipline. It's not intended for losing weight, but you do shed a few pounds, which I believe is mainly inflammation. The first time I did it, in my early twenties, I was so inspired by how healthy and renewed I felt that I continued to do it religiously every year. My enthusiasm for the master cleanse has been so contagious and at one point our entire household was on it, including Alberto and Blanca. I promised Gigi I'd do it with her before she shoots her upcoming Guess campaign. The interesting thing about being a chronically ill mother is that no matter what your struggles are, your mommy duties never stop. So even though

I'm having surgery, I will keep my promise to Gigi and start the cleanse today.

My next season of the *Housewives* is filming, and the producers are following me to the hospital. I'm so nervous that I barely notice the film crew. David and I arrive and meet Dr. Piro in the pre-op room.

"It's graduation day! We're taking the port out," he says. "The disease is under control, but it's gonna take a long time to recover from the psychological damage that this did because it takes a piece of you." *How is he making those assumptions?*

"I feel like I'm getting into better times," I say.

"Think of this like the beginning of the next phase to help recover from all that," Dr. Piro says. I turn my focus inward. *Is this the end of my journey? Is he right?* Instantly, I start to cry.

"I feel like I've lost my balls, you know?" I tell David. I feel scared and somewhat defeated. Even though I always keep up a good front, if I'm really honest with myself, I know that my body is giving me very different signals from what my mind is trying and wants to believe. Deep inside, I can feel that this isn't an ending at all. *More than anyone in the world, I'm desperate for my health journey to wrap up right here, right now, but my body feels like a toxic waste dump.* Other Lyme patients have told me that their doctors made similar comments; even the most brilliant doctors are not educated on this disease. This is exactly why I feel compelled to write this book.

May 16, 2013
Difficult does not mean impossible,
it just means you have to work harder!
#determinedtokicklymesass

The last season of the *Housewives* ended with my realizing there was something wrong with my brain function after a dramatic fight. So

I can't say that I'm excited to start filming again. It's overwhelming to think about working on the show while my recovery is still my full-time job. However, quitting isn't an option because I am under contract, I need to honor my commitment and this job is my financial independence. These things, along with adrenaline, help me force myself to go to work and get me through the two-, three-, or four-hour shoots. I am also grateful for all the amazing things in my life. And by now my illness has been going on for so long that the ending must be right around the corner. *I mean, who in the world gets sick for years? I've never heard anything so crazy.*

I recently learned about the spoon theory, a metaphor to help those who are chronically ill conserve their energy and use it wisely. You have a certain number of spoons each day, and when you use them up, you're done. You can't add more. The metaphor offers a way to accept, understand, and avoid feeling inadequate about your limitations while you fight to recover. So I use this metaphor to navigate filming, very consciously and carefully managing my spoons and don't do anything else but film the show during this time. If I film in the afternoon or the evening, I stay in bed all morning. If I film in the morning, I stay in bed all afternoon and night. *God, I am so glad someone thought of this spoon thing. It's so simple but so helpful.*

One time, the cast and I are doing a magazine shoot at Kyle Richards's house. I haven't driven a car since my accident, so thank God Alberto can take me. I'm having a really bad day with that earth-pulling exhaustion, where I can't even put one foot in front of the other. Rather than go into Kyle's house, where all the girls are doing hair and makeup, I choose to lie down in the backseat of the car to conserve my energy until they're ready for me on set. *This is the only way I can make it through.* It's strange to me, because if someone was sitting in *my* driveway and not feeling well, I would go out and say, "How are you? Why don't you come into the house, take the guest room, and relax until we start?" But Brandi Glanville is the only castmate who comes outside to see me. Nobody else goes near my car, not even to offer a glass of water.

Although I try not to be, I'm hurt by the lack of simple things like this from women who are supposed to be my friends. Lisa Vanderpump *says* she is my friend, but she seems to only be my friend more when the cameras are rolling and not when they aren't. I have been in and out of hospitals and clinics in the previous year and a half, trying to find a cure for a disease that has been incredibly debilitating. I understand that my sensitivity is heightened because I've been sitting on the sidelines and not at my best, but Lisa visited me only once during this time period. She says it is because she's overwhelmed with her workload. But it's interesting to see that, as busy as she is, she found a way to show up in the middle of the day to see David get his star on the Hollywood Walk of Fame a few weeks earlier. This is when I realized she is a different kind of friend, a Hollywood friend.

Without cameras rolling, I clearly feel the lack of compassion of this group of women. They are my coworkers on a reality TV show, which, although it may seem more glamorous and interesting, is no different from a job at a bank. There, you see your coworkers during business hours and maybe have a coffee with them once in a while, but you don't share your private life with any of them. This is how it is with the women on the show. I don't view them as close friends because I'm not intimate with them in any aspect of my life. I don't really trust them with my heart because sometimes they become so volatile that I am afraid that anything I share with them can potentially end up on national TV, so I have my guard up. I have my real life with real friends and my show life with show friends. It's a strange way to live, but this lack of authentic intimacy seems to be normal in this environment. To be honest, I haven't really been able to fully participate so I try to go with the flow. The times that I have to attend all-cast events during this season are the toughest for me. The noise and stimulation are hard on my brain. This is why I choose to live in a quiet cocoon isolated from the outside world, which is the exact opposite of what is required of me as a housewife. I am supposed to be this glamorous woman who lives a fun and exciting life, yet

I can barely get dressed and deal with whatever drama is brewing in the moment.

My word retrieval is so slow that, even though I attempt to participate in conversations, I'm better off just staying out of the fray. Brandi is for sure the craziest cast member, but she also has the most compassionate heart in the group and is sensitive to my struggles. With the little energy that I have, it becomes harder and harder to listen to the women fight over mostly unimportant things, so I learn to let things roll off my back. I become more timid as time passes. *Who am I? Will I ever be normal again?* I can't help struggling with these question as long as the answers seem to be unknown. As crazy as it all feels at times, I never lose my laser-beam focus: my quest to find a cure for Lyme never leaves my mind. It's sad to learn as time goes by how many people suffer from invisible chronic disease, but it's also good to know that I'm not alone in this journey.

Fan mail starts pouring in, and I get lots of messages on social media from suffering and debilitated Lyme patients. The hard part is that they're looking to me for answers that I don't have. I share how I feel on social media, but I am afraid to discuss my treatments because I don't want people to waste their money on the crazy expensive things that I have tried without success. Several celebrities who are battling Lyme reach out to me through David, and it's fascinating to learn how many suffer in silence. This reminds me of a very famous person I met along the way, who told me that if she talked about her Lyme publicly, it would ruin her image and the sales of her beauty products. It left me stunned and speechless, because a thought like that never crossed my mind. *Wouldn't this just make her more human?* I don't know, and I guess it's best not to hold any judgment around this for everyone should do what feels authentic to them. I just feel that the more people who speak up, the faster a shift will come about. Regarding my own path, I feel spiritually enlightened. God gave me this life because I'm strong enough to live it, and I'm determined to turn my mess into a message.

Some people question how I could be sick when I "look so good." At one *Housewives* party, one of the women asks me how I feel.

"Not so great," I say. "I'm just trying to keep it together."

"But you look pretty, so it doesn't matter how you feel," Kyle says. I know she is joking because she says it with a smile, but the words ring true. That's the frustrating part of any invisible disease: how you *look* has absolutely nothing to do with how you *feel*. Lyme patients can be in treatment for years and still look quite normal. One day, a castmate questions how I can run through Beverly Hills for an on-camera scavenger hunt if I'm actually sick. Here's how: I spend 45 minutes to create a 10-minute scene because it's part of my job. I am disciplined and learn to push within my limitations. I now realize that most people have no clue about what it takes—how much energy and effort—to do things that look so simple and easy on camera and that *most* can do without blinking an eye. Resting for a *week* to film for a *few hours* and having to recover afterward is my new normal, and, although it's hard, I have to accept it. When it comes to parties this season, I am always the first person to go home, and I get a lot of flak about it from the other women. It's probably hard to understand that once I leave those parties, my nervous system is so amped up that I curl into a ball in the backseat of the limo, sweating with tremors and severe exhaustion. Nobody knows that I'm hanging on by a thread and just trying to keep it all together. You can't really understand unless you live it.

July 6, 2013
Praying for the one and only important thing in life.
#Health

In the middle of filming the show, it's time for Gigi to leave for New York to start college and her career as a model. She's always been extremely driven and is excited to take on both tasks. It's crazy how eighteen years with your child goes by so fast. I'm going to miss her desperately. It's going to be hard not to see her smile every morning at breakfast and have her energy in the house. She's such a bright light, loving, fun, and motivating for all of us, as she always goes after what she wants. It isn't the first time that we'll be apart, but this time it's for real. On the other hand, I'm excited because Gigi is the first person in my family to go to college, and I like the idea of her getting a degree. I was blessed with the opportunity to model, travel the world, and make a lot of money at a young age, but I never found my way back to college. I also feel confident that I've given Gigi the tools and foundation to make a life for herself.

"I know you're going to take New York by storm and hit the ground running," I tell her while we pack her room in Malibu.

August 11, 2013
Treasuring every moment I can
with my @gigihadid in NYC.
#nextchapter #baby1off2college.

A week later, I fly with Gigi to New York to help her move into and furnish the apartment we found online. I spent plenty of time thinking carefully about how to best manage and use my energy, because setting up her new home is a huge task. I ordered the furniture from various Web sites and had all her linens purchased, washed, ironed, and shipped to New York before we left. Tom ordered all the cleaning supplies and groceries. Although this living situation is clearly the right choice for Gigi, it's hard on my relationship with David. He thinks she should experience dorm life and that I'm spoiling her by getting her an apartment. But Gigi is going to be working and starting a serious modeling career. She needs to be in a place where people wake up at six in the morning for work, not in a dorm where teenagers could be partying all night. Maybe I'm not familiar or comfortable with dorm living because I didn't go to college, but I still want Gigi to be in a secure building with a doorman so I don't have to worry about her. I worked in New York when I was her age and saw too many models get into dangerous situations because they lived in unsafe places. To me, the extra cost of a doorman building buys me peace of mind. Perhaps it sounds extravagant but Gigi has always been very frugal; she doesn't care much for clothes or fancy items, probably because she spent the first eighteen years of her life in the barn and on the volleyball court.

I am carving out a little space in the big melting pot that she can call home, a grounding pad so she can focus all her energy on becoming a financially independent young woman while getting her education. Even though Mohamed lives a big and fancy lifestyle, that does not define our children. I purposely raised them away from Hollywood in a far more realistic lifestyle that feels authentic to me. It was important to me that they went to public school, where we became part of a wonderful and normal community. I always made them aware that their dad's money wasn't their money and that if there is anything about that lifestyle they desire, they must work for it. I'm always shocked by the attitude of entitlement that you often see in children from wealthy families. Gigi, Bella, and Anwar are very well aware that they have to make their own money starting at the age of eighteen and learn to survive on their own by the time they turn twenty-one. The training wheels are off by then, which I consider an extraordinary blessing considering that Mohamed and I both came from very humble beginnings.

I feel really sick as I move Gigi to New York and don't have much energy, yet I push through to fulfill my obligation as a mother. I schlep from Bed, Bath & Beyond to the Container Store, move furniture, and hang paintings. Finally, she's settled in and the time has come to say good-bye. I wish I could stay for six months, because leaving Gigi is a lot more difficult than I ever imagined. Well, I guess I don't really know what I imagined, but I do know that even though millions of moms send their children to college each year, it's still not easy when it's *your* child—especially the first one leaving the nest. An hour or so before I leave for the airport, Gigi and I are snuggled up on her bed talking about last-minute stuff.

"I should have written a manual, like a checklist of all the things I need to talk to you about before you start college," I say.

"What?" Gigi asks, laughing.

"I have about a thousand things in my head right now that I still want to tell you," I say. I feel the tears in the corners of my eyes.

"Like what?" she says. I pause to think.

"Well, did you know that you should save your receipts when you get your hair and makeup done because it is tax-deductible?" This is the first silly thought in my head, and it sounds funny, not deep like the kinds of things you'd imagine you would talk to your child about before she leaves home. But that's it: the things I want to discuss are all over the place from serious to simple.

"Yes, Mom. I know," Gigi says. "I already made a folder for that." *Of course she has! What am I thinking?* I need to relax, because there is no reason to doubt Gigi, a perfectionist who is always on top of her game and certainly a lot smarter than I was at eighteen.

"And Mom, if you want to tell me something, there's the phone and FaceTime and we can text," Gigi says with a touch of sarcasm in her voice. "I'm not dying; I'm going to college. I promise you I will be fine."

"I know you will be," I say. When I was young and modeling far from home, I had to go to the bank and get a roll of quarters to call my mom in Holland from the pay phone on the street. There were no cell phones or any of that sort of technology, so my momma couldn't reach me even if she wanted to. I feel confident that I have given Gigi the tools to survive in this world. Leaving home is part of growing up, and I know my angel is definitely ready to spread her wings and fly.

September 27, 2013
Unfortunately not a very glamorous cover
but a story that must be told for those who can't be heard.

My life back in L.A. continues to be on the sidelines, solely focused on my recovery and trying to crack this code. *Why is this so hard?* I often ask myself. I speak to numerous Lyme patients from all over the world to continue to educate myself and share information. From talking to Avril Lavigne, who can barely get out of her bed in Canada, to fans who write me from the Australian Outback, I know that we *all* ask ourselves that same question: *WHY is there no cure?* I often feel defeated, but every day I find a way to hold a space for gratitude, because I do know I'm lucky even though I'm wrestling these terrible circumstances. One day Avril stops by my house with her mom for a cup of tea. Her light sensitivity from Lyme is so severe that she can't even take her sunglasses off when we are sitting in the living room, even though my blinds are closed! Avril's mother has been taking care of her, and I can see the fear in her eyes. I feel so much compassion because there's nothing more devastating for a mother than not being able to fix your child. But we nurture and support because that's what we do for our children.

It's a tough first quarter for Gigi in New York. She is juggling work, school, dating, and a first heartbreak. I've spent most of my days in bed since she's left, so I've been unable to visit her. Although we connect several times a day by text and FaceTime, it isn't the same, and I can feel the sadness in her voice. One day when we FaceTime, it's the middle of a dark and extremely cold winter day in New York City, and Gigi is not herself. She's crying over little things that usually would not bother her, and even though she has a fever and has been ill with what I think is a flu and exhaustion, something doesn't feel right. I call Marc.

"What's the best holistic clinic in Gigi's neighborhood?" I ask him.

"I don't know anyone down there, but the most amazing guy is on Fifty-fourth Street," Marc says. "I'll find out if he can see her."

"Okay, thanks. Then please text me the address," I say.

"My long-distance pharmacy is running out of ideas, my love, so I need you to get in a cab uptown and go get checked out," I tell Gigi. She sees Dr. Lee, a Chinese doctor, for acupuncture and special herbs, which clear up her flu but not her exhaustion. Somehow she is not jumping back into life like she usually does, so my mommy intuition tells me that she really needs me right now. I go to sleep worried and wake up the next morning with my mind set. I impulsively ask Paige to book me a flight to New York for that afternoon. I spend most of my time here resting in Gigi's bed, but at least we're together. Although she didn't ask me to come, since she knows that traveling is difficult for me and doesn't want to bother me, she is happy and grateful that I'm here. David feels otherwise.

In fact, this is one of the biggest blowups we've had. He's furious that I have come to New York two days before our wedding anniversary. But I am in survival mode right now and doing my duty as a mother, caring for the child I put on this planet, so it's hard to understand what is going on with David. The disconnect hurts and is very confusing to me. However, when my child needs me, *nothing* else in the world matters. I am running on empty and just trying to feel the best that I can.

David is not communicating well and gives me the silent treatment for several days. He actually comes to New York for work while I'm here, but he ignores my texts. Having someone disconnect from me in a relationship is the worst feeling, which is clearly a leftover from the abandonment I felt from my father's sudden death. On the plane home from New York, I feel not only physically ill but also emotionally sick because of the unnecessary stress from my marriage. Something has to shift. Although I lost the ability to let my words flow freely over the last two years, writing is my only outlet, so I attempt to put my thoughts to him on paper. After all, who am I going to talk to? I'm not ready to admit that my marriage is not what we hoped it would be. I love this man, but I can't express myself to him, and he is shaking my world right now. It's truly been a rough road for both of us. I know I am not what I used to be.

My Love,

You pulled away the only lifeline I had which was YOU! I counted on you because you promised me you would be there for me. I begged you to please never abandon me again and not only did you do it, you did it at the worst time in my life.

I honestly will never, ever understand what I did to you to deserve this. I have not been the greatest wife due to my illness and the inability to keep up with your busy schedule. But I never stopped caring for you the way you deserve to be taken care of. You still had a loving home. You will never understand the true meaning of these words unless life brings you to your knees one day. If you could spend one day in my brain or my shoes, I'm not sure what you would do.

So I apologize if I wasn't focused on where you thought my focus should have been. But trust me, I am just trying to endure the punches life is throwing at me, every single day, day after day for the past 400–500 days of my life while keeping you all happy and taken care of.

I have nothing left to give. All there is left is to make it out of bed in the morning, love those close to me, and find a cure for this disease that is slowly killing me. Besides that, nothing matters anymore, David. I apologize if this is just a big ramble, but I am just writing as it comes to me.—Yo

Here, I share only a fraction of the letter with you just so you get a sense of my state of mind. The rest is personal and private. Obviously, there is much more to the story, especially the difficulties in managing a blended family. But even with this letter, David and I don't get to the bottom of what happened. Instead, I learn to shelve my problems in the hope that I can resolve them one by one when the time is right and my energy returns. I'm starting to lose my voice, I feel introverted, and I lack the ability to rock my world in order to make a point or stand my ground, which is far from the righteous and outspoken woman I used to be. But I need all my energy focused and directed on my own little world, the cocoon that is keeping me safe for now.

Chapter Six

....

I DIDN'T REALLY KNOW HOW STRONG I WAS UNTIL BEING STRONG WAS THE ONLY CHOICE I HAD LEFT.

Although I have more profound male friendships, I'm blessed with a small core group of women whom I trust and value very much. I usually don't discuss my marriage with anyone, but I talk to Paige and do confide in my girlfriend Kelly at this time because she loves my husband and is supportive of our union, and I like that. As a good Christian girl born and raised in Chicago, she values marriage in an old-fashioned way. This particular day she drives down from Beverly Hills to visit me. We drink tea and lie on the couch in the living room, talking for hours. I share what happened the past couple weeks, and she suggests that David and I see her therapist. It feels good just to vent about all the things that have been bottled up inside me to someone who is nonjudgmental and an honest, loyal, kind, and authentic spirit. I'm grateful for our rare friendship during a time of my life when I feel very isolated. It's strange to feel this disconnected and unable to pull out of it, but I need to choose the road of least resistance. I crave peace in order to deal with all the changes in my life.

Once David's friends and colleagues notice that I'm not attending parties and big events anymore, they know something is really wrong. Many people kindly start contacting David, suggesting various treatments, doctors, and approaches. This is how we find out about the Paracelsus Clinic in Appenzell, Switzerland. Craig McCaw, a friend of ours from Santa Barbara, knows several chronic Lyme sufferers who were treated there with great success.

Paracelsus, one of the largest alternative medicine clinics in Europe, has a mostly holistic approach to various chronic and degenerative conditions, which they've been treating for more than fifty years. Their goal is to understand you as an individual, not label you with a disease, and then to focus on the *cause* of your illness and not just your symptoms. Their medical director is Dr. Thomas Rau, who started his career specializing in rheumatology and internal medicine but switched to a more alternative approach when he realized that his patients weren't getting better with traditional medicine. This resonates with me so much. I'm excited and hopeful. David is supportive of this and makes plans for us both to go to the clinic right after filming ends for the *Housewives* in a few months. The plan is for David to spend the first week with me then my brother, Leo, will come from Holland to keep me company for two additional weeks as I continue my treatment.

We order Dr. Rau's book and decide to go on his anti-inflammatory food plan, which is primarily fruits and vegetables, rice-based foods, onions, and no fish or meat. If you really want to eat meat, it has to be organic and grass fed. The food plan is an important part of the clinic's program, and I stick to it rigidly for three months. After all, I'm not going to leave my children for three weeks and travel all the way to Switzerland to have Dr. Rau tell me to go on a special diet or that my treatment isn't working because I have a lot of inflammation in my body. No! I want to arrive in Switzerland 100 percent committed to this diet and say, "I've done *my* part. Now, what can you do for me?" I don't want them to use inflammation or my diet as an excuse for why they can't fix me.

On September 22, David and I fly to Zurich. On the plane, I write in the diary that I've kept sporadically throughout my journey.

My Diary
September 22, 2013
Memory loss, hard time focusing, not absorbing info, no word re-
trieval, loss of strength in my hands, pressure in my brain, no en-
ergy to exercise, no period, loss of muscle mass, cramps in my hands
and feet, hair loss, difficulty participating in life. One good day
every ten days.

The night we arrive, we go to the hotel and straight to sleep because our first morning at the clinic starts early. We meet with Dr. Rau, who interviews and examines me extensively. A nurse does metabolic, genetic, and blood tests.

"I've been following your diet religiously for three months," I tell him.

"I can tell. In fact, I'm amazed by your results. You're my star patient," he says. "If you don't mind, I'd like to hang up your labs to show other patients what they can accomplish."

"Of course," I say.

Dr. Rau does many of the same blood tests I already had in the United States to look at things like my cholesterol, thyroid, liver enzymes, heavy metals, trace elements, old viruses, toxins, and other imbalances. However, he looks at them from a different perspective. One of Dr. Rau's tools, which is not used regularly in the United States, is darkfield microscopy. This looks at my live blood under very high magnification to see individual cells, infections, and internal stressors. The clinic also uses thermography and hair mineral analysis to check for heavy metals, which they say is more accurate than blood tests for these things.

Dr. Rau is the first person to actually explain my fluctuating eyesight, which goes from okay at times to just seeing shadows. Losing your eyesight is a big deal, and normally it would be the first thing you'd tell your doctor, but I'm battling so many other symptoms that I forget to tell Dr. Rau about it. But I don't need to. When he examines me with a special light, he actually sees that the Lyme has attacked my optic nerve. *I told you so!* I've seen various top ophthalmologists in L.A. and insisted something was wrong with my sight, but no one believed me. They said my eyes were fine and that I only need a mild prescription for reading. I also share with Dr. Rau that on and off over the years, I have taken Xanax to help me sleep and calm my nervous system, which seems to speed up at night. Dr. Rau is not happy about this and switches me to melatonin. We also discuss the dangers of Botox.

"With your brain issues, it should be obvious that you never inject anything in there ever again," he says with a strict Swiss accent. I nod politely as I have a total aha moment. *Of course I shouldn't do that! What am I thinking? What is the world thinking? Who purposely injects TOXINS in her brain for vanity?* In the moment, my body starts sweating. I feel embarrassed, reckless, and like the dumbest person on Planet Earth. *Why did I do these things to myself without really thinking about them intelligently?* I'm ashamed of my lack of judgment and appreciation for all the beauty God gave me naturally. *Why didn't I honor that?*

My mind is going a thousand miles per hour. The Botox discussion hits home, and it's not until David nods at me that I come back to the conversation they're having about the laxatives I use for my chronic constipation. Dr. Rau thinks I should stop these immediately as well. He also suggests that I switch my synthetic thyroid medication to a glandular formula.

Paracelsus also has a holistic dental department because Swiss biological medicine considers this a crucial part of a well-rounded approach to health care. All patients go to the dental department when they arrive. I walk into my mandatory appointment feeling a little bit annoyed because I've already spent a lot of time and money on my teeth. *I'm ahead of the game on this one.* As a child, I took painstaking care of my teeth. Yet, no matter what I did, I had cavities in every single tooth. My brother barely brushed and has perfect teeth. Go figure! When I arrived in America as a young model, I had a mouth full of dark mercury fillings. Ten years ago, I finally had the courage to get my whole mouth fixed. I had the fillings and my wisdom teeth removed, plus a few root canals. So when the clinic tells me I need dental work, I brush it off with a laugh. *What could still be in my mouth that's affecting me?*

"Right now, I'm just focusing on my Lyme," I tell the dentist.

"Well, your teeth are connected to your Lyme," he says. "You have metal-based crowns, cavitations, and root canals." *I've never heard the word "cavitations" before, and whatever they are, I'm not dealing with them now. I need to focus on one thing at a time.* All the treatments I've done and special clinics I've visited have been very expensive. Having work done on seemingly healthy teeth seems extravagant, and I'm cautious not to do too much. Once again, I can't help feeling frustrated with the fact that I've paid for health insurance my whole life, yet it doesn't do me any good when I really need it. Of course, I know I am privileged and I'm not complaining. But it's the principle that matters to me.

Don't we all deserve answers for this? Should wealthy people get better medical treatment than others? The answer is no, of course not, and that question haunts me every day of this miserable life I am living. Chronic Lyme isn't cured with high doses of antibiotics. I think I have proved that point by now. This whole thing is a mystery. Being in an international clinic, I meet Lyme patients from all over the world, further proving that this is a global problem. Anyway, as much as this frustrates me, I have to save myself before I can save the world, so with that in mind I focus on my own little life one day at a time.

I show up at the clinic every day of my three-week stay here around eight in the morning, and they tell me my treatment schedule for the day. Most of the treatments focus on detoxification, restoring my digestive system by healing my intestines and GI tract, and strengthening my immune system with a diet to restore my body's ideal pH balance. These treatments include IV cocktails with homeopathics and infusions of a special saline solution with high doses of vitamins B and C and folic acid. It's the first time I'm introduced to ozone therapy directly into the vein, which boosts oxygen in cells and tissues to speed up the healing process. This powerful treatment has been around for hundreds of years, yet it's not approved by the FDA. Paracelsus also does a form of acupuncture called neural therapy, where acupuncture points are injected with specific homeopathic remedies and procaine. The idea is that because these points, which are determined using Chinese meridians, are very specific, the remedies are more effective and boost the body's ability to heal itself and reset the autonomic nervous system.

Another very interesting treatment is hyperthermia. After they place an IV in my arm and a thermometer in my butt, I go into what looks like a closed tanning bed device that raises my body temperature to about 103 degrees. The process takes three to four hours with a nurse by my side monitoring every step of the way. She supports my body with IV fluids and homeopathic remedies as needed. Thankfully, I can communicate with her through a small window right above my head because my body is wrapped in silver foil blankets to keep the heat trapped inside my ailing body. It feels extremely claustrophobic inside this cylinder. The heat makes me feverish and weak as I drift in and out of a strange mental state with intense shaking and sweating one minute and shivering with chills the next. It's an out-of-body experience. However, I focus on all the positive effects this treatment could have for me. The theory behind this treatment, the most intense one that I have done thus far, is that when the body creates a fever, the heat should kill all the viruses, Lyme bacteria, and co-infections. In today's society, the minute we have a fever, we rush to take a fever reducer, but I'm learning that if we just allow the immune system to fight the fever rather than block it, we may benefit more. Burning the bugs? YES! Let's kill them and get them out of here. It sounds perfectly realistic. At the end of these treatments, I feel like a truck ran over me and I want to sleep for days.

I eat mainly at the clinic's restaurant, where all the food is vegetarian, low-sodium, and specific to Dr. Rau's anti-inflammatory diet. I do my first forty-eight-hour liver cleanse, which consists of sugarless, organic apple juice, saltwater flushes, and an olive oil–lemon cocktail. This enhances the liver's ability to get rid of waste like excess cholesterol and certain proteins. I'm fascinated by the amount of bright green and yellow liver stones I expel into the toilet. Of course, I immediately google "liver stones" and "liver cleanses," and happily realize that this is just a normal part of cleansing. I've heard of liver cleanses throughout my life, but I never thought I needed one because I don't drink much alcohol and always lived a pretty clean life. Today this proves me wrong. Colonics at Paracelsus, as at Sponaugle, are an important part of treatment. I also learn about electromagnetic frequency (EMF), which comes from things like cell phones, computers, and lights, and how it affects the body. Paracelsus has machines that measure the EMF in your system, and I have extremely high levels in my body.

In general, my Herxheimer reactions are intense. I know this is helping me make progress long term, so I try to focus on getting through it one day at a time, and having a positive attitude. The days are long, so by the time David and I get back to our hotel room each night, I just want to crawl under the blankets and hide. I'm exhausted from always being exhausted. We sleep with the windows wide open because I love the smell of the fresh mountain air and the soul-soothing sounds of nature and silence without any traffic noise. It reminds me of a sweet childhood memory—my mom used to crack my bedroom window at night, even when it was twenty degrees below zero.

I meet some amazing patients from all over the world who have inspiring stories and one common goal. Everyone is suffering greatly, yet everyone wants to live. Since we all need simple connections of love and understanding while far away from our homes, we form a supportive community. Paracelsus treats many things besides Lyme, including cancer, autoimmune diseases, chronic fatigue, and Epstein-Barr, just to name a few. This may seem like a wide range, but the doctors here agree that it all comes down to the same thing: a nonfunctioning immune system. To treat the immune system, you have to focus on the gut, which is your entire digestive tract, including every part of your stomach ending in your small and large intestines. This is where 70 percent of your immune-system cells live. Even though I've used my gut as an intuition compass my whole life, it's here that I learn that the gut is *literally* the brain of my body. If mine is not healthy, I won't recover from whatever disease I'm fighting. Having an unhealthy gut puts one at risk for an array of health conditions. In contrast, healing the gut strengthens the immune system, something that's crucial for anyone who suffers from chronic illnesses.

David does some basic treatments in the clinic, and we have a nice and much needed week together. We get along easily, just like the good old days. Our different perspectives on family support during challenging times and very different beliefs about healing and medicine are starting to affect us. Nevertheless, we're happy to be together in this magical little town, and even though we have separate treatments during the day, we enjoy our short nature walks at night and make the best of the circumstances life has thrown us. My goal when I got to the clinic was to get strong enough to walk back to the hotel rather than drive. On David's last day here, we accomplish this together. Although at a slow pace, I push with all I have because I thrive on these small accomplishments. The mountains are so beautiful and inspiring, the smell of cut grass makes me feel close to nature, and walking past the cow farms happily reminds me of my childhood. At one point, we stop so David can take a picture of me in the grass. All I want to do is roll in it and feel that strong connection to the earth.

David and I have only one weekend together, and he insists we visit our friends the Manoukians, who have a beautiful home in Gstaad. Although I'm sick, shaking and sweating with fever after a four-hour hyperthermia treatment, David is determined to see them. I just want to take a hot bath and crawl into my comfy hotel bed, but instead I'm lying in the passenger seat of our little rental car, quietly crying from utter exhaustion as we drive for almost six hours through the mountains. I'm just trying to be a good wife. *But what's he thinking? It's like pushing a child who has a 103-degree fever to get out of bed and take a road trip.* My lack of brain function makes me more and more passive. I just can't deal with any debate or disagreement, so instead of standing my ground, I've started to let things slide. I also never want to be a difficult sick person or bother anyone, so trying to go along with my husband seems the right thing to do. I feel sorry for him since I can see him struggle because he does not have me the way he used to.

We arrive in Gstaad right after dawn. Our friend's home is beautiful, although I see very little of it because I go straight to one of the guest rooms and crash, exhausted and sick as a dog from the long and winding roads in the Swiss Alps. My girlfriend Tamar is a kind friend and makes sure I have all I need, but I literally don't get out of bed for twenty-four hours. Only out of pure respect for our gracious hosts do I summon the energy to have a bite to eat with them, but I spend the rest of the weekend in bed. We drive back to Paracelsus Sunday night.

David leaves the next morning, and Leo arrives. I'm excited to see him—he is a great source of strength and comfort for me. Although he hasn't been able to come to America to see me since I fell ill, I always feel his unconditional love, and there is nothing better than having my brother beside me at this time. Whenever I am with him, no matter how much time has passed since we saw each other last, I realize that no one makes me laugh more than Leo, no matter what the circumstance. Laughing is something I don't do enough of these days. Leo pushes me to walk from the clinic to the hotel every day. We do so hand in hand, just as we did when we were young. Sometimes, we reminisce about our childhood; other times, we just listen to the sounds of the birds and the silence of nature, which remind us of times we spent in the woods as children.

This last business year has been tough for Leo and Liseth, who have three children, Joann, Lizzy, and Ian. More than ever, this is the perfect time for us to be together and for him to rest as well. Leo joins me on the Dr. Rau diet and is really impressed with how good he feels after just one week. He leaves Switzerland with so much excitement about healthy eating that he brings home Dr. Rau's cookbook and the various spices and herbs listed in it to encourage his entire family to try the diet. Leo is introduced to this change in lifestyle and takes it very seriously because he sees me sick. I guess we're not open to getting educated about or paying attention to things until someone you love gets hurt.

The three weeks in Switzerland are a great learning experience and the various treatments definitely strengthen my overall health and give me more energy. Yes, I made progress. But is it good enough to get on with a productive life? No. It seems like all the treatments I've done so far create certain shifts because they improve my strength and lower my inflammation, but unfortunately this doesn't last. I leave Paracelsus with thousands of dollars' worth of biological medicine that I can't buy in the United States, like homeopathics for my IVs, injectables, pills, and a complex protocol. But it's hard to integrate this into my day-to-day life at home. I'm sure this is difficult for anyone who is sick and even tougher when you're dealing with brain dysfunction. I'm overwhelmed and confused. I have trouble putting all the pieces of the protocol in action. The bottom line is that Paracelsus wasn't a magic bullet for me, and I'm learning that even the best clinics in the world cannot cure chronic Lyme. There is very little magic in the world of the chronically ill. Believe me, these are sobering realizations.

October 5, 2013
Getting knocked off my socks by
#LymeDisease last year was the most
humbling experience in my life so far.
#SelfReflect #Searching4ACure

One morning downstairs in the kitchen, I gaze out my favorite window at the beautiful blue ocean that forms the backdrop to my countertop, which is covered with countless bottles of medicine. I'm annoyed by how this reminds me of my unsolved puzzle. It's difficult to understand or accept that I can work diligently and yet none of the hard work is paying off. I'm not just upset about my OWN health. The longer I travel on this journey and the more research I do, the more I learn about the many Lyme patients whose lives are destroyed. *Hundreds of thousands of people deal with this silent killer, but nobody can help us? Helllllooooooooooooo!*

Knock, knock! Where is everybody? Why isn't anybody standing up for what is right? Why isn't anybody answering questions about this mysterious disease? And where is the Centers for Disease Control (CDC) in all of this? Why are their guidelines more than a decade old? It's so disappointing to think of all the celebrities and rich folks in this country who have Lyme and, as a result, could use their platforms to raise awareness and help our cause in the same way they have done for AIDS and cancer, among others. Many of these people share their stories with *me,* yet they don't want to share them with the world for fear that it might tarnish their careers. Ironically, this could actually be the most important contribution that we make to the world! I agree that it's not fancy or glamorous, but it's morally the right thing to do for our children and their children. Staying quiet just adds more power to the invisible chronic-Lyme snowball that tears people's lives apart!

All of this brings out the rebel in me, the side of me that says, "Fuck you all." Excuse my French. I'm going to find a cure for this disease, and nothing and nobody is going to stop me. I will not allow anyone to shut me up or shame me into silence, and I'm not going to rot away behind closed doors either. Instead, I will continue to talk, post, and blog about it until my message is heard. *This is a living nightmare without an end in sight!* I can't even put into words the frustration I'm feeling right now. I just want to scream from the rooftops until I find someone who is willing to listen and has the power to make a change for all of us. I do feel extremely cautious about sharing details of the privileged and expensive treatments that I've undergone. I don't want anyone to waste money on treatments that are not the cure we are all looking for. Writing this book gives me an opportunity to share, and you can draw your own opinions about things that might resonate with you. Of course, always with the advice of a medical professional.

Chapter Seven

....

I DON'T WANT MY PAIN AND STRUGGLE TO MAKE ME A VICTIM. I WANT MY BATTLE TO MAKE ME SOMEONE ELSE'S HERO.

B ack home means back to business wearing the mommy, wife, and property manager hat again. But my body and brain continue to decline rapidly. I need a new plan of attack, so I call Dr. Piro to discuss my persistent brain issues. *Once again!* He refers me to Dr. Bradley Jabour, a nationally recognized neurologist who has been a professor and chief of neuroradiology at UCLA Medical Center. He's said to be a pioneer in various kinds of MRIs and scans to evaluate neurological disorders of the brain. This sounds like something that could give us new information, so I make an appointment immediately. The functional MRI that Dr. Jabour does reveals inflammation and inactivity in the left frontal lobe of my brain and my decreased brain function. It's around the holidays, and this is the best Christmas present I could get! Obviously, damage in the brain sounds scary, but at least these results validate that I have not lost my mind. My brain function *is* lacking because of the inflammation from the infection. This is what I've been saying since the first day I got sick. *I told you so!* I'm grateful to receive this news because it gives me a new direction to fight. Even though I'm not sure what it all means, things can only go up from here. At times, it's challenging to find the purpose in the cards life has dealt me and make sense of it all. Yet I have no choice but to accept my new normal as I continue to visualize the energetic, athletic, and multitasking woman I once was. I'm starting to forget what it feels like to be her.

Even though Dr. Jabour admits that he's never treated anyone with Lyme brain, he thinks that I can benefit from something called TMS, which means transcranial magnetic stimulation therapy. He is conducting a clinical trial on TMS and has a 70 percent success rate, so I feel lucky to be able to participate. For six weeks, Alberto drives me to the clinic every day except Sundays. With a special high-tech tool, the doctor can see my brain on a screen to accurately pinpoint the underactive area. His sweet nurse marks this with a blue pen and then aims a magnetic-pulse device on that spot. The magnetic pulses stimulate areas of the brain that are underactive in patients with brain injuries or disorders. It feels like a woodpecker pecking at my brain. It hurts a little, but it is more annoying than painful, especially after an hour and a half each day. The treatments are exhausting, and I keep falling asleep during them. However, the nurses want me to stay awake because I'm instructed to read a list of words and envision a specific thought to go along with them.

On my Bravo blog, I write, "Unfortunately I won't be able to write a blog as my brain is out of order at the moment. I have started an intense treatment to try to repair the damage the Lyme has caused neurologically. Unfortunately, I'm experiencing worse symptoms than before the treatment started. But I was promised that it would get worse before it gets better. My apologies for not being able to pull it together—hope to be back at it next week." However, things get only a *little bit* better. After the six weeks, my mood seems calmer and my brain function is a little more accessible, but, once again, it doesn't last and certainly is not a cure.

I miss my horses. I miss my life and all things familiar to me, so on my way home from one of my TMS treatments I stop to see Bella ride at her barn in Calabasas. Even though I gave up horseback riding when I moved to Malibu, I love to sit ringside surrounded by the familiar smell of the horses. I have so many happy childhood memories associated with this scent that it instantly puts my soul at ease, providing a calmness and realness that I cannot get anywhere else in the world. My girls and I built a lifelong foundation, and one of our deepest bonds was created around our horses and the responsibility of taking care of them. Both Bella and Gigi are nationally ranked equestrians in their age divisions, but Gigi never thought of making it her career while Bella always did. The barn is her happy place, and her whole life's focus has been on horse showing and building a future around that. We talk about finding a college where she can bring her horses, and she dreams of and works toward participating in the Olympics as well as being a professional equestrian. I support that dream because it has always felt right in my gut.

Nevertheless, when I watch Bella ride that day, something feels off. She gets very winded after jumping her round, something she is trained to do and has done her whole life.

"Bella, are you okay? You're so so out of breath, my love," I say.

"I don't know, Mommy. I've been feeling really tired lately. But I'm just trying to power through it," she says, smiling. I leave the barn puzzled and a little bit worried, but not on my game enough to take action.

A week later, Bella calls me, crying, from a horse show at the Los Angeles Equestrian Center to tell me that she had a bad crash and hurt herself.

"It's okay, my love, that happens to the best of us," I tell her. But when she gets home that night and shows me the enormous bruise that covers her entire right thigh and buttocks, I practically have a heart attack. Never in my thirty years with horses have I seen a bruise that big. I call her trainer, Jenny, the next morning to find out what happened, and that's when I discover that I'm clearly not the only one who is concerned. Jenny feels that Bella's performance has gone down over the last three months for no apparent reason. This is shocking. Just one year earlier, I bought her Lego, the horse of her dreams, and they were a winning combination everywhere they went. *So is it the horse? Or is it Bella? What's going on?*

I start to watch her more closely. Even though she *looks* fine, her performance tells a very different story. Bella has been horseback riding and competing since she was three years old. It's as natural to her as walking. When you jump horses, it's all about rhythm and counting, and your brain needs to be on fire in order to perform. But Bella's brain seems to have lost the perfect count it always had, and she's making calculation mistakes. I let it go on a little bit longer, but one day I wake up with this strong intuition that I have to take her off her horse so she can take a break to regroup and figure out what is going on. For now, riding six days a week requires too much from her both physically and mentally.

I'm afraid to tell her because I don't want to break her heart, but I also don't want to lose my child in a riding accident.

"Bella, you need to take a break and start focusing on other things," I tell her.

"What do you mean, Mommy?" she says, with tears in her eyes.

"I don't mean to sound insensitive," I say. "But I think something is off with your riding, and we need to figure out what that is." She is devastated. *But how can I let her make one more mistake? How can I let her fall one more time?* She listens to me and stops riding but feels like her whole world has come crashing down. The thought of not being able to fulfill her dream is a huge blow to her self-esteem, and she gets really depressed. She's losing not only her dream but also her identity. It's hard for Bella to imagine who she is when she's away from her horses and out of the riding britches and dirty boots she has worn since the day she could walk. This is the start of a rough time for my baby girl.

It's an overwhelming time for me, too. Not only am I trying to keep my own head above water, but I also have to figure out what is wrong with Bella. Dr. De Meirleir happens to be in Reno doing clinical research at the University of Nevada. He diagnosed me and changed the path of my journey, so I know that I have to take Bella to see him. I don't want to waste time taking her through the traditional medical system for fear of missing a proper diagnosis. I pull it together and fly her to Reno. Our appointment is that afternoon.

"Bella, can you share your symptoms with me?" Dr. De Meirleir asks.

"Brain fog, exhaustion . . . ," she says politely. Then she turns to me. "What else, Mommy?" It's hard for her to remember her symptoms, a frustrating situation I know way too well. Therefore, I made a list for her on my iPhone before we got to the appointment.

"Shortness of breath, trouble focusing, and pain along her spine that is so severe she sometimes cries herself to sleep at night," I read from my list. He takes a long time examining her and does extensive blood work for various tests that are done only in European labs.

Six weeks later, results reveal that Bella has neurological Lyme also.

Even though she grew up in the barn, I never saw a bull's-eye rash on her or a tick, for that matter. This is devastating news, and I feel trapped with a sense of helplessness like none I've ever felt before. *Now I have not ONE, but TWO children with Lyme and no cure.* Having seen the suffering of many children during my journey, I'm distraught, to say the least. It's one thing to be sick *myself*, but when my children get diagnosed, knowing there is no cure, THIS IS A GAME CHANGER. Of course, I'm scared to death, but this news motivates me to fight like I've never fought before. I know that it's up to me to figure this out and keep them going. *I'm going to scour the earth until I find a cure for them.* I feel very alone in this because David is busy in the studio and Mohamed is not good at dealing with illness. He's highly sensitive and can't deal with the suffering of his loved ones, so instead he's in denial about what has been really going on.

This brings me to one fascinating part of raising a child with an invisible disease that the outside world does not understand: Bella can rest for sixteen hours and then get up and go hang out with her friends. There, she snaps a selfie of the thirty happy minutes of the day when she's able to lift her head off the pillow and posts it. This creates a very different perception of reality and immediately gives people an opportunity to judge. "See? I told you she is fine. She looks happy in that selfie." Or, "If she can go out to dinner, she can go to school." The list of critical comments goes on, but no one should judge a child's journey. People don't seem to understand this, but it may be part of "you don't get it until you get it."

Regardless, it's *my* job to be my children's guiding light and, hopefully, lead them to victory.

Dr. De Meirleir prescribes a combination of different antibiotics for Bella. Initially, I'm panicked, so I start her on them. But we stop after three days because her Herxheimer reactions are so severe and my intuition isn't sold on this protocol. Long-term antibiotics have not proved successful for me or anyone I know with chronic Lyme so I feel extremely cautious about treating my children with these drugs. I worry about ruining their guts with a long-term antibiotic protocol. I'm starting to use my own experience to try to help guide their treatment as best I can as their caring mother, so I begin both Bella and Anwar on a holistic protocol with antibiotics such as silver, a regime of herbs to treat Lyme, and IV protocols to boost their immune systems.

In the midst of this, the holidays are coming, and all I want to do is hide under the covers and wake up on January 1 because I feel completely shut down with anxiety and exhaustion. However, mommy duties are calling, so once again it's time to pull up the bootstraps and try to keep it together and create some sort of normalcy in the midst of this storm. I force myself to go with Alberto to buy a tree. Not having this traditional symbol of the holidays would disappoint my children and *really* make me feel like a loser mom. It takes me five days to do the same decorating that the old Yolanda used to do in one afternoon. Still, once it's finished, it feels like a huge accomplishment to see my children's lifelong Christmas treasures hanging on the fresh-smelling branches of our ten-foot tree. The house feels somewhat normal because it looks beautiful and festive, but I have to admit to myself that I can't do much more than this. I used to start shopping in November, but there's no way that I can run around to buy presents. I feel bad for being such a downer, yet that all seems so meaningless to me right now. I talk to the children about this and they understand. The circumstances of our family life with Lyme are affecting everything, and they're feeling it. Still, instead of feeling sorry for themselves, they decide to volunteer and serve food at the homeless shelter in downtown L.A. on Christmas Eve, which puts everything in perspective and makes me so

My greatest
accomplishment,
my life...

My childhood in Holland with my horses
and connected to the earth.

So proud of the dress my mom sewed
for me and the haircut I gave myself.

Momma and Pappa, Ans and Gerard van
den Herik, on their wedding day in 1961.

My beautiful Momma after a long day
of sorting potatoes at the farm.

My brother, life partner, and best friend,
Leo van Den Herik, in 1965.

My first soul mate and spirit animal, Gino.

My first photo shoot, with tears in my eyes, while learning how to smile on command.

That powerful feeling of strength and endless energy.

The unexpected career that made me a financially independent teenager.

Excited about my first *Vogue* photo shoot in Australia.

Straight from the barn to the runway for Dutch designer Frans Molenaar in Amsterdam.

My mom, my foundation, and the woman who taught me discipline, my work ethic, and perseverance through life's tough times.

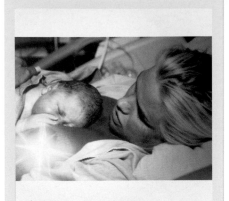

One of the three best days of my life, the birth of my son, Anwar.

Aspen winter wonderland with Baby G.

Gigi with her rescue pony, Rocky Daddy, at home in Aspen.

Baby Bella.

With Gigi in Mexico, pregnant with Anwar.

Just the three of us, waiting for baby Anwar to arrive.

The ones that made my life complete.

The sugar of my life.

A bond like no other,
my baby Bella's third birthday.

On our way to Holland to see Oma.
Photo by Gigi.

My three musketeers starting the
journey of life together.

Our first Halloween in Santa Barbara.

A precious Anwar and Mommy
moment in time.

Home in Santa Barbara and doing
what I love best.

Retreating to the life I knew and wanted
to pass on to my children.

Anwar and Lucky, my fourth child.

Getting the Dutch ice skating
roots activated.

Decorating gingerbread houses and
building our family traditions.

My mini me, Gigi.

Finding solace in the place I've found comfort since I was a little girl.

Passing on the passion of taking care of an animal you love.

Digging in the dirt, looking for magical crystals.

The unbreakable bond of sisterhood.

Grateful for my Momma's support during the transition to my life as a single mommy.

Obsessed with theme table decorations.

My friend Tom Hahn.

Lucky 23 and captain of her high school volleyball team.

Looking to the universe for answers on Ellie's ALS diagnosis.

Fast forward to a new life in Malibu.

Paige, our sisterhood has exceeded anything we could have imagined the day we met at the Santa Monica car wash.

The persistent puffy round circles under my eyes that appeared every three to four weeks.

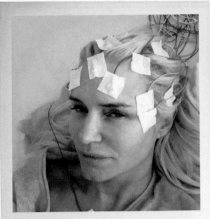

Turned inside out at Cedars Sinai in 2012.

The fridge that became famous.

The beginning of my journey with my port and high doses of IV antibiotics.

Sick but on mother duty. God forbid there would be a Christmas without a tree.

The show must go on: Looking good, feeling bad.

Finding signs of love and inspiration
anywhere I go.

Paige, my twin from a past life.

The only constant and
unconditional thing in my life.

Jaymes, my amazing sister-in-law
and fellow Lyme warrior.

I often craved solitude and a
space where I could find my
fading inner voice.

When your brain is offline and you can't
find the words you're searching for.

My obsession with organic,
homegrown foods.

The Lyme Research Alliance gala in
Connecticut, 2013.

My spirit angel and the reason why I'm
on a relentless search for a cure.

Bella and Lego, the winning
combination.

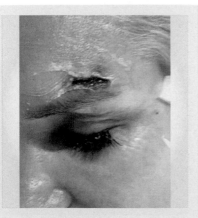

Middle-of-the-night bathroom collapse.

Happy Dutch girl, grateful for the
thoughtfulness of family and friends.

Supporting the local farmers at Sunday's farmers market.

When life gives you lemons.

Girl talk with my bestie, Ellie.

With Gigi on set of her Guess shoot.

Visiting the New School with Gigi in 2013.

The importance of giving back at the homeless shelter downtown L.A.

Taking a break from treatment to smell the grass in St. Gallen, Switzerland.

2012 *RHOBH* premiere right before I collapsed behind that wall.

Switzerland, contemplating my journey and connecting to my childhood memories.

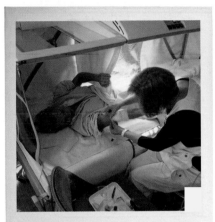

The hyperthermia treatment at Paracelsus, Switzerland.

The misleading impression of an invisible disease.

Twin warriors.

2013 *RHOBH* premiere party.

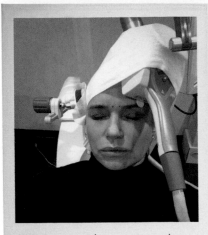
TMS transcranial magnetic stimulation.

Richard Helfric's 150 pills
a day protocol.

Pushing to keep normalcy in my home
at Christmas 2013.

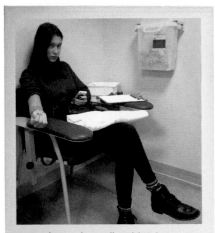
Enduring the endless blood tests.

Dropping Gigi off at college in NYC.

Anwar, the unwavering guiding light in darkness.

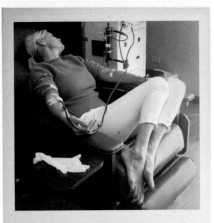

RHP in Tijuana, Mexico.

At St. John's with my sweet angel.

No matter how tough the journey, we never stopped laughing.

Stem cell treatment in Tijuana, Mexico.

My binders with medical discoveries.

Nyepi, the silence I'd been searching for.

Bali, a spiritual journey and the exploration of my own soul.

Salutation to the universe, feeling deep gratitude for being guided.

The beauty of a simple, white water lily.

Seeing older people work the rice fields reminded me of the physical power we all have.

Grateful to see and feel the strength of this amazing animal.

Chapter Eight

....

SILENCE

M y next attempt to get better is probably the most hideous protocol of this entire journey. It's recommended by my dear friend Chris Cortazzo, whom I love and respect very much. His mother has survived cancer.

"Richard Helfrich brought her back to life after chemo," Chris says. "She's been in remission for ten years now." He hands me four books by Richard Helfrich about rebuilding the immune system. Although some of the treatments and protocols I do may seem crazy and are way out of the box, I don't do *any* of them on a whim or haphazardly. Tom is my quarterback in the research department. He helps me look up any ideas and we carefully weigh their pros and cons. So, of course, Tom and I do some digging on Richard. We learn that he drastically changed his own health after being diagnosed with cardiomyopathy, a serious heart condition. Using an alternative approach, Richard healed his heart over the course of five years. In the decades that followed, he says he's used a similar program to change the lives and health of thousands of patients. It makes such a huge difference when you work with doctors and practitioners who have battled their own war. Somehow it humbles them and makes their heart grow with compassion. It's a beautiful thing to see or better said to feel, proud. They come home late that night tired, inspired, and grateful for the lives they live. I'm thrilled with this free pass and the pressure it takes off me. It makes this year's Christmas more about togetherness, cooking, watching movies, and being grateful for all the important things that money can't buy.

like there is a deeper understanding when they have walked a similar journey.

"Give me one year and I'll put your disease in remission," Richard says after he reviews my medical records. *Another fucking year?* "Just know that my protocol isn't for sissies. It takes a committed and dedicated soldier who's consistently willing and able to take 150 pills a day."

"I'm no sissy, but *150 pills?*" *Then again, how can I argue with someone who is doing the protocol himself?*

"They're spread out over breakfast, midmorning, prelunch, lunch, afternoon, dinner, and bedtime," he explains. "You also take ten different herbal tinctures, three times a day." Discipline has never been my problem, and, honestly, I would eat tree bark for six months if it would help me get well and move on with my life.

"Well, then, I'm your soldier," I say. My only moment of hesitation is when I learn that his protocol costs thousands of dollars a month. My financial resources aren't endless, and I've already spent a great deal of money on treatments over the last few years. *But what choice do I have?* I'm battling a disease that has no cure, and I don't want to go back on antibiotics or other conventional pharmaceutical drugs. This holistic approach seems like one of the few options left. After I begin this protocol, I show the seemingly endless bottles of pills to my mom via FaceTime one day.

"Have you lost your mind?" she asks, startled. *Yes! I HAVE lost my mind and I'm trying to find it again.* I'm not going to lie, swallowing all those pills feels very unnatural to me, especially on an empty stomach in the morning. But as I follow Richard's strict instructions, I learn how to make it work. For example, somehow my stomach tolerates the first thirty pills of the day as long as I take them with a glass of papaya juice. It's a very intense protocol, but I'm an obedient soldier, and I will not miss one single supplement or drop. *Ever!*

After five months, I have more strength, can function a little bit better, and have slightly more energy. Instead of being in bed *all* the time, I'm in bed for three days and up for one. On the good day, I push myself to walk down the driveway, although this lands me back in bed the next day. I also notice that my skin, which has been dry and rough since I got sick, looks healthier, and my hair is getting thicker and not falling out anymore.

That said, it hasn't cured my Lyme yet or given me back my old life. I always say that one day I'm going to put on my sneakers and run from L.A. to San Francisco! I am praying for a Forrest Gump moment because I feel this urge to run off all the failures that I've experienced since the day I collapsed mid-push-up in the gym before my wedding. I actually keep my sneakers at the front door, ready for that particular moment to come. But after all these months on the Helfrich protocol, I still don't have my Forrest Gump moment or anything close to it.

February 11, 2014
More determined than ever.
#Alive #Blessed #Grateful

This reality is quite different from what they say on the *Housewives* finale. The summary about my life since filming stopped says, "On the verge of beating Lyme disease, Yolanda is ready for her next challenge . . . moving closer to Beverly Hills. She and David have listed their Malibu home." I'm certainly not on the verge of beating this disease. My brain hasn't made much improvement since this journey started. However, we *are* selling our Malibu home. Its magnitude and the overwhelming responsibilities that come with running it are more than I can handle. We have help, but I'm still in charge of it all. The beautiful lemon orchard and rose gardens that I used to love tending to are now monsters of pressure. Not only do I feel trapped in my brain, I also feel trapped in this big, beautiful house. With David's recording studio in the basement, there is lots of traffic in and out of the house and music going six to seven days a week. As I've mentioned, the pre-Lyme Yolanda loved this kind of activity, but the new me can't take it. Most of the time, I hide upstairs in my bedroom.

This is a very lonely existence, but it's the only one I have. The only person who can relate is Ellie, who has been living with ALS for more than three years. She is now trapped in a paralyzed body with breathing and feeding tubes, yet she still has perfect brain function. ALS is the most brutal disease I've ever witnessed and heartbreaking to watch. Ellie and I have a strong bond of motherhood, and our common thread is to stay alive for our children and find a cure for our diseases, although my sentence is by far a less onerous one than hers. I FaceTime her often, especially since she's the only person I know who is not running around and busy with life. She's always there when I call, and we often joke that we're the only two losers in bed all day.

"I wish we could merge your sharp-as-a-whistle brain into my still-functioning body and make one perfect person," I tell her. I always encourage her to set goals and find a reason to live.

I try to do the same, and right now my goal is to figure out my next move on this journey. The outside influences and noise are too much for me right now, and I really need silence to think about it. I dream of going somewhere quiet and doing nothing for a week, no treatments, no responsibilities, nothing. It may sound strange, but I can't find a silent spot in my own brain anymore. The Lyme cycles create this shaking engine in my brain that I can't still or slow down. It's hard to think, and I desperately crave humble quietness where there is no crazy life buzzing in the background. I am longing to connect with the earth and the ocean so I feel grounded again.

Around this time, a close girlfriend invites me and David to her house in Bali, and this seems like the perfect plan to get the silence I crave. Since I'm starting to have some better days, it's just what I need. I also feel connected to Bali. My grandfather fought in the war in Indonesia, my mom lived there for a year, and my Uncle John and Aunt Alie are Indonesian, so I love the influence of this culture I was raised with. I want to simply throw on shorts and flip-flops and get lost in space and time without Lyme. I want to eat some of my favorite childhood dishes—satay, gado-gado, and homemade nasi goring—just like I used to eat at my Aunt Alie and Uncle John's house growing up.

The trip seems even more ideal because David is having a concert in Jakarta.

"I can go with you to your show, then we can go to Bali together," I say.

"I can't go. I have to work," he says. Normally, I wouldn't go without David, but something is calling me to Bali, and I know I have to follow my intuition about this trip. When David says no, I ask Paige.

"Sure. If that's what you need, I'll go with you," she says instantly.

"Why would a woman need to go on vacation with a girlfriend?" David asks when I tell him.

"Why *not*?"

"Have you read the book *Eat Pray Love*?" David asks.

"Of course I haven't read it because I *can't read*!"

"The divorced author travels to Bali and meets a man who eventually becomes her husband," he says. *I just want to get away from my life and get lost in a culture that's familiar to me and eat the food I love. The last thing on my mind is meeting somebody. I'm looking to meet myself!*

"I want to have this experience with *you* as husband and wife, but you have all these excuses: you don't like the beach, you're too busy, you can't take time off from work," I say. *How can I build with someone who's constantly blocking me from building?* Typically, I'm all about keeping the peace and would try to fix things between me and David, but something inside me remains stubborn. I insist on going.

A few weeks later, I accompany David to his show in Jakarta. Paige meets me there and together we fly to Bali. My friend's driver picks us up at the airport, and we make small talk with him as we travel to her house.

"It's a good thing you came today," he says. "Tomorrow, the airport will be closed."

"Why?" I ask.

"It's Nyepi," he says.

"Nyepi? What is Nyepi?"

"It's the Hindu New Year. Our day of silence where you reflect on your life, pray for forgiveness, and contemplate how you'll do things better in the new year," he explains. *Day of silence?* "The streets will be empty because we're not supposed to leave our homes, and all the shops and everything else will be closed. You can't use electricity or phones and aren't supposed to talk for twenty-four hours."

My jaw drops as I look at Paige. *Silence. OMG. I asked for silence and look what I'm getting: a WHOLE ISLAND in silence!* I'm stunned, but I also believe that there are no coincidences in life. Before we left California, no one knew what I was talking about. *I* didn't even know what I was talking about. I wasn't sure why I was drawn to Bali, but clearly the stars were aligned and I'm supposed to be here.

"You are such a little witch," Paige says to me, giggling. Even though my once stellar intuition has felt dim lately, I am extremely grateful that we're here in this moment.

March 30, 2014
Praying for health and happiness
before the day of silence tomorrow.
#Nyepi #HinduNewYear #BalineseCulture

Once we arrive at the house and settle in, I prepare for my day of silence. I ask our host for a pen and a stack of paper, and then we walk to the charming little town nearby to get candles. It's a warm, gorgeous night and the energy on the streets is electric. A beautiful carnival goes by with the most amazing bright-orange and red costumes. I love getting lost in a crowd of local people who have never seen a *Housewives* show.

I feel the spirit of their beautiful religion and this special holiday cele-
bration. It's magical.

"I'm taking Nyepi very seriously," I tell Paige, who loves to chitchat all
day long. "So don't talk to me tomorrow for any reason." I say this jok-
ingly but she knows I mean business. I go to sleep excited to see what the
next day will bring.

The following morning, I wake up around six thirty and immediately
notice how quiet it is and how quiet I feel. All of a sudden, there is space
for the sound of God's creatures, minus all the overwhelming noise of
today's modern world. I haven't felt this kind of silence since I lived in
Holland as a child while biking to the barn on the quiet country roads at
dawn. I realize how much I miss that peacefulness and I feel such gratitude for those simple memories. Then I bring my mind back to Nyepi.
What a blessing to have permission to live in silence for a day, the
silence that I have been yearning for for so long but somehow haven't
been able to find or give myself. The sense of responsibility that I have to
my husband and children always overrides anything *I* need. It's been a
long time since I've been alone with my thoughts and I'm loving every
minute of it.

After meditating for a couple of hours, an amazing sense of clarity
comes over me. I pick up the paper and pen and just start writing. A
whirlwind of words pours out of me. I don't even know what I'm writing,
but I do so without thinking or sparing anyone's feelings. I spend the entire day just purging my thoughts and emotions, meditating, and taking a
few brief naps. The words are authentic and true to me. It feels good to
just let them flow without reading or correcting anything. The end result is
twenty-three handwritten pages of pure thoughts and feelings. For someone who has been so bottled up, this endless stream of words is thrilling.
I share some, not all, of the writings here because there are parts that may
be hurtful to some people, don't move this story along, and are deeply
personal between me and David. Out of respect to our journey together,
I will leave it at this.

March 2014
6:40 A.M.
The Day of Silence
I don't know much about the Hindu religion, but I like this Nyepi Day and I love the idea of today being the first day of my Yolanda van Den Herik New Year. Stripping away all the belonging and titles I have accumulated over the past 50 years and try to reach deep to remember what it's like to be me. Immediately, my children come to mind, but I must redirect the thought and remind myself that today is going to be about ME, which is easier said than done. I would like to acknowledge all the things that I could have done better in the past and plan on how I want to hopefully live in the future.

As I am laying in a small single bed in a 10' × 10' hut, my big fluffy bed at home seems so far away. I needed this distance away from that life in order to separate me from it. My life, my husband, my children, my job, my responsibilities to family and friends have become an unexplainable pressure to me. My life is too big.

I just got this craving for Starbucks coffee, but without electricity, I might as well forget about any cravings today. Bali is on lockdown. Nobody is allowed out of the house, no electricity, water, shower. Even the airport is closed. It's just perfect!! I have been asking for quiet time. Well, God provided and gave me the most silent day I will probably ever experience. It's magical. I have never not talked for a day. How amazing that everyone on this island is having quiet time in their homes with their families contemplating their mistakes this past year and their dreams and goals for the upcoming year. What an extraordinary gift of their culture and religion. I am honored to be here.

I have not lived, but just existed for these past few years. I never stopped a minute, let alone a day to think about how it made me feel, but rather choose to be in constant battle mode with blazing guns to fight the spirochetes that have attacked my brain so severely that it literally has brought me to my knees. I often wonder if I have the strength to continue to fight this battle on top of the usual pressures of life. Sometimes, the thought of taking my own life seems the only way out of this, but thank God my sense of responsibility for my children will always override that feeling of awful desperation. I have to remind myself that I have come a long way, to which seems an endless recovery, but I do know that last year at this time, I could not even get out of bed. It's the mechanical part in my brain that seems to be stuck in first gear. I feel like I have the coping skills and intelligence of a 10-year-old. My confinement within the walls of my own brain is suffocating because the slightest outside pressure shuts it down so recalling memories or participating in any debate of intelligent conversation is almost impossible.

The more noise around me, the smaller I feel. I have very much lost my sense of self and it's hard to remember what it's like to be me with the freedom and the ability to do what I like and what makes me feel good. I have clearly come to a dead end on this road less traveled and I want to stay in this little hut until I find my compass. I feel this great urge to reevaluate my life and all those in it, but have not had the tools to do so. I need to purge and visit all the topics in my life that are blocking my spiritual being from shining bright.

David: How do I all of a sudden feel trapped by the most quality human being in my life? I feel empty and lost all drive to try to fix all the issues that have broken our bond. It's not because I don't want to, but because I don't have the ability right now to do so. The little energy I have left, I need to get out of bed in the morning and just try to get through my day the best I can, just one day at a time.

Since the death of my father, I have never given my heart fully to anyone until I met David. I loved him deeply and completely until too many disappointments during this vulnerable time chipped away my respect for him and our union. I am not sure if this is the end of our journey together or if we can rebuild from here. My heart is so

*closed off at this moment that I can't feel a true sense of where I am
at. I can't imagine my life with someone else. But I can also not imagine being emotionally stuck in a relationship that doesn't seem to
work anymore.*

The next day, I wake up overcome with a deep sense of relief, but
also with sadness for being stuck in my head for so long. *How did I get
here?* The girls and I sit around and share our personal experiences
from Nyepi. Of course, I'm the only one in this group who actually was
silent.

"I've been in survival mode and lost the ability to communicate from
the day Lyme confiscated my brain," I tell them. "The everyday fight to
keep my head above water took away so much joy in my life."

"I know this sounds crazy, but I think we should do mushrooms," says
Paige. "They supposedly open up your brain." Of course, being the researcher that I am, I immediately google this type of mushroom and learn
that it's organic, natural, safe, and, most importantly, legal in Bali. It's believed to enlighten the brain and expand the user's consciousness. One
report said that psilocybin, the active chemical in magic mushrooms, supposedly has the power to rearrange the brain's neurons so that new connections are made between them, and accessing the neurons becomes
easier, which brings clarity and a fresh perspective. I was born and raised
in a country where soft drugs were legal, but I never did them. Part of this
was because I was always very health conscious, but also because I don't
like to be out of control. *Well, if I am going to do drugs at my age, this
sounds like the perfect one.* So off we go on a mushroom hunt and soon
find what we are looking for.

When we come home, we sit in the outdoor kitchen watching Paige
slowly brew the mushrooms into a tea that she pours into water bottles for
our not-so-ordinary tea party. It turns out to be the funniest experience of
my life. According to my friends, I become a hilarious stand-up comedian.
Paige has known me over two decades and says she's never seen me this
funny. I talk up a storm and laugh at myself and the craziness I've been

through in the past couple of years through self-deprecating skits about the housewives, how David married a lemon, and how fucking ridiculous my whole world has become. I laugh my ass off with tears running down my cheeks for more than six hours until my jaw and stomach hurt. They are the kind of belly laughs that I remember from childhood but somehow left behind when I became an adult. I mostly laugh at how stupidly serious and responsible I am and have been my whole life.

"Fuck trying to be perfect all the time and always doing the right thing at all costs," I say. *I have a major realization: if I die tomorrow, I'm not going to get a gold medal because I've only had a handful of boyfriends or hosted the perfect dinner party. I'm not going to get a gold medal for being the perfect wife. There's no award for being a good girl at the end of this journey. I need to start living my truth!* I think about my life in Hollywood and realize that I hate it. My disdain for superficial Beverly Hills is the reason I packed up and moved to Santa Barbara when Mohamed and I separated. *Now, twelve years later, I'm back? Why? How?* I feel so trapped by the big life we have at home: all the social obligations, charities, my job, and my house. None of it matters to me anymore. What used to bring me joy and make me happy has vanished, and all that is really important is my health and my children's health, and a way out of the hell that I've lived since I got sick.

All of a sudden it starts pouring rain, bringing our six-hour laughing marathon to an end. I walk over to the outdoor shower, which is built in a beautiful pond filled with water lilies. They seem like the most gorgeous things that I've ever seen, so I sit on the shower floor with the hot water pouring over my head and I am mesmerized by the very clear view of a white water lily that seems magically lit by a spotlight. Water drips slowly from its leaves and everything is clear and colorful in a way that I've never seen before.

I only sleep for a couple of hours that night, and when the sunrise wakes me around five o'clock, I feel strangely positive—or maybe just spiritually awakened. I also have a great sense of gratitude for all that I've experienced in my three short days here. I want to feel the dirt beneath my soles so I go for a barefoot walk through the rice fields, where I see women in their seventies or eighties bending over and doing hard physical labor. It inspires me and reminds me how strong we really are. It gives me hope that one day I will be gardening, growing, and eating my own organic vegetables again. There's something so grounding about strolling slowly in the heat, sweating, and just taking in *life* after feeling as if I've gotten so disconnected from the earth and life itself. I feel great clarity about what is real and important in the world. I still have the same joint pain, exhaustion, and all my other ailments, but I finally start to feel and understand that my emotional well-being is a very important part of this puzzle in uncovering the mystery of my chronic disease. Far away from my life, I finally tap into my higher consciousness.

Riding on an elephant has always been a dream of mine, so Paige and I go to an elephant sanctuary, not a tourist place, but one where they rescue elephants from all over Asia. They are so big and breathtaking and I never understood how anyone could harm these beautiful creatures just for their tusks. Sitting on top of the elephant, I'm in awe of the sturdy strength of his body beneath me. *Aren't elephants supposed to be lucky? Maybe some of his strength will rub off on me.*

The whole time I've been in Bali, David hasn't called me or responded to any of my texts. Still, when I get home, I feel excited and invigorated, and I want to share the twenty-three pages I wrote. *I'm hoping this will help David understand who I am deep inside and my vulnerabilities. Maybe sharing it will bring us closer.*

"I would like you to read this; it's raw and unedited," I say, proudly holding the thick stack of handwritten pages out to him. "It's my truth without worrying about hurting anyone's feelings or offending anyone." I assume he will be excited that I've had such an enormous breakthrough in my writing, but he's not responsive or engaging in my joy.

"It will tell you all you need to know about how I've felt these past couple of years," I say.

"I can't right now," he replies, shaking his head. I'm disappointed because David knows that I haven't been able to write like this these past three years and how painful that has been for me. *Maybe he's scared to read the truth because he doesn't want to deal with the consequences of what I have to say or even open that box. The lid is on. It's safe where it is. This shouldn't surprise me because that's how he deals. Yet I'm handing him this long piece of writing, one filled with my deepest emotions and thoughts, and he won't look at it? If you truly love someone, don't you want to know what's inside the other person? The light AND the darkness? The good AND the bad?* I don't know if he ever read it.

Chapter Nine

....

YOU CAN BREAK DOWN A WOMAN TEMPORARILY, BUT A REAL WOMAN WILL ALWAYS PICK UP THE PIECES, REBUILD HERSELF, AND COME BACK EVEN STRONGER THAN EVER.

People, both friends and strangers, often tell me about Lyme-related treatments and cures, and I'm grateful for all the suggestions as I navigate the dark maze of the unknown. Most of the time, my intuition says, no, no, no. Occasionally, however, one of these suggestions feels right in my gut and I want to know more. This happens one night when David comes home from a charity event where he saw the TV producer and director George Schlatter.

"George has been struggling with his health for a long time, but now he looks fantastic," David says. "He wants to talk to you about this doctor in Tijuana."

The next day, I call George, and he tells me about Dr. William Rader, whose focus is on an embryonic stem cell treatment that he practices in Tijuana because it's not legal in the U.S. George sends me Dr. Rader's book and a video, where Nancy Reagan praises this treatment, which is being used for various things like Alzheimer's, brain damage, and autism. I do my best to read the book, which means going over the same page multiple times and highlighting what makes sense to me. I've always been fascinated by stem cell therapy, so I'm intrigued. I research Dr. Rader, and although I read some negative things, I see that many celebrities have gone to see him and benefited. *These people have access to the best. There must be something to his treatments.*

Even though I've had *so* many disappointments, I still get excited every time I hear about something that sounds promising. Somewhere deep inside it feels as if I *am* going to crack this code before my time on Planet Earth is up. I *am* going to figure this out and find an affordable cure for all. I'm determined not to leave any stone unturned. My next step is a trip to Tijuana. And I'm hopeful.

May 23, 2014
On my way to Napa with my
six hundred pages on stem cell research.
#MedicineOfTheFuture #Cure4LymeDisease

Once again, Paige is the Thelma to my Louise, and she joins me on this new adventure. Following the instructions we get from Dr. Rader's clinic, Paige drives us to a hotel in San Diego near the Mexican border. Here, we park the car and wait for a van to pick us up. We're with a whole group of people, a mix of every age, race, class, shape, and size. The sense of desperation and hopelessness is thick in the air, and it's clear that many of these people are here as a last chance to stay alive. Some are first-timers like me; others are returning patients who had positive results from previous treatments. When we board the van, I sit down next to a woman who looks as if she's around my age.

"My daughter was her high school's star basketball player with several offers from colleges when she got *so* sick that she couldn't get out of bed," she tells me. "But after her treatment with Dr. Rader, she was up in two days and on the hotel treadmill. Now I'm here for myself." This calms my nerves about the total madness of going with a bunch of strangers in a crowded van to cross over the border into Tijuana! It's a mind-blowing experience, and for what we paid, I should be flying in and out of Mexico by private helicopter. After driving for about an hour, we pull up to what looks more like a hotel than any of the clinics that I've been to. Then I realize that it *is* a hotel and that Dr. Rader's office is hidden in its basement down a long hallway with old, peeling paint on the walls. *How did I get here? Have I lost my mind?* I doubt my decision for a split second, but when there are no answers to your chronic illness, you become relentless and desperate. When you're desperate, you do crazy shit that, in another frame of mind, you might even call irresponsible. I've become part of this down-low community of people who practice underground medicine that is not approved by the FDA. I'm in do-or-die mode.

After thirty long minutes with too much time to debate my decision to come here, I'm brought in to meet Dr. Rader, a mysterious but very kind man with pasty white skin. He asks if I have any questions and, after a brief exchange of words, he orders his nurse to give me an IV. After a lot of poking and prodding, she can't find a vein that works in either of my arms. My veins are tired and overused. *Is my body telling me not to do this? Is this a sign?* The nurse covers my arms in heating pads, which is a trick used to dilate the veins. I'm also dehydrated, so after I drink a couple of bottles of water, the nurse finally finds a vein and runs some IV fluids. The actual treatment is a simple intramuscular injection of stem cells in my butt. Then, along with other patients, I'm placed in a hyperbaric chamber that almost looks like a sauna. I gaze around the room, stunned and overwhelmed at the number of sick people here. *Why is everybody sick these days? And why so many sick children and babies when they're supposed to be healthy and living life? Is it our water? Our food? Our toxins? Our air?*

The whole experience feels very secretive and strange especially as we're led back to the van and dropped off close to the Mexican border. One of the patients asks the driver why he's leaving us here.

"This is as far as I can go," he tells us. "From here, you have to walk back into the United States." *Walk across the border? I didn't even know that you could do that from one country to another.*

"But here are some passes for the VIP line so you can cross it more quickly." The driver hands us the passes and we go on our way. I thought that was nice until I learn that this doesn't exist. There is one line and one line only. All we can do is wait like everyone else in the longest line I've seen in my life, one so endless that vendors have set up stands where you can actually buy things like shoes, hats, and toys, and you pass all these pharmacies while you move along the line. *This is probably the ultimate low of my journey. I've really fucking lost my mind! But there are people in wheelchairs, so who am I to complain?*

It feels like a scene straight out of the *Dallas Buyers Club,* a movie that actually inspired me and got me thinking that a cure could be in Mexico, a place where doctors can practice freely without being limited by the FDA. The rare times that I've been out and about in the last year or so, people have recognized me from the *Housewives.* That's fine at Starbucks or the mall, but not when I'm crossing the Mexican border on foot after doing a treatment that's not legal in the United States. *Imagine the TMZ headlines! All I can think of is Blanca telling me how much her friends in Mexico love the show.* To go incognito, I wear a baseball cap and sunglasses and immediately pull the hood of my sweatshirt tightly over my head, even though it's a blazing-hot day. Sweat runs down my face to my neck and all the way to my waist. I feel exhausted and faint. I am miserable and Paige is annoyed, but we have to make our way back to the car so she can drive us home.

June 28, 2014
Crossing all borders as the quest for a cure continues.
#LymeDisease #TijuanaMexico #DallasBuyersClub

A couple of hours later, we finally step foot on American soil, and a different van picks us up and takes us back to the hotel parking lot in San Diego. We're all pissed off, irritated, tired, and hot, so the rest of the ride is pretty silent. Once we arrive and get off that bus, we walk through the parking lot. I've never been so happy to see Paige's car in my life! The second we get in, she blasts the air-conditioning and I lie in the backseat with my familiar blanket and pillow and fall asleep for a couple of hours. When I wake up, I'm feeling hopeful. *Maybe THIS will be the treatment that works.*

"The Coffee Bean?" Paige asks, referring to our ritual of stopping there for our guilty pleasure: a vanilla-ice blended drink.

"Of course," I say. *Yes, these drinks are full of sugar and not beneficial for my health, but once in a while we just have to let it fly!*

Initially, the stem cells give me a definite lift and I feel stronger. My inflammation goes down noticeably, my brain feels a tiny bit more open, and the unexplainable chronic cough that has plagued me for years goes away. Unfortunately, these results last only a few weeks, and my blood tests, which I always do to see how a treatment is working, don't show much improvement. For example, my white blood cell counts are still really low. Any benefit is anti-inflammatory but not permanent, so I wouldn't recommend this stem cell treatment for any other Lyme patients. Maybe it's good once you are in remission but for me, right now it's yet another expensive disappointment. I know the treatment is beneficial for many other conditions, but I file it under "waste of money" and "not a cure for Lyme" and trudge on. I continue to research with the help of Tom and listen to word-of-mouth suggestions and leads on different doctors and treatments.

At a Bravo photoshoot, Marcello La Ferla, Bravo's creative director, tells me about his close friend Mario who has been chronically ill for eight years. Mario went to see Dr. Jose Antonio Calzada, also in Tijuana, and is making a lot of improvement at the clinic there. I'm intrigued, because not only am *I* struggling right now, but so is Bella. I am treating her holistically with vitamin drips twice a week, herbal Lyme medications, and a miniprogram from Richard Helfrich, but she isn't feeling better and it's heartbreaking. I research Dr. Calzada, who practices both holistic and

Western medicine, and learn that he also uses darkfield microscopy. During your visit to his clinic, they detox your body and prepare it for his recommended protocol, which includes vitamins, supplements, and stem cells. I decide to take Bella to see him because something has to shift. I have to find relief for my baby girl.

A car service from L.A. to Tijuana is really expensive, so I decide we'll drive there ourselves. I haven't been behind the wheel of a car for a very long time, so Bella drives. I'm the co-pilot and try to guide her with Google Maps, but it's my first time using it, and, according to her, I'm not a very good navigator. Finally, Bella stops the car and has me drive so she can guide us instead. We're fine for about half an hour, but the minute we cross the border into Mexico, Google Maps shuts down. I try to stay calm, but it's not easy. Here we are, two girls with Lyme brain driving a Land Rover in Tijuana. *The blind leading the blind. I have no business being behind the wheel of a car at all, much less at ten at night in a totally unfamiliar place.* I'm determined to help my baby girl no matter what it takes, but this was obviously not a smart move. The streets are pitch-black and we seem to be in an unsafe part of the city with no clue how to get out of it. I call David.

"We're lost," I say.

"I know," he says with panic in his voice. "I've been following you on Find Friends, and all of a sudden it disconnected." Luckily, Alberto is home and, using Google Maps on his phone, gives us directions. I drive with a knot in my throat and sweat dripping down my neck from nerves. Finally, we reach our hotel. I'm trying not to show Bella but I am so relieved that I feel like crying and I'm about to have a meltdown. *What was I thinking? I feel so alone in this journey. My decision-making is obviously not on point anymore. I'm led by a heart of desperation and nobody seems to understand how sick my baby girl really is and clearly they are not supportive in my quest to cure her.*

The next morning, we wake up early and walk across the street to Dr. Calzada's clinic. When we meet with him, he explains the information that he's gathered from our blood smears. Interestingly, he tells us that Bella's and my blood smears look very similar.

"Bella's red blood cells are clumped together, something called the rouleau effect. Her blood cell activity is compromised because of bacterial and viral infections, and some red blood cells are misshapen because of parasites," he says. I'm overwhelmed for her but I give her a big hug and promise we are going to fix this problem.

It's Bella's first experience at a clinic, and, being the warm old soul that she is, instead of worrying about her own diagnosis, she shifts the focus and makes friends with the suffering patients in the treatment rooms. She starts asking questions and seeing other people's struggles puts things in perspective for her. I also think it's the first time she understands the harsh reality that there is no magic pill that will restore her health and that this is going to be a journey. Nothing is instant in the world of the chronically ill, a lesson that took me a long time to learn. At the end of the week, we go home with a three-month protocol of herbs and European injectable peptides. They have some benefits for Bella, but again this isn't a cure.

In the midst of all this, I start filming my third season on the *Housewives,* something that some people question. "If she were *really* sick, why would she do a TV show?" they say. But my decision to stay on the *Housewives* is pretty straightforward. First of all, I'm not a quitter or someone who goes back on my word. I signed a binding contract for four seasons, and, as a responsible human being, I take my commitment to Bravo and Evolution, the production company that shoots the *Housewives,* very seriously. Second, I have bills to pay and people to support, so in terms of a job this is the best-case scenario, with four months of filming and eight months off. I couldn't find a better one if I tried! The perception of my life from the outside looking in probably leaves room for speculation from people— including members of my big, unconventional family—about why or if I need to work. But my life isn't what it appears to be. Maybe if I had a husband who said, "It's okay, baby. You rest and get better and I'll take care of your bills," I wouldn't feel as much pressure to make money while I'm struggling with my health. But that's not the case. Although David is generous in so many ways, I don't have the financial luxury to retire and just be sick.

I'm also a very positive person by nature and believe that as long as I keep searching, a cure is right around the corner. *I don't feel well now, but I'll be better in the next day/week/month, so I can get through.* I simply force myself to pull it together the best that I can, I carefully count my spoons, try to put a smile on my face, and go to work with gratitude for all the great things in my life. Of course, that doesn't quiet the negative noise around us from people who judge my journey, and by now support from a lot of people who I thought were my friends has died down. People were very empathetic and rallied around me during the first few weeks, even months and first years that I was sick, but the truth is that most people got on with their lives—and seemed to think that I should, too. They just stop checking in. This is hurtful and really hard to wrap my head around because I come from such a different culture. Maybe my expectations of friends and family members are too high because I'm willing to do so much for them.

It's hard to comprehend that so many people whom I *thought* were my true friends were just "friends." And I'm sure I am not alone in feeling this way. On this journey, I've met other chronically ill people at doctors' offices and clinics, and you can read the disconnection and loneliness on their faces. This is *so* sad because being chronically ill makes you feel alone *enough.* Coming to terms with some of the friends and family members who have not shown up forces me to take inventory of the people in my life. It sounds cliché, but during this dark time I learn who my real friends are and understand their capacity to love and support. My core group is small, but they're mighty. They don't say, "Let me know if you need anything." They figure out what I need and show up without asking.

July 16, 2014
Coming back to life . . . mind, body, and soul.
#NeverGivingUp #LymeWarrior

I try to focus on getting through filming and my current health protocol of supplements, stem cells, a very strict gluten- and dairy-free diet, and doing the hyperbaric chamber and colonics twice a week. Then one afternoon when I'm home in bed, my brother calls.

"Mom has uterine cancer," he says. "The doctors are going to do a complete hysterectomy and then a special form of internal radiation for eight weeks." I'm shocked and devastated. But I'm not surprised because my mother hasn't felt well for a long time. *I knew something had to be wrong.* Obviously, my first instinct is to get on a plane ASAP, but I'm not feeling well and have several *Housewives* obligations. Unfortunately, I can't juggle both. Although I'm not with her when she has the surgery, friends in the community step up, taking turns cooking meals for her each day. A few weeks later, I'm able to go see her. I hire someone to check in on her every morning and bring her fresh eggs from the farm.

At the same time, Kyle and her husband, Mauricio, are taking a family vacation on a yacht in Majorca, Spain, part of which will be filmed for the show. Since Holland is only an hour and a half away by plane, they invite me for the weekend. I've known Kyle for a couple of years, but not very intimately, so I think this will be a great opportunity to spend time with her and her family in a more substantial way than we have while filming for the show. Once I arrive, everything is great. I have always connected with Mauricio, and I enjoy getting to know their beautiful, kind daughters, who are a pleasure to be with. I also enjoy spending time alone with Kyle. I love her interest in our European culture, and our more intimate talks, which we've never engaged in before, feel very genuine. We're both devoted mothers, and each of us has a daughter leaving for college in the fall. We enjoy the breathtaking natural surroundings, being on the water, and the delicious food.

On my second day, we're sitting at the table and about to start lunch when my phone rings. The caller ID says "Home," so I know it's David, and the minute I hear his voice, my gut tells me that something is wrong.

"I didn't want to tell you now . . . ," David begins, pausing. *Is Bella sick? Is Anwar okay? Is it Gigi?*

"What? What?" I say, interrupting him. *It's something serious.*

"Well, Bella . . . ," he says.

"What about Bella?" *What?! Just say it.* My heart sinks into my shoes. I get up from the table and go down to my cabin to get away from the cameras when he says, "Bella was arrested for a DUI." I can't catch my breath, and the adrenaline starts rushing through my body. It's like a train ran over my heart. *DUI. Drinking and driving. OMG.* My "what if?" button goes from one to ten in a split second because my greatest fear has always been the thought of losing one of my children in a car accident the way I lost my father. *What if she had hurt someone? What if she had crashed and died?*

"I wanted to wait 'til you got home, but unfortunately it's already on TMZ and the Internet," David says. "I figured you'd find out." I'm devastated by Bella's choices but she is safe. The worst part is that I'm being filmed as I find out this horrible news and even though I go into my room and shut the door, they continue filming. Even though David is holding down the fort in L.A., I disagree with his parenting style and all I want to do is get on a flight home and hold Bella in my arms because she is scared and devastated. Being so far away makes me feel helpless. Unfortunately, the next flight isn't until tomorrow. I've barely digested this news, so I'm not ready to share it with Kyle and thousands of Bravo fans. I take off my mic and ask the producers for permission to get off the boat so that I can walk and pace until my nerves calm down. I do my best to hold it together and not have a total meltdown in front of everyone, but back in my room I cry my way through a box of tissues.

Since I have been a single mom who raised Bella for most of her life, I immediately blame myself. I take it personally and doubt my parenting skills. *Where did I screw up? We talked about the dangers of drinking and driving a thousand times.* I have always told my kids that I'll pick them up anytime, day or night, no questions asked. They should never get in a car with someone who's been drinking or drive drunk themselves. A million thoughts go through my mind but the truth is that Bella has been an extraordinary child for seventeen years. She is edgy but lived a very disciplined life as an equestrian competitor, so this reckless choice is so shocking and disappointing. Her integrity and philosophy of life is always so right on and far beyond her years so her decision is hard to understand and a blow to my confidence as her mommy. But then again, Bella is human, and being a mother is discovering strengths you don't know you have and dealing with fears you never knew existed.

I talk to Bella most of the night on the phone until I get her three best friends to go over to my house to watch her because she is devastated. Early the next morning I catch a flight back to L.A. My emotions run high and I am so scared that I just break down and cry the entire way home. The other passengers probably think I'm some loony who lacks control, but I'm overwhelmed with a feeling of vulnerability that I have never felt before. Midway through the flight, I open my laptop and try to write Bella a long letter. Initially, it's difficult to put my thoughts together and process all that's happened in the past twenty-four hours, but I have to accept the fact that Bella made a human error. *I still make mistakes and I'm over fifty; expecting my children not to make them is unrealistic and unfair. It's up to me to show Bella the lesson here as well as the consequences.* I write about how much she means to me and how fatal this mistake could have been. I tell her how grateful I am that she didn't hurt anybody or herself, and that she needs to know that I will have her back 24-7 and 365 days a year, through the good times and the bad.

When I get home, she tells me what happened: Bella and her friends had a bonfire on the beach and were drinking wine. When they needed bottled water, she volunteered to get it and, although the gas station was close enough for her to walk to, she chose to drive. Social media, celebrity Web sites, and tabloids spread the story like wildfire. Of course, Bella is mortified and ashamed of her actions. She has to appear in court, where they suspend her license for a year and put her on six months' probation. She also has to do twenty-five hours of community service and attend twenty-five hours of AA meetings. I don't want to punish her for making a mistake but it is my duty to teach her consequences for her actions so I sell her car and make her pay her own legal fees from her lifelong savings account. And I also take away her phone for a month so that she is completely removed from social media and its toxic effect. Interestingly, after the month is over she actually thanks me. She feels reconnected to her real life in the now, looking forward and around rather then down at her phone.

Five weeks after this incident, it's time to take Bella to college in New York, where she was accepted to study photography and fashion at the Parsons School of Design. I already rented an apartment for her near Gigi's apartment and with a roommate because her Lyme protocol is a lot to handle and I don't want her to live by herself while in treatment. When we arrive in New York, I spend several days setting up Bella's apartment, organizing her closets, hanging pictures, and running to the Container Store, as I had for Gigi just a year earlier. This is part of my job as her mother, but it takes every ounce of strength that I have to push through because I feel sick and extremely exhausted. Bella and I also have a meeting with IMG. Earlier this year, I organized test photo shoots for Bella to start building her portfolio. The shoots were hard for her because she never really feels well, but we came well prepared. I've already gotten calls from several other modeling agencies but like Gigi, Bella feels that IMG is the right place for her. They have been following her development and are thrilled to sign her. She gets signed that day. This is all a very new direction for my baby girl and although she is still heartbroken over having to give up her riding career she is open to new beginnings. I'm grateful for this opportunity and it feels like things are falling into place and the universe is pushing her to move on from her riding career.

Bella is happy when she comes back to the apartment after her first day of classes. I'm putting the final touches on the apartment, hanging our family paintings on her wall, and am scheduled to fly back to L.A. tonight.

"I have something for you," Bella says as the two of us sit down on her bed.

"What is it?" I ask.

"A card." I open it and read these beautiful words.

Dear Mommy,

Please believe me when I say that, from the deepest part of my heart, I'm sorry for what I did. I know there is no excuse and the only thing I want is to gain back your trust and show you that I'm still the good girl you have had for 17 years and that I'm the girl that you raised me to be. This one incident is a big mistake that I take very seriously, but please trust that this doesn't define who I am as a person. I love you.—Your Forever Baby Girl

Tears are rolling down my cheeks by the time I finish reading this meaningful note. I am touched by her words and the fact that she nailed my trust issue. I think she's learning and growing from this experience.

"What happened doesn't mean you're not a good mother, just that kids make mistakes, you know?" Bella says.

"I get it, Baby. I *still* make mistakes and I'm fifty! So, yes, I know that." Bella has always been my mirror; somehow, she always has words of wisdom at the right time.

"Mommy, I learned my lesson," she says. "Don't worry about me being here in New York." When I took Gigi to college last year, the experience was new for me, and I panicked about a lot of things that I don't even think about with Bella. But leaving her is hard because she's suffering greatly from her Lyme symptoms. Combine that with her DUI and I feel insecure about letting her go. Yet when I read her card and talk to her, I realize that my insecurities about Bella's "not being ready" are *my* insecurities, not hers.

In the next two semesters at Parsons Bella works very hard, determined to be a straight A student. But she is also booking a lot of modeling jobs and doing Lyme treatments. This would be a lot for a healthy person to keep up with, let alone a teenager battling chronic Lyme disease, and she doesn't have the stamina for it all. I really feel she is pushing herself to the limit and is about to break down if I don't step in.

"Bella, a modeling career might not be here forever," I tell her. "But you can always go back to college and further your education later." Mohamed doesn't really interfere with my parenting style but he is dead set on all three kids going to college, so I have to support him on that. But I also know my business and, as I advised Gigi, I truly believe that if you hit one sweet spot in this career, you grab it with both hands and go for it. If you let it pass, it may never come again. I discuss it with her treating physicians and get a doctor's note so that Bella can take a leave of absence from Parsons and put her studies on hold while she focuses on modeling and, most importantly, getting healthy.

It's also time for me to refocus on *my* health. My friend Laurie recommends that I see Aaron Cameron, a naturopath and holistic health practitioner who uses all sorts of unique devices, like the Rife machine, a high-frequency healing device. He works out of his garage in Malibu, but despite this humble and interesting kind of "office," he's had great results with other people who were sick, even a few Lyme patients. When I meet him, I really like his way of thinking and his passion for holistic medicine. Three times a week, I go to his garage and I'm on the Rife machine for hours at a time. But after three months, I'm not making enough progress, despite my dedication. Still, I respect Aaron's insight, so I'm interested when he tells me about an Australian doctor practicing in Mexico who helped both Aaron's mother and father get better when they were ill. As I do with every treatment and doctor, I research this doctor. He did a clinical trial with a well-known Los Angeles hospital. I'm intrigued by his AIDS theory and research, but then the story gets a little fuzzy. Apparently, he invented something at this hospital but was somehow out of the picture when they were close to finding a cure. Still, the pros outweigh the cons and I like his philosophy, which goes back to healing the immune system to fight cancer, AIDS, Lyme, and other immune disorders. So in mid-September, Anwar, who doesn't want me to go alone, flies with me to

Zacatecas, northwest of Mexico City. It seems like the middle of no-where, and feels like another crazy and very mysterious adventure. We check into the hotel and I am told to wait for the doctor, who works at a laboratory but doesn't have an actual office in the city.

Waiting in my hotel room all day gives me a lot of time to question my decision to be here. I think of many reasons to pack my bag and leave, but I am driven to find a cure. It's now five o'clock and the doctor is still not here. Around six we decide to go for a walk and explore the town. I love the vibe of this beautiful, authentic little village. We have a nice dinner and it's obvious that people just seem to live and enjoy their simple lives with a lot of music in their hearts. When we get back to our room we are ex-hausted and about to fall asleep when I hear a knock at the door. It's now ten o'clock. The doctor comes into my room and shakes my hand. Even though I already spoke to him on the phone many times, he explains his treatments. *He seems like a very intelligent man.*

He proceeds to give me intramuscular injections of holistic remedies and some special skin gel in a syringe for my face. It all seems bizarre, like another scene from the *Dallas Buyers Club,* but I have faith and I trust Aaron's research on this and the fact that he had his very proper Cana-dian parents treated here, so I'm trying to go with the flow.

"I've been going to small villages here in Mexico to help local people who have cancer, and they're healing," he says. "But I've also had a lot of celebrities travel to me, like Charlie Sheen." *If people with access to the best are coming to see him, there must be something to it.*

For the next three nights the doctor comes to my room at ten to give me the same injections.

"What's so magical about ten o'clock?" I ask him.

"I like to travel when I'm not seen, in the dark," he says. Some nights the oddness of it all hits me, and I wonder if this is all worth it. *Yet what choice do I have after all these years besides dabbling in this world of underground medicine? The best medical system in the world has failed me. I'm desperate!*

Yet, despite my hopes that this treatment will be the One, the only benefit is a short-lived anti-inflammatory response and a little boost in my energy. Besides that, I am pretty much back to square one. I am discouraged and file this under "Waste of Money" and "Not a cure for Lyme."

September 14, 2014
Sometimes discouraged but still
determined to find a cure.
#LymeDisease #ZacatecasMexico

At the end of September, the *Housewives* season is about to wrap but not without an all-cast trip. I'm struggling through my days but I am so excited because we're going to Holland! I think it's the perfect time to take the cast and crew to see where I was born and how I was raised and to learn more about me and my country. I often feel like a fish out of water with this group of women, and sometimes I'm sure they view me the same way. Maybe they'll understand me better after meeting my family and experiencing my culture. When we arrive in Amsterdam, I'm thrilled to be home sweet home and surrounded by the smell of my country, the food, and the language. This is where I feel most complete. The first day we walk around a bit and then go to an all-cast dinner at a cute restaurant near our hotel.

To start the trip, I give a little welcome speech and suggest we go around the table and see if anyone has something to share that will connect us on a deeper level. "I know you all heard that Bella got a DUI and you are talking about it behind my back, so let me put it out in the open. The thought of what could've happened to Bella shook the core of me, and although this has been a very unfortunate experience, I have no shame around it. I am just very scared for Bella about the backlash on social media once this airs on TV. I'm sharing this with you because I think sometimes we try to hide these things from each other and pretend that every-thing is perfect. Well, guess what? *I'm* not perfect. None of us are and neither is my family."

Perhaps talking about vulnerable things like this can connect us on a more spiritual level. In Beverly Hills, it's rare to find people who show the true core of who they are as human beings, yet this is so important to me and has gotten even more so as I struggle with my health. I just can't con-nect with the whole superficial thing and am not good at playing the game. Unfortunately, the mention of a DUI leads to the topic of alcoholism, and then Lisa Rinna and Kim Richards get into a fight. When Kim implies some-thing negative about Lisa's husband, all hell breaks loose. This certainly isn't the warm and fuzzy moment I hoped for. Voices are raised and wineglasses are flying through the air. The whole situation is embarrass-ing and unsettling. It's not a great start to the trip. *How are we going to continue the week together after that explosion?* We go back to the hotel, but, instead of sleeping and getting the rest I need so much, I'm up late talking to the different women involved and trying to play peacemaker. I feel responsible because we are in my country. I'm already exhausted from the long flight and not getting enough sleep is added stress and not great for my health.

The next day, I wake up with a migraine, a stiff neck, and severe joint pain, symptoms that have become common for me after long flights. But when I look out the hotel window and see Amsterdam's charming canals, I get so excited to be home that I take three Excedrin Migraine pills, have a stiff Dutch cup of coffee, and try to push through. I'm not the only one feeling out of sorts. Several of the other women are shaken up from last night's insanity, and there's a clear divide among the group. Still, we all have obligations to our *Housewives* contract so quitting is not an option. Instead, we focus on a long day of filming in Papendrecht, the small town where I grew up. Here, I lead the girls on a bike ride to look at my child-hood home, the windmills, and the beautiful natural surroundings. We end up at my mom's apartment, which is nice and cozy but very small—so trying to squeeze the whole crew and all the women inside is comical. My mom is excited to have us and serves coffee with my favorite Dutch cream hazelnut cake. I happily get through that day on pure adrenaline and my excitement about being home.

But I pay for it the next morning when I wake up feeling like I was hit by a truck. I can't move or get out of bed. The exhaustion is so debilitating and the pain is unbearable, not something a few Excedrins can alleviate. I just never know when it's going to hit me like this but I am sure the emotional stress from the first night and running around for so many hours yesterday have me down for the count. Unfortunately, this is the name of the game with Lyme. I push it too hard and use more than one day's worth of spoons, and this is the result. It's sooooo frustrating. I'm sad and disappointed. All I want to do is run around Amsterdam with the other women and share our famous french fries and pancakes, but unfortunately I can't pull it together and need to stay in bed. I call the producers to tell them that I can't work today. They are clearly disappointed because it kind of screws up our story line but I think they know me well enough by now to know that if I could I would. In order to stay on story, we have to film me telling someone that I need to rest in bed today, so Kyle comes to my room to shoot that scene. After the crew and Kyle leave, I burst into tears and have a full meltdown with frustration. Before I got sick, it never occurred to me that my body could let me down like this. I used to drive it like a fast and furious Ferrari, my foot on the pedal, full speed at all times. I thought my energy was an endless resource. But now I'm depleted from this never-ending fight against Lyme and the rest is just a faint memory.

I stay in bed all day while the women visit the Anne Frank and beautiful Van Gogh museums, shop, and have lunch—all the things that I wanted to do, too. That night, we film our second dinner scene downstairs on the terrace of our hotel with my brother, Leo, and his wife, Liseth. Even though I don't feel well, I pull up the bootstraps and show up to work, excited to see my family and for them to spend time with the cast. We end the night by taking everyone for a stroll to the red-light district, one of the oldest areas of Amsterdam, which serviced the sailors in the early 1800s. It makes me so happy to walk the streets in the dark listening to people speak my language, and being with my brother always puts a smile on my face.

When I return home from Holland, I decide to stop Richard Helfrich's protocol with the 150 pills a day.

"You're the biggest warrior that I've met in thirty years," Richard says. "You've been so diligent."

"But after swallowing thousands of pills, this warrior can't swallow one more," I tell him. His protocol strengthened my overall health more than anything else I've tried so far. Blood tests show that my liver function has improved and my hormones are perfectly balanced. But my thyroid is still off and my white blood cell count, although a tiny bit better, is still very low. So is my CD57, which is a natural killer cell that's attracted to Lyme bacteria. A low CD57 means that the Lyme is more chronic and mine is 23. Plus, my Lyme tests are still positive, so even though this protocol helped, it isn't a cure. My blood tests aren't supporting the fact that I'm killing spirochetes or making progress toward ridding my body of this disease. I've given it my all religiously for almost a year, but in my opinion the needle is not moving like it should be.

Anwar is also not feeling well. His symptoms flare up on a regular basis, so I take him to Dr. Allen Green, a new holistic doctor in Santa Monica. It's fascinating how many doctors I've taken him to with no results, but a mother never gives up.

"I have been very successful in treating chronic Lyme with low-dose immunotherapy (LDI)," Dr. Green says. "There are minimal side effects." LDI works by desensitizing the immune system to the bacteria we are treating and helps the immune system become more balanced by reducing inflammation caused by foreign invaders or allergens. As a result, this helps fight pathogens more effectively. It's given by an injection under the upper layer of the skin every four to six weeks. Anwar wants to give this a try and also starts going to Dr. Green's office twice a week after school for IV drips. Unfortunately, the first LDI injection knocks him off his feet with a 102-degree fever. He is also crying from severe joint pain and uses three boxes of tissues trying to clear his sinuses, which have been bothering him for the past two years despite doctors and test results saying he's fine. But even though this is a tough time for him, he pushes through, and we start to see some improvements in his health.

By November, my symptoms are worse, and managing the big house in Malibu, which is on the market but yet to sell, is too much for me. I no longer see its beauty; all I see is pressure. I can't run it anymore, it's running me. Having full-time staff in the house can be very stressful because everyone needs direction and my brain can't handle it. I just need to be quiet and left alone until I can figure out the next step in my health journey. Because I feel best in small spaces, I decide that David, Anwar, and I should move to David's condo in Beverly Hills. It seems like a perfect solution for this moment in time.

"Let's live in the condo during the week when I have my treatments and come back to Malibu on the weekends," I tell David.

"If you leave this house, you're not coming back," he says in an angry voice. Of course he doesn't want to leave his home, but I'm also in survival mode and this is the only choice I have. David moves to the condo with me, although he makes it very clear that it's against his will. He is not able to express himself and I am stuck in my head so our communication is at a standstill. *Does he really think I like this change? Why can't he just understand that this is what I need at this point in my healing journey?*

Chapter Ten

....

THERE IS NO FORCE MORE POWERFUL THAN A WOMAN DETERMINED TO RISE.

I've made many friends throughout my journey in the Lyme world, members of a club that none of us wants to be part of. One of these friends is my fellow Lyme warrior Ally Hilfiger. She's had Lyme since she was a child and has suffered on a unique journey. When I met her, she was close to remission and feeling better than she had in a long time but still raw. She is on the board of the Global Lyme Alliance and is very active in the search for a cure. One day, we're talking over a cup of tea.

"If I ever have to do another treatment, I will go and see this stem cell specialist in Korea," she says. Ally's a smart cookie so I respect her judgment, especially knowing she has tried so many protocols herself. I'm desperate for a new plan of attack. I've been sick for three years now, and my symptoms seem to be getting worse. But most important, I have two sick children. My determination to heal them motivates me. I'm on a mission to find smart doctors anywhere in the world who can possibly help solve this problem. *They have to be out there. Maybe this specialist is one of these doctors.* Ally gives me his contact information, and he and I start to communicate by e-mail.

November 15, 2014
Mission Lyme disease back in action.
#ExhaustedButDetermined #IChooseToBeUnstoppable #MustFindACure

His philosophy is not to fight the Lyme, cancer, or whatever illness you have; it's to fix your immune system so the *body* can fight these conditions on its own. He has found that sick cells in people who are chronically ill keep producing and copying sick cells, and once you're in this chronic state, you can't get out of it. He takes your own blood stem cells and then, in the lab, separates out the healthy-looking cells and treats them to grow and multiply. Once reintroduced into the body by IV, these new and healthy soldiers should make new and healthy cells. It's definitely an out-of-the box treatment for Lyme, but my gut tells me that it makes total sense. My brain might not be as intelligent as it used to be, but a lot of my decisions are made using my intuition and the research Tom does for me. Intuitively, rebuilding my immune system feels right, especially since my blood tests show extremely low natural killer cells, which are crucial because they are the ones that destroy infected cells.

I call some references and when I talk to several patients with cancer and other chronic immune disorders, who have seen this stem cell specialist, they praise his treatment. Some even claim that he saved their lives. The only critique is that he's not easy to deal with, but working with a difficult personality seems like a small price to pay to feel better. I actually love the Asian culture and very much respect their work ethic. The bigger price is the actual cost of the trip, which is very expensive when I add up the air-fare, hotel, and the treatment. I hesitate. *But what good is money in the bank if I'm too sick to enjoy it? Or, even worse, if I'm dead? God's given me this journey for a reason. Why sit in America at a dead end?* Once again, I pray that it will be the answer. Although David isn't too keen on my going to Korea, he knows there's no stopping me at this point. Of course, when I tell Paige about the treatment, she decides to come with me, not just to be my wingman, but because she still has lingering Lyme symptoms herself. Korea is a long way away, and I'm so grateful to have my best friend with me.

It's a freezing-cold day when we land in Seoul. After spending a night at a hotel, Paige and I go to the clinic. At my first appointment, the doctor does an array of genetic testing with fancy computers. Then he draws my blood, which he'll use to grow my stem cells in the lab for six weeks. At that point, I'll have to return to Korea to have them injected back into my body. From many generations of doctors and educated in America, he seems highly intelligent. For the next seven days, I report to the clinic every morning at nine for treatments, including vitamin drips and immune modulators. The treatments are exhausting, so I don't have the energy to do much else except go to the Korean Spa at night for body scrubs and to use the infrared sauna. No wonder Asian woman have the most beautiful skin in the world, they care for it with so much dedication.

November 19, 2014
I guess you fight through the bad days to earn the best days of your life.
#LymeDiseaseAftermath #RebuildingTheBrain
#StemCellTherapy #MedicineOfTheFuture

Although most of the other patients don't speak much English, we still form bonds with one another because, whether they have cancer, Lyme, or any other chronic condition, we're in this maze together, trying to fig-ure out our disease and find a way out of our suffering.

There is one sweet Korean woman who is about seventy years old in the treatment room next to mine. It's clear that she's losing her battle with can-cer, and it's heartbreaking to hear her young family deal with the sadness of this reality. There are also a few English-speaking children at the clinic, and when I talk to their parents, I wonder if this stem cell treatment could be good for Bella and Anwar, too. It seems pretty noninvasive; so if it works, it's worth bringing them all the way here.

The truth is, worrying about Anwar and Bella keeps me up at night, and I feel completely alone when it comes to their health. Mohamed doesn't understand what they're going through. How can he? He isn't there when the children are crying in the middle of the night from pain or spend hours on the couch when they'd rather run around with their friends like normal teenagers. I guess it's hard for him to accept or understand how three people in his family could be sick with the same disease. So the weight is only on my shoulders, my sick shoulders. I figure out how to have the kids' blood taken in the United States over the next few days and FedEx it to the clinic here. This way, Bella and Anwar won't have to come to Korea twice. Instead, they can return with me in January when our stem cells are ready.

I don't feel any significant improvement but am hopeful that I will when I return and get the stem cells reinjected. In my Bravo blog, I explain that I'm writing from Seoul and that "I have learned to adjust to my new normal, the rebel inside me is just not able to accept this silent disability. Lyme disease has become a fast-growing epidemic worldwide. I'm determined to help find a cure and figure out a way to share knowledge with the millions of people struggling with this debilitating disease."

November 22, 2014
I am driven and motivated to think outside the box and
recognize the diverse points of views in global medicine not only
to cure myself but to pave the way for all my fellow Lymies battling
this poorly acknowledged debilitating disease.
#ChronicNeurologicalLyme
#StemCellTherapy #MyHealthJourney

While I wait for my healthy cells to grow in Korea, life goes on in L.A. The first weekend in December is the premiere of *Selma,* the Martin Luther King Jr. movie that Oprah produced and appears in. Although I'm sure that it's going to be amazing, I'm not feeling well and in no shape to attend a red carpet event but David feels differently.

"It'll be a nice weekend for you in your favorite place, in a beautiful hotel," David says. He's referring to the fact that the event is in Santa Barbara. What he doesn't understand is that when you're sick, all of that doesn't matter anymore. In this moment, I don't care about my favorite place, my favorite hotel, or my favorite woman, Oprah. I just want to get well. Nevertheless, David talks me into going and we drive the ninety-five miles from L.A. to Santa Barbara and check into the Bacara Resort and Spa. The first day, the movie screening is at the beautiful Arlington Theatre, where my children used to perform their school plays. I have many fond memories of our happy, healthy lives here. When the movie starts, all the lights turn off but the screen is so bright that I have to shield my eyes for a minute and the sound is loud and overwhelming. I try to buffer it with the earplugs David brought, but every sound is like nails on a chalkboard to me. *I can't sit here for one more minute.*

"I have to leave, but you stay. Okay?" I whisper to David. "This is too much for me to handle."

"How can I stay? I drove you here," he says sharply. I'm not happy about leaving either. It's rude and embarrassing to get up in a theater so quiet that you can hear a pin drop, one full of people who are riveted by what they are watching. *Selma* is a profound movie, and the little bit I saw was incredible, but my brain can't take it. We walk to the car in silence, and the second I get in, I start bawling. *I can't even sit through a movie. Something that requires nothing of me!* Back in the room, I climb into bed frustrated and upset. Tonight is a big dinner at the hotel to celebrate and honor the movie. *Maybe if I just lie here for a few hours, I'll be okay.* When it's time to get ready, I pull myself together and go with David to the dinner which is in the ballroom just down the hall from our room.

It's less daunting than getting in a car. *I can always come back to the room if I don't feel well.*

We do the red carpet and make our way to our table with some familiar faces like Magic Johnson. When we sit down, David starts talking to Magic about the immune system.

"What's your best advice for someone battling chronic disease?" David asks, referring to the HIV that Magic has lived with for more than twenty years.

"Keep on walking," Magic responds. "No matter *what*, you have to keep walking."

"*See?* I told you so," David says, turning to me, implying that if someone living with HIV can keep walking, I can, too. That's easy advice to give when you're feeling well or your illness is controlled by medication, but I literally *can't* walk. Of *all* people, David knows that I've always been hard-core about exercising so it's hard to understand how he could doubt my perseverance. This is hard for me to watch happen because even though a lot has changed, my character and core values are still the same. The old me didn't think anything less than four or five miles was even a workout! I've been an athlete my whole life. I'm used to pushing my body to the limit so it's hard for me to accept that I don't have a motor anymore. There is nothing to push. It's not mind over matter. I physically can't do it. Unfortunately, when you don't look ill and you are battling a disease most people don't know anything about, it's hard to comprehend how paralyzing and debilitating this truly is. I'm annoyed and irritated, both at his insensitive comment and at myself for not feeling well. *Fuck this. I'm having a glass of wine. Maybe it will cheer me up.* I can't even remember the last time I had a sip of alcohol, but I don't care. Oprah starts to make a beautiful speech about the movie, acknowledging iconic civil rights heroes, but only a couple of minutes into it, the whole room starts spinning. I feel dizzy and faint. *I'm going to throw up. I have to go.*

"I'm going back," I quickly tell David as I run from the table down the hall to our room. I make it to the bathroom just in time to violently throw up. I climb onto the bed fully dressed because the room is spinning. I curl into a ball and pray for this awful feeling to go away. *I'm pushing myself too hard to please David, to do the things he wants me to do. What's wrong with me? And what's wrong with him? We both know that I'm in no shape to do any of this.*

The next morning, I feel not only sick but totally embarrassed. I e-mail Oprah, apologizing for being so disrespectful and getting up in the middle of the movie *and* her speech. We go to her house for a beautiful brunch with an amazing choir and the entire cast from the movie before driving back home, where I get into bed immediately. A few days later, David pushes me to take a walk, probably because of the advice he got from Magic.

"Come with me to CVS to get razors," David says. "It's just a few blocks."

"It's not that easy," I tell him. "I don't feel like getting dressed."

"It's fine, it's dark," he says. "We'll go slow." The thought is daunting, but I want to give it a try. I'm wearing my pajama bottoms and throw on a big sweatshirt. The store is only two blocks from the apartment, but it takes monumental effort. When we get there, I go inside, but after a couple of minutes the glaring lights, bright colors, and loud music starts to bother me and it makes me feel light-headed.

"I'll wait outside," I tell David. I pull my hoodie up over my head and sit on the stoop of the handicap ramp right outside the double doors. A group of women in their twenties come strolling down the sidewalk and pass me when one of them turns around.

"Do you know where the Seven-Eleven is?" she asks.

"Yes. Make a left at the corner onto Westwood Boulevard and walk two blocks. It'll be on your right."

"Yolanda?" she says. "Are you Yolanda from *The Real Housewives*?"

"Yes," I say. It's funny how people recognize my accent before they recognize my not-made-up face. I go out so infrequently that I often forget that people recognize me from the show even in my pajamas and a hoodie.

"Can we have a picture?" the woman asks.

"Sure," I say. I'm obviously not looking too cute, but I don't have the heart to say no.

A few days later, one of the top Lyme specialists in the world reaches out to me. As I've mentioned, people constantly contact me through e-mail or social media to tell me about the latest Lyme treatments. Some are opportunists, but many are just great people who want to help, and I feel lucky that one of these amazing and legitimate people is Dr. Richard Horowitz from New York. He's one of the most Lyme-literate doctors in the world and he practices Western medicine with a lot of success. Although he can't diagnose or treat me without me flying to New York to see him in person, he offers to review my records on my behalf and for Dr. Piro.

"Send me all your medical files since the day you got sick, everything," he says when we speak briefly for the first time. *Little does he know who he's dealing with! If he knew, he probably wouldn't offer.* I have four binders with my test results and doctors' reports, which we scan and e-mail to him. Because I can't read or comprehend much information, Dr. Horowitz is kind enough to send me his book *Why Can't I Get Better?* on audio and I start listening to it on my laptop over and over again as I try to work my way through all the important information it conveys.

One week later, Dr. Horowitz sends me a written summary of my whole case that's more brilliant than anything any other doctor or health-care professional has provided within the past three years. I'm grateful and thrilled to get his opinion and point of view. The frustrating part is that I've given every doctor I've seen on this journey this *same* information in advance of my appointments. But most of the time, they don't take the time to look at more than a few pages, if any, before I arrive. Dr. Horowitz, on the other hand, went through every piece of information and every test I'd done with a fine-tooth comb. We FaceTime to discuss his recommended treatment plan.

"When they did that spinal tap at Cedars-Sinai in 2012, they should've known that those encephalitis cells were a sign of Lyme," Dr. Horowitz says. "Anyone who is Lyme educated would know that." *What?* It is frustrating to learn that I'd seen some of the best doctors in L.A., who, because they're not Lyme educated, gave me a week of antibiotics and sent me home with a chronic fatigue diagnosis, and never retested me for Lyme. I feel so helpless.

"Does this mean that I could have been helped years ago?" I ask.

"Yes," Dr. Horowitz says.

"Encephalitis? Is that part of Lyme?"

"Yes, but Lyme is really just one part of your problem," he adds.

"Is that why I've made such little progress?" Right now, it's almost three years since I got sick and almost two years to the day since I was diagnosed with Lyme, and I've reached a new low. Although I didn't think it was possible, I feel sicker than before. I'm weak and spend most of my time in bed, forcing myself to get up only when Anwar and David leave or come home. Even that is hard to do.

"There's a whole army that has invaded your body, and you need to start taking them down systematically," Dr. Horowitz explains. "You're not just fighting Lyme and co-infections, like babesia with possible exposure to Q fever, another tick-borne infection, but you also have evidence of heavy metals and mold toxins, with detoxification problems, nutritional deficiencies, mitochondrial dysfunction (i.e., a problem with the energy production inside your cells), multiple hormonal abnormalities, chronic insomnia, an imbalance in the part of your body that controls your blood pressure, called the autonomic nervous system, as well as your being deconditioned. These are all part of the sixteen-point Lyme-MSIDS model that you are learning about in my book. And there is also the problem of 'persister' cells and biofilms. These are cells that are resistant to the long-term antibiotics which you have taken. Specialized medication and natural therapies are needed to address that." *I'm confused. I don't even know what I'm fighting anymore.*

Dr. Horowitz works with Dr. Piro to create a very clear plan of attack using antiparasitics and antimalaria medication for babesia. I am very goal oriented so I am happy to understand my next move. I'm appalled and infuriated though by how expensive these medications are. Just *one* bottle of Mepron medication is two thousand dollars and my daily Bicillin shots will be three thousand dollars per month, and none of it is covered by my health insurance! I want to scream from the rooftops how wrong this is. *I'm blessed to be able to afford this protocol, but what about the people who CAN'T afford it? They are forced to self-medicate with alcohol and drugs to numb the pain and suffering of their disease until they slowly die or kill themselves to get out of their misery. There's something morally wrong with this picture. God, if I get out of this, I'll be your humble servant and fight for the Lymies in the world to find a cure that's affordable for all.*

I start this new protocol a few days before Thanksgiving. Forty-eight hours into it, Mr. Herxheimer hits me hard, but I don't complain because I think that David is over my being sick and of course so am I. Although my life is so isolated, I'm more and more connected to my inner spirit and strength. I learn to focus on myself without feeling guilty and I am consciously letting go of anything and anyone toxic in my life. My focus needs to stay on my reason for living: my children. They're truly the only thing that keeps me fighting. Even though they don't always understand why I can't get better, my kids never let go of my hand or question my journey or our journey together as a family.

My love and support of them never stops, and my girls consistently return this love and support, even though they're flying all over the world for work. Anwar and I are very close. He's got my back at all times. He gets what I am going through and works relentlessly on his own recovery. Often, we sit on the couch and have our IVs together and talk about life. I have always known that he is an old soul, but during this difficult year he's really starting to tap into his own spirituality, perhaps because I'm becoming more enlightened about my own. He has surrounded himself with a great group of friends who are discovering the higher consciousness and purpose of life. It's a beautiful thing to watch.

I get up with Anwar every morning to make him breakfast and see him off to school. I make an effort to perk up my voice and put somewhat of a smile on my face before he leaves the house because I know he's extremely sensitive and deeply connected to me. But as soon as the elevator door closes, I get back in bed and rest. I often FaceTime with Ellie, who lives in Paris, where her daughter Gracie is at the American University. Supporting her in her courageous battle with ALS inspires me and always puts things in perspective. I also try to reach out to two or three of the hundreds of Lyme patients who contact me each week asking for any advice or direction. Some of the e-mails leave me in tears, especially the sick teenagers and desperate children who ask me to help their moms or dads who have Lyme. Although I can't do a lot, somehow giving back and helping other people makes me feel better.

One night I'm watching an episode of the *Housewives,* which began airing recently but was filmed months earlier. I was at Brandi's housewarming party, and it's a sentimental moment for me because that was the absolute *only* day in the entire year that I felt somewhat of a spring in my step and had enough brainpower to speak with a clear train of thought and give a toast. I'm proud of Brandi for creating a happy home for her two little boys. Her journey hasn't been easy, and I admire her strength.

Regardless of my struggles, I keep my commitment and fly to New York because I'm scheduled to go on *Watch What Happens Live* to talk about my third season on the *Housewives.* These appearances are part of my job. After flying, the inflammation in my brain severely affects my eyesight and brain function. *I'll feel better tomorrow, after a good night's rest.* But I wake up feeling awful and petrified to go on a show that, as the name implies, is live. I can barely focus on finding the words to speak a proper sentence. *But I can't cancel after Bravo has flown me out from California. Who says no to Andy Cohen?* Plus, I'm staying with Bella and want to show my girls that sometimes we have to put on a brave face in order to honor our commitments. My word is only as good as I am, so off I go to the *Watch What Happens Live* studio on this freezing-cold December day with my girls by my side.

"I've had a flare-up in my Lyme brain and I'm afraid I won't be able to talk much," I tell Anthony, the producer, and Andy.

"Yeah, you don't seem like yourself," Andy says.

"I'm worried that my brain isn't working well enough to respond to questions on the spot, especially on live TV," I tell him.

"Please don't worry about it," Andy says kindly. Thank God he is compassionate enough to show me his questions in advance so I can mentally prepare. But even then, I don't know if I can do it. I settle into my chair on the set next to the other guest, actress Anna Kendrick. Immediately, the lights in the studio bother me, but I take a deep breath to calm my nerves. *Just make it through without crying.*

"I wanted to know how your Lyme disease is going," asks Liz from Massachusetts, a viewer who calls in to the show.

"Well, I'm struggling at the moment. It's been a long journey. Every day I wake up trying to figure out how to get over this and today especially is not a great day," I respond. "But unfortunately, these are the cards that life dealt me, and I'm going to figure this out because there are millions of other people suffering just like I do."

"Thank you so much for standing by your commitment to come on the show tonight, because I know when I went into your dressing room, you weren't feeling well," Andy says. "And I know that you've been going through it really hard for the last couple of months. I'm so sorry, because in the show it seems like you were so strong this season when you were filming."

"I guess that's the most frustrating part of this disease: you look so normal from the outside. It's not like people with cancer, where you can tell they're sick," I say. "Lyme is a silent killer and an invisible disability." With Andy and Anna's help, I make it through the best that I can. When I leave the studio, I go straight to the airport and fly home.

Midway through the flight, I have difficulty seeing and feel a severe migraine coming on. I get home at three in the morning, and by the time I wake up at eight, I've lost 70 percent of my eyesight. My limbs are burning, and my brain function seems like that of a two-year-old. By that afternoon, I end up at St. John's hospital, on IV fluids, Medrol, and pain medications.

My Diary
Dec. 19–23, 2014 at St. John's Hospital
Realizing that I'm in the midst of a badass relapse. Nothing in me has the strength to keep it together. Experiencing absolute loss of words, slipping into an abyss with a feeling that I am slowly dying. My body doesn't belong to me anymore. Something confiscated my brain.

I'm released from the hospital two days before Christmas. Despite my extreme joint pain and feeling totally debilitated, my girls are coming home for the holidays and I want to keep our traditions alive, even if *I* barely am! I invite our entire large blended family to our Malibu home for Christmas dinner. I also invite my wonderful sisters-in-law Jaymes, Maureen, and Mary Lou and brothers-in-law Ian and Marty. All of them have been right by my side during this journey. They're always a great help at our annual Christmas dinners, and I love the family cooking in the kitchen together. I decide to make things a little easier and order the entrées from a local market while we cook the special dishes ourselves. All I want for Christmas is love, health, and happiness.

December 25, 2014
All I want for Christmas is what money can't buy.
#LoveHealthAndHappiness
#MyMostPreciousBelongings @gigihadid @bellahadid @anwarhadid

David is scheduled to go to Miami tomorrow to record an album with Andrea Bocelli. He'll be there for a week and insists that I come with him.
"I really feel horrible," I say. "I'm not sure if I can travel."
"You'll be okay," he says. "We're flying private, and once we get there you can just sit by the pool and relax." Even though David has seen me

sick and struggling these past couple of years, it's still hard for him to understand that this is not a sit-by-the-pool-and-recover kind of thing. Trying
to be the good wife, however, I go with him. I wear sweatpants on the
plane, and the second we arrive at the hotel, I get into bed. Yes, it's a big
bed in a beautiful suite overlooking the Atlantic Ocean, but unfortunately
none of these luxuries matter to me anymore. I may have a different view out
my window, a different ceiling to stare at, and different lightbulbs to count,
but I still feel terrible. After weeks of antiparasitic medications and Bicillin
shots, I get hit hard with an array of difficult symptoms. Besides a severe
chronic cough, my hands are trembling, my fingers and toes are gnarled,
and my body alternates between shivering in a cold sweat and breaking out in a fever. If I'm not in bed in the hotel, I'm naked and curled up in
a fetal position on the bathroom's cold marble floor. It seems to be the
only way to soothe myself. I also experience severe anxiety for absolutely
no reason. Oddly enough, smoking raw tobacco on the balcony seems to
be the only crazy thing that calms my nervous system. When this absurd
craving first hit, I researched it and learned that, back in the day, Native
American Indians used tobacco for its powerful parasite-killing properties.
So rather than hit the whiskey bottle, I smoke out of utter desperation to
soothe myself. *I trust that my body craves what it needs.*

When I was healthy, I often walked barefoot on the beach to charge
my body with ions. Tonight, our second night in Florida, I have a strong
urge to do that and connect with the earth. I feel so disconnected from
any and all aspects of my life, as if something has confiscated my being
and all I can do is surrender, hold on for dear life, and pray. *Maybe I
need to be closer to nature.* When David returns from the studio late that
night, I ask him to take me to the beach. He's always pushing me to move,
so he's happy to come with me. My balance is off, I'm weak, and my bones
are burning like fire. I can barely get one foot in front of the other. As I
reach the shoreline, I take off my clothes and slip into the dark blue ocean,
which is cool and comforting. The waves gently wash over my naked body,
and I can feel the current tugging at me. Tears pour out of my eyes, roll
across my cheeks, and meld with the salt water as I try to still my mind to

become one with the water's ebb and flow. *God, please just take me in a wave. I can't live like this for one more day. Please carry my body away. I just want to disappear.* My next thought is a clear image of my three children. It shifts my consciousness immediately and it's the only thing that keeps me from letting myself drift off and drown. I lift my head out of the water and hear David's panicked voice in the distance.

"Yo, what are you doing?" he yells. I can't tell if he's irritated or scared with the time that it's taking me to float and go through my own thinking process. He doesn't understand my connection with the earth or my spirituality. Sadly we are existing on two very different vibrations. The freedom of floating in the cool water without pain for a moment felt so good. If David wasn't so tired from work and in a hurry to get back to our room, I could stay here for hours.

My Diary
December 28, 2014
In Florida and unable to leave my bed. Impossible to function or make any decisions. Feel 100 years old. So disappointed that I can't figure this out. Spent whole day in bed, staring at ceiling with no brain function. Unable to write my blog. Very stressed about it, because I can't pull my thoughts together.

It's New Year's Eve, and David and I are invited to Andrea and Veronica Bocelli's house for dinner. I can barely stand up, but David insists that I get dressed and he picks me up from the hotel at eight P.M.

"Even if it's just for a little while," he says. "You've got to get out of the room." I agree. It's New Year's Eve after all, but I feel unstable and my hands are trembling intensely. A strong force of something is controlling me but it's not me. I push myself to get up and go. Of course the other guests are dressed up beautifully, but a T-shirt, shorts, and no makeup is all I could pull together; my looks are honestly the last thing on my mind these days. I'm happy to see my dear friends and their kids, but I'm anxious and have a hard time communicating.

"I love you so much, but I have to go," I tell Veronica around nine thirty. I want David to stay because it's New Year's Eve, so their driver takes me back to the hotel. I crawl into bed and bawl my eyes out. *I'm not living. I am just existing in a body that no longer belongs to me.*

My Diary
December 31, 2014
I've lost my life. Worst New Year's Eve ever.

Chapter Eleven

....

I FOUGHT TO LIVE, I LOVED, I LOST, I MISSED,
I HURT, I TRUSTED, I MADE MISTAKES,
BUT MOST OF ALL, I LEARNED . . .
AND WITH THAT KNOWLEDGE I CHOOSE TO
MOVE FORWARD, ONE DAY AT A TIME.

On January 2, I fly from Miami to meet Bella and Anwar in Korea. Our stem cells, which have been growing for weeks, are ready. Mohamed is not on board with this decision. *Does he think I'm schlepping all the way to freezing Korea for fun? Thousands of miles from home? Thousands of dollars out of my pocket?* I'd fly to the end of the earth to find a cure for Bella and Anwar and nothing and nobody is going to stop me. My children know that I'm educated about every move I make and that I would *never, ever* do anything to harm them, but their father's support would be a great source of strength for them right now.

Truthfully, it's taking every last drop that I have to go to Korea. My latest protocol is taking me down, and I'm struggling. If my children were not meeting me there and I hadn't spent so much money on this promising treatment, I would cancel this trip. But this isn't about me. It's about my kids and my commitment to their health, and with Anwar's limited school holiday schedule, there is no other time we can go. David flies with me to Seoul because I'm not feeling well enough to go on the seventeen-hour flight alone. After one night, he continues on to Singapore, where he's shooting *Asia's Got Talent*.

On our first morning in Korea, Bella, Anwar, and I go to the clinic to meet the stem cell doctor. We get IV drips of vitamins and minerals. These are said to help our stem cells absorb better when they're injected back into the body. At the end of each day, we return to our connecting hotel rooms, practically crawling into bed feeling miserable, not only from jet lag and treatments but also some crazy flu that just hit us like a ton of bricks. To make matters worse, Seoul in the winter is cold and dark, and so are my children's moods. They're tired, sad, and angry, at times wondering why they have to spend their school break in a clinic in Korea. They are not connecting with the doctor so I'm having a difficult time motivating them. I try to shift their perspective to one of gratefulness and remind them—and myself—how blessed we are to have this chance to get well. I'm trying to keep it together in front of my kids and decide to take a break from my current protocol for a couple of days.

On our fourth night, we go back to the hotel, too tired to do anything. I'm walking to the bathroom to pee, when I collapse. I wake to Anwar trying to lift me off the floor and hear Bella talking on the phone. She's trying to get someone from the clinic to come here. My heart is beating out of my chest and I'm shivering.

"Can you turn on a hot bath?" I ask Anwar. He nods, then goes into the bathroom. Once it's ready, I climb into the tub still wearing my pajamas. The hot water running over my ice-cold body feels so good. Twenty minutes later, there's a knock on our door and it's the nurse from the clinic. She doesn't speak much English, but kindness is universal and her warmth and smile calm me a bit. She takes my temperature and blood pressure. Somehow I understand it when she says that my blood pressure is low and I'm severely dehydrated. While the kids get me tea and cookies from the hotel, the nurse hooks me up to an IV. She sits patiently by my bed until the middle of the night, when my vital signs return to normal. It's a pretty low moment for the three of us, who are horribly sick in a strange country where we don't know anyone. Still, we manage to endure all our treatments until the end of our eight-day stay.

January 5, 2015
Another day at the office, tired but determined to turn
this mess into a message for all my fellow Lymies whose voices can't be heard.
#ChronicNeurologicalLyme #WeMustFindACure
#ProperDiagnostics #AffordableForAll

From Korea, David wants me to meet him in Singapore. I'm torn. Of course, I want to see my husband, but I'm in no shape to go anywhere besides my own bed. I drop off Anwar and Bella for their L.A. flight and walk through the airport like a ghost. *Why didn't I go home with them? That's the intelligent thing to do.* Then I walk to my own gate and board a plane to Singapore.

Each morning, I manage to get up with David and go with him to the set of the show, about forty-five minutes from our hotel in Malaysia. I help him get dressed and ready, and then, once he starts filming, his manager and my dear friend Marc Johnston, who is like a brother to me, accompanies me back to the hotel.

"I think I'm dying," I tell Marc one morning on our drive. "I don't think I'm going to win this."

"But you *have* to. Your children need you. We need you," he says in his sweet English accent. Back at the hotel, I get into bed. *I could sleep for weeks. My body is tired, SO tired, after twelve hundred days fighting what feels like a losing battle.*

David sets up appointments at the best hospital in Singapore. Our hope is that their testing is different from what I've had everywhere else. *Maybe we'll get a fresh perspective from minds in a different part of the world.* The doctors are amazing, but the test results are the same: Lyme, co-infections, autoimmune disease, and thyroid disease. Together we return to L.A., where I get back into my fuzzy white robe, feeling totally and completely discouraged, about not only myself but also my children. My great effort managing their cases feels like a failure, and I don't have many more options for treating them. Long-term antibiotics didn't work for me, so why pollute Bella's and Anwar's young bodies, especially their guts, with these medications? Why subject my children, who are already weak from the disease, to anything without hard-core proof?

Like so many of the treatments I've tried, the stem cells give the kids and me a lift in overall energy. But they're not a cure for Lyme and it unfortunately doesn't fix our immune systems like the doctor suggested. I consider the trips to Korea a big waste of time and money. I always hoped that if I could do fifty things together it would make me 100 percent better. I know I should view each one of these experiences as a building block, but I'm getting really disenchanted. I'm worse than I've been in all the years that I've been sick. Once I get home, I resume my protocol, but again the die-off reaction is unbearable. It's interesting how much better I feel when I take a couple of days off from the antibiotics and antiparasitics, something doctors refer to as "pulsing." But I need to finish this course if I want results. At the same time, I'm doing all sorts of holistic things—the hyperbaric chamber, ozone treatments, colonics, coffee enemas, Epsom salt baths, and lymphatic drainage massages. *Why does it seem like nothing is helping? I've probably done eighty hyperbaric chamber sessions, but they make my symptoms worse.* Everything is off, including my appetite. I've barely eaten in months, mainly nibbling on green olives and radishes—that's all I'm craving. And I still long for silence in my brain, which feels shaky. Some nights I need to take two Xanax just to sleep and calm my nervous system.

My Diary
I feel like I've been in this abyss for the past two months and I can't get out. When is it going to end?

I often sit on the floor of our tiny balcony smoking my raw tobacco. I love watching the young children running around the playground next door. Their seemingly endless energy is a joy to watch. There's also a church here and on weekends I sit in my white robe on the balcony and watch people dressed up in their Sunday best. I'm envious but it makes me happy to see others live the life that I can't be part of.

One morning, I wake up with my head pounding intensely and the bones in my lower body on fire. *I'm going to throw up.* I move as quickly as I can to the bathroom, which isn't quickly at all. After barely making it to the toilet, I lie down on the cold bathroom floor. *I feel like I want to die. I can't possibly get through another day. God, please take me. Please!* I pull my cell phone from my robe pocket and call Paige in Santa Barbara. When I hear her voice, I just start bawling.

"I feel like I'm dying and I can't live like this for one more day. Please come here and don't leave my side. I can't take care of myself anymore."

"I'll be there in an hour and a half," she says.

"Honestly, I feel like there's a demon inside me, some monster that has taken over my gut," I tell her.

Paige arrives like a whirlwind of fresh air. It's only been six weeks since I last saw her, but I can tell she's startled by my appearance. My skin has a yellowish cast to it, I have black circles under my eyes, and the muscles on my calves have atrophied so much that my legs are bony sticks poking out from my robe.

Because David is traveling, Paige sleeps next to me, watching my every move and doing anything she can to bring me comfort. She goes to the market, makes chicken soup from scratch, puts fresh flowers around the apartment, and picks up my prescriptions from the pharmacy. She clears off the kitchen counter, organizes all my medications, and keeps a log for Dr. Horowitz detailing my nausea, blurred vision, dizziness, vomiting, extreme exhaustion, and other severe side effects. After a nurse teaches her, she gives me the daily Bicillin shots to treat my bacterial infections. When I want to know more about my medications or symptoms, Paige does the research. She even deals with the annoyance of calling my insurance company because she is enraged by the amount of money I've spent on medical care for Bella, Anwar, and myself. With three children of her own and a job, I know it's not easy for Paige to take off all this time to be with me but she's a trouper, and I need every ounce of her strength.

In the midst of this horrible relapse, the *Housewives* producers call me. I need to reshoot an interview for the show giving my opinion about what happened when the women and I went to Holland. David and I already moved out of our Malibu home, but we have to shoot there so it's consistent with the other interviews I've done for the show. I skip my morning medication because it will knock me out and cause a Herxheimer reaction that I cannot handle right now, and then Paige drives me to Malibu. She grabs an orange dress from my closet, thinking the bright color will give me a lift and makeup and hair will be there as well. I need all the help I can get to look somewhat healthy.

"I can tell you don't feel good," says Dusty, my makeup artist. " 'Cause even that orange color doesn't brighten your face." Having to recall what happened on the *Housewives* Holland trip is hard, but forming an opinion and articulating it seems like an insurmountable task.

"Yo, you can get through this. Think of how strong you've been," Paige says on the drive back to Beverly Hills. "You've fought so hard. You've come so far."

"I just don't know anymore, Paige."

"You're also the nicest sick person I've ever met," she adds, trying to make me laugh.

"I know you have to leave soon," I tell her. "But before you do, please find me a caregiver. I need a brain, someone who understands the Lyme journey and can help me get better."

"I'm on it," Paige says.

I need someone to take control of my life and my health care, because I can't put it together anymore or fight for myself. All these medications are confusing. *When do I take them? How much do I take?* I also don't think David wants to be a caretaker anymore. He says he isn't going anywhere and that we're in this together until the end. But lately he's been less and less involved and sadly our lives seem very far apart. I admit that I'm not the person he married three years ago. He wants his lively, sexy, funny, and intelligent partner back, and I understand that. Yet I'm trapped in the cocoon of my paralyzed brain and am barely able to live in my own skin, let alone go out to fancy parties and live someone else's life. My world is small because small is all I can handle. *I miss being me. I don't even remember what it's like to be normal or function in this world.*

At one in the morning, I wake up with severe night sweats. I go out on the balcony in my underwear and lie down because the cool stone against my skin is the only relief I can find, and I gaze at the stars, with a deep desire to connect with the universe because it feels as if my connection to everything else in my life is gone.

"God, I need a surrogate brain, someone to think for me and lead me through this. God, please help me," I say out loud. "Please, I beg you."

Paige starts talking to various friends and people in the Lyme network about finding some help. The issue is that I need more than just a typical nurse. I need someone who understands chronic Lyme, which isn't easy to find since some of the best doctors in this town don't understand it. I also need someone who can make sense of my complicated protocols and can look at my case intelligently and help take me to the next step because I am stuck. After a few days, Paige narrows the list of potential candidates down to three women and plans to interview them downstairs in the lobby of our apartment building. But after the first meeting, she comes upstairs.

"I was waiting on the couch when in walks this sweet blond woman in a bright dress. I literally felt like Mary Poppins arrived," Paige tells David and me, her voice full of excitement. "I want to see what you think. Can I bring her up?"

"Yes," David says. Minutes later, Paige walks in with a woman whose beautiful spirit and kindness fills the room immediately.

"This is Daisy White," Paige says. Daisy walks over to the couch and hugs me. Instantly, I feel a connection.

"I have Lyme myself, but it's in remission," Daisy explains. "Since then, I've made it my mission to help others get well as a health advocate."

"What's a health advocate?" David asks.

"I help execute your protocols and figure out which tests to do and how to interpret their results. I keep track of where we've made progress and where we haven't, help prioritize your treatments, and figure out the next step in your journey," Daisy explains. *That's exactly what I need. Taking care of myself has been a full-time job. I can't do it anymore.*

I look at Paige and nod.

"I've learned to use various tools, like computers, scanning devices, and different types of muscle testing. My goal is to make sure you're headed in the right direction. For Lyme patients it's so easy to lose our way because we can't tell the difference between a Herx that's helping or one that's setting us back," Daisy adds. "I'll help you find your way." My gut says she's the one and David agrees to hire her for six months to get me over the hump.

"Great," David says.

"So you would need me on Mondays, Wednesdays, and Fridays?" Daisy asks.

"No. I need you every day."

"Okay," she says.

"My biggest worry is my children, I need help getting them well," I say. This strikes a deep chord and the floodgates of tears open. Daisy tears up as well.

"I will," she says. "I can."

"I need help making sense of all of this." I point toward the stack of binders on the coffee table.

"Can I take those home with me?"

February 10, 2015
It's during the worst times of your life that you
get to see the true colors of the people who say they care

about you. Thank you @1437paige for showing me the
true meaning of a twenty-year friendship.
#IamBlessed #BestFriendsForever

Over the next few weeks, I feel better knowing that Daisy can help me steer the ship. She recommends that I see Dr. Dietrich Klinghardt, who is internationally known for his successful treatment of chronic illness and one of the most well-respected, Lyme-literate doctors in the world, one who has survived Lyme himself. He practices for most of the year in Europe but works out of his Seattle office for a couple of months a year. We schedule an appointment for March 10th.

In the meantime, Daisy introduces me to the ZYTO machine. We use it every two weeks to understand my progress. I'm a bit skeptical at first, but, as I stick with it, the things that come up are so dead-on that they seem undeniable, and it definitely gets my attention.

February 12, 2015
I am going to find my way out of this maze and find a cure for
not only myself but also for all my fellow Lymies.
#NoteToSelf
Minutes turn into hours, hours turn into days, days turn into weeks,
weeks turn into months, and my months have turned into three years.
#Misdiagnosis #ChronicNeurologicalLyme #MoreDeterminedThanEver
#MyHealthJourney #LymeDiseaseAwareness
Much love and a big hug to all of you fighting your own battles
with chronic illness.

On Friday, February 13, I wake up at three thirty in the morning and can't fall back to sleep. I go into the living room to lie on the couch, where I realize that I'm strangely awake and alert like some heavy fog has lifted from my brain, a clarity I haven't experienced in years. Even the tremors in my hands feel less severe than usual. It's such an obvious shift that it almost feels eerie. *Is God working his magic? Have my prayers finally been heard?* I'm not sure what is going on but I'm up and still have a few hours before I need to wake Anwar for school, so I decide to prepare and boil coffee for my enema. *Today I'll do it before my colonic instead of after.*

A few hours later, Daisy drops me off for my eight o'clock appointment in Santa Monica at the Gentle Wellness Center with France Robert, my colon hydrotherapist. France is another one of my guardian angels, whom I also call my "colon whisperer," a title she deserves after thirty years of experience in this unusual field. I lie down on the table and gently insert the tube. *Just another day at the office.* Then she turns on the colonic machine.

"Look! Look!" she screams seconds later. I quickly turn around to find France pointing at the glass irrigation tube connected to the colonic machine. Inside, we see a huge creature, about sixteen inches long and so wide that it fills the entire circumference of the tube moving through in perfect slow motion. It has octopus-like suctions all around it and what looks like a big head on each end. France is in such shock that she doesn't even think to stop the machine so we can study it and take pictures. Instead, it gets sucked away, and we stare at each other in astonishment. *I can't believe the big, fat monster that just came out of my ass!*

"In thirty-three years, I've seen a lot but I've never seen anything that big," France says. Well finally, there is a payoff after being tortured by some of the strong medications I've been taking. *My own sense of having a demon monster inside of me wasn't that far off. I'm fascinated but disgusted. Where did this come from? How long has it lived inside of me? Are there more? Is this the cause of my disease? Is this the end I've been waiting for?* I immediately text Daisy, who's at the Chinese tea shop next door getting me a ginger tea.

"Oh my God. A monster came out!"

"That's fantastic," she writes.

"Fantastic? Are you crazy?"

"Yes. This is progress!" *Who knew progress would be a sixteen-inch monster coming out of my ass?*

"Did you take a picture?"

"No. It went too fast!"

"Because you did a coffee enema earlier this morning, there was no stool in the lower colon so the parasite came out in this perfectly clear water and was easy to see," France says. Daisy picks me up, and we spend the rest of the day researching parasites and looking for pictures online. I mentally scan my whole life. *Where did I pick up that ugly monster?* I've taken pristine care of my body since I was a teenager. When I get home, I immediately tell Blanca about the creature. I'm so disgusted, but also strangely excited, hoping this is the culprit of my three-year nightmare.

"Growing up in Mexico, my mother gave us antiparasite medication four times a year," Blanca says. "It was preventive." I'm shocked; I've never *heard* of taking antiparasite medications preventively. I'm desperate to understand what just happened, stressed, and scared, especially after browsing the Internet and seeing images from the parasite world. It's truly mind boggling. *After all the parasite testing I've done in the last three years, how did everything come back negative? How did they miss this?*

Of course every time I go to the bathroom after this day, I'm obsessed with what is coming out of me. I start doing colonics three days a week with special herbal enemas for parasites. I set up a parasite lab in the guest bathroom with disposable gloves, a tray, cups, and sticks, and I literally start dissecting my own poop. I must have been a scientist in a past life because I feel the deep urge to understand this. I want to collect these parasites, take pictures, and send them to different labs for testing. I've kept a chronological photo diary from this entire journey as I worry that my failing brain will not be able to remember my discoveries, and I am not going to leave this chapter out no matter how much shame I feel around it. I photograph some of these disgusting things next to a plastic fork to show their actual size. A particularly fascinating one is skinny like a shoestring and about twenty-two inches long. *It's like finding aliens in my own body! The only word I can find here is FASCINATING!!*

I use the Internet to identify them, although there's very limited information on this subject. I don't know why I used to associate parasites with being dirty. It's hard to believe I have them because I've always been neurotic about being clean and have a lifelong ritual of showering twice a day. Nevertheless, once I educate myself, I learn that parasites have nothing to do with personal hygiene. Every person supposedly has microbes in his or her gut but in a healthy environment, they should live in harmony with your gut bacteria. In my case, however, they seem to be running the show and have taken control of my body. *It's like I'm being eaten alive from the inside out.* This seems to be is a big part of the puzzle, but there is no overnight solution and unfortunately I don't feel much better.

In the midst of dealing with the monsters living inside of my body, Bella calls me crying from New York about the severe pain in her spine and joints. I feel so helpless and reach out to Dr. Joan Fleischman, a friend I made in the world of Lyme sufferers who lives in New York. She and her two children are battling this disease, too, so she's extremely understanding and compassionate about our situation. The last time I was in New York, I took Bella for an appointment at Dr. Fleischman's office, so she is kind enough to make a house call to Bella's apartment. She starts treating Bella with the coil, which is the same principle as the Rife machine and can cause severe die-off reactions. I feel helpless being so far away.

"Please come home so that I can help you," I tell Bella. I'd feel safer with her here.

"Mommy, I don't want to give in to being a sick person," she says, determined to stay in New York and push through her symptoms. "I need to keep trying to be a normal teenager and be with my friends." In all honesty, I don't have a magic pill for her, so I accept whatever it takes for her to keep herself going. She is such a tough cookie and she motivates me to keep fighting for a cure.

Just a couple of weeks later, it's almost time to tape the *Housewives* reunion show. I'm vomiting and really ill with nausea and tremors from the hard-core parasite protocol I have been on. The day of the taping, February 20, I feel horrible and am coughing with a deep, knife-stabbing pain in my lower abdomen. I have a massage at 7:30 A.M., but it doesn't help. Dusty is coming to do my hair and makeup but I feel trapped in a body that doesn't even belong to me. The reunion is part of my contract and commitment to the show; backing out isn't an option in my mind but getting dressed isn't either because the fatigue is so severe. When Daisy walks in, I'm wearing a nightgown and curlers.

"I'm going like this," I tell her. In my pajamas means that I only need to change my clothes once. I am conserving my spoons. The second we arrive at the studio, I'm ambushed by cameras. Who knew they'd want to film my arrival? Not me, because I'm in an old white nightgown. "If you'd warned me, I would have worn cuter pajamas," I joke with the crew.

Once inside the studio, I slip on an old dress I'd grabbed from my closet and lie down on the couch in the dressing room. Andy comes in to say hello and sees that I'm obviously not myself.

"Just do the best you can," he says.

Once we start taping, it's almost impossible to push through. The subjects my castmates are discussing and debating seem insignificant compared to my daily health struggles. Despite my best effort to be there, I don't feel like I add much to the conversation.

"Yolanda, how are you feeling?" Andy asks.

"I'm trying to weather the storm and just came back from Korea, where I had stem cell treatment that's not available here yet," I say. "I fight and pray every day."

"What do you think about a viewer saying she's worried that you're receiving erroneous treatments?" he says.

"There are people in my family who deny my disease. So *that* hurts. But a stranger doubting what I go through doesn't mean anything to me,

because none of those haters have walked in my shoes, know me personally or have seen my medical files," I respond. "So who are they to
judge?" Although I exist in a safe cocoon at home, I feel so raw and
vulnerable, and being here without full access to the "search button" in
my brain makes me insecure. Two hours into the typically twelve-hour
taping, I need to stop. The effort and energy it takes to come up with
somewhat intelligible answers is like pushing a car without gas. *I feel so
hopeless.*

"I'm really sorry, but I have to go back to bed," I tell Andy and the
other women. When the reunion show airs, I have to write my blog.

Hello Bravo lovers,
First and foremost, thank you so much for all your love and support
during my crazy health journey. Please know that it is a great source
of strength and that it really means a lot to me. I also appreciate
your kindness and compassion in understanding that I have not been
able to blog. Getting well is my full-time job these days. It took me
a while to learn the true meaning of patience and surrender, but I
have finally accepted that healing doesn't happen on our schedule.
It doesn't have a clock or a calendar.

The diagnosis isn't simple, either. A late-stage chronic Lyme dis-
ease patient probably doesn't just have Lyme disease. Unfortunately,
this situation is like peeling an onion with many layers of problems. I
won't bore you with the details of my diseases collected throughout
my life journey until the day I got sick now almost three years ago.
One funny story gives you a sense, though, of the long-term journey.
At twelve years old, I raised a premature baby cow on our farm,
because her mom had died. I bottle-fed it every day, let it suck on
my chin, and babied it until it was stable. I just recently found out
that little love gave me Q fever, which has been a low-grade infection
throughout my entire life.

The path forward isn't completely clear. As I turn each corner,
new obstacles arise, but I am a determined warrior, and even though

this has brought me to my knees, I know God often uses our deep-est pain as the launching pad of our greatest calling. So even though my life may not be perfect for now, I try to find a blessing in every day. Watching my children grow and establishing themselves into the world is my greatest joy and drive to continue to fight until I find my cure. Unfortunately I had to miss watching Gigi and Bella walk Tom Ford's fashion show right here in town a couple of weeks ago. I've waited my whole life for that exciting moment, but while I couldn't be there in person, at least today's technology allowed me to live-stream the show from bed. I've cried my eyes out for missing so many precious moments as their careers take off, while I've been forced to watch from the sidelines with great pride, inspiration, and hope for a front-row seat one day in the near future.

And, unfortunately, I am far from alone. Lyme disease is a major epidemic of the twenty-first century, and I am sure that in the years to come, as people become more aware and educated about this disease, you will come across someone in your inner circle who is afflicted with this. In some ways, it's like AIDS in the early 1980s. I am going to make it my mission in the coming years to help find proper diagnostics and a cure affordable for all. There is so little acknow-ledgment and understanding from the world at large for this and most chronic invisible diseases, for that matter. That's why I like to say that you don't really get IT until you get IT.

Throughout this journey, I have finally, after fifty-one years, met the true core of my being. I understand pain and suffering in a dimen-sion I never knew existed. I am finding my own strength at its best, yet in the worst time of my life. I am getting to the most raw and vulnerable part of me and it has changed my perspective towards life and human beings for the rest of my life.

All of this brings me back to the reunion. It was nice to see all the girls, even though, for obvious reasons, I have been extremely disconnected and pretty much living on a different planet for now. My overall take on the season is that we must all try to be kinder than necessary, because those hardest to love need love the most. Some people come into our life as a blessing, while others come into our life as a lesson, so love them for who they are instead of judging them for who they are not.

It's obvious that some of the women's behavior is a true reflection of how they feel about themselves, and for that, I have great empathy and compassion. The issues at play here are real-life struggles, so remaining open to things with which we don't agree allows us to see that there is always a resolution to a situation if we are willing to make the effort. Everyone matters, so I don't feel the need to compete and keep pointing out other people's imperfections in order to feel better about myself. Since today's world has enough critics, I choose to be an encourager where possible (while also telling friends what they need to hear, and not just what they want to hear) and treat everyone as if they were what they should be and hopefully help them become what they are capable of becoming.

I think it's important for all of us participating in the Housewives journey to remember that just because someone has inflicted hurt upon us, it does not give us the right to do the same.

Anyway, thank you for supporting our show the way that you have. I hope you continue to tune in for the three-part reunion. I am sending you lots of love from my healing cave and hope to see you all next year.

Remember, character isn't what you have, it's who you are.
—xoxox Yo

February 28, 2015
Didn't wake up feeling great or too cute, but I WOKE UP . . .
#CountingMyBlessings #DeterminedToFindACure
#ChronicLymeDisease #MyHealthJourney

I am on a course of Biltricide, which is a medication to treat tapeworms and flukes. It's very strong and makes me feel incredibly sick, but life still goes on around me and I force myself to participate wherever needed the most.

My Diary
March 5, 2015
Sick as a dog, but got up and took Anwar to get his driving permit. I couldn't let him down as I knew he needed me there.

March 7, 2015
David leaving again for 18 days again. I'm sad and don't understand how you justify leaving your sick partner behind. I could never do that to him. No energy to debate it though.

March 8, 2015
Bella has to go to Paris. She has severe fatigue, pain, and is feeling insecure. Wish I could keep her home longer, but work is calling her.

On March 9, Daisy and I fly to Seattle for my initial appointment with Dr. Klinghardt. We have found a rhythm for managing my day-to-day care. She has been an angel sent from heaven who has taken me by the hand and is leading the way. When we walk into Dr. Klinghardt's cluttered office, I instantly know that he and I are a perfect fit.

"Let's sit!" he says with his German accent. I feel connected to him the minute we start talking—our Dutch and German backgrounds give me a safe and familiar feeling. Daisy gives him a rundown of my medical background, current protocols, and most recent test results.

"Okay, let's put you on the table." Dr. Klinghardt gestures toward the treatment table in the middle of the room. "Yolanda, do you know about muscle testing?"

"Yes, I am just starting to learn about it from Daisy."

"Oh, good. Indirect testing uses another person's arm to help us see and ask your body if certain tools or treatments are working and if the body is improving," he says. "It gives Lyme patients a compass as to what is making you strong or weak, which pathogens might still be in the body— fungal, bacterial, viral, or parasitic—and how toxic the body is.

"You have a mouthful of metal-based crowns, and they're blocking your healing," he says.

"This doesn't surprise me because I heard this at Paracelsus a couple of years ago."

"All that metal is preventing your immune system from doing its job and causing toxicity, which the bacteria bind to like a magnet," he says. "This accounts for a lot of your strange symptoms, especially with your brain." *Finally, someone has a reason for my brain issues!*

"Your brain is retrievable though," Dr. Klinghardt says.

"Are you sure??" I say. *I don't want to cry, but I feel a wave of tears coming on.*

"So the gut is testing weak," he adds. "Must be some creatures in there." *Creatures?*

"Daisy, can you show Dr. Klinghardt the pictures of my parasites?" I ask. I am expecting him to be shocked, but he just nods when he sees them. *He doesn't seem impressed at all.* Apparently, this is very common for chronically ill patients.

"We'll work on the parasites, but they're only a small piece of the bigger picture," he says.

"Has she had neural therapy to all scars?" he asks Daisy.

"Yes, thyroid especially," Daisy says.

"Every scar is an interference field to the body's functioning at its best. It's also a place where bacteria and viruses can live, causing the body to hold on to illness," Dr. Klinghardt explains. "Your tonsils and teeth also cause interference fields or focal infections. We need to address all these issues in order to help you heal." He injects my tonsils with procaine but tells me this is just a bandage. Eventually they need to come out but there is a pecking order of other layers to clear before that. *Tonsillectamy? At my age? Scary thought.*

I promise Dr. Klinghardt that I will start his protocol immediately and will be back in six weeks to see if I have made any progress. He tells me it will take me about two years of dedicated work to get back to perfect health. It sounds like a long time but I like the confidence in his voice when he makes this statement although I won't believe it until I see it.

At this point, many people in the Lyme community know who I am because of the show and they often thank me for talking publicly about our misunderstood disease. As I walk through the waiting room, a beautiful woman looks up and jumps out of her seat when she sees me. She walks right over, giving me the biggest hug.

"Thank you for bringing awareness," she says.

"Where are *you* in your journey?" I ask. I've learned that being chronically ill is a journey with many chapters so it's very normal for patients to ask one another where they're at.

"Thank God, I just finished the parasite chapter," she says. "It's been about six months."

"Really?" I say, not wanting to sound too excited but clearly *very* interested. Then she pulls out her iPhone, swipes through her photos, and holds up a picture of a huge parasite. I'm stunned. *Oh my God! This is crazy, it's identical to one that I passed!*

"What do you know about it? What is it?" I immediately feel connected to her and it's good to know that I'm not alone.

"There is a book by a Russian scientist about rope worms. You'll find yours in there," she says, writing the name of the book on a piece of paper. The second we get back to the hotel, Daisy googles and orders *Helminthes: Known and . . . Unknown* by N. V. Gubarev. *What are the chances of running into someone who holds the information that I need more than anything right now? Is there such a thing as a coincidence? Life has truly brought me to my knees but God is good and that's all I know in this moment.*

Home from Seattle, I experience a little bit of a shift since my appointment with Dr. Klinghardt. Daisy and I are driving to my colonic and I actually notice the sun on my skin, a sensation of well-being that I haven't felt for a very long time. I start researching and understanding what I'm really dealing with. Once the book arrives, I can't put it down. I read it over and over and compare the photos on my iPhone with those in the book. The author calls parasites "our invisible universal enemy." In one part, he writes:

> Our body is an ideal habitat for millions of parasitic organisms. For them, our mortal bodies are a universe where they may splash about in lakes of blood, urine and lymph. They may dwell in alimentary masses in an intestine, may feed at numerous restaurants in our oral cavity and revel in lakes of saliva, etc. Oh, yes, the parasites feel well and comfortable; unfortunately, we cannot say the same ourselves.

The book explains why getting rid of these worms, also known as Helminthes, isn't as simple as excreting them. Some are large, so they counteract the movement of your intestines that occurs when you go to the bathroom. They're also strong and elastic, so they can hang on to the walls of your intestines. Gubarev explains how they can create symptoms that can easily be confused with many other conditions, such as pain in the chest, legs, and arms; frequent colds; headaches; skin problems like pimples and psoriasis; hair loss; bloating; and sinus issues. The book not only identifies various worms but also has natural enema recipes to help remove them from your body. These recipes use both common ingredients such as lemon juice, baking soda, and milk as well as less common ones such as special mint leaves, sea buckthorn, and messmate leaf. Daisy orders all the ingredients to follow the Gubarev treatments.

It's hard to imagine where I got so many parasites. Most likely I contracted them while traveling the world as a young model. When I was shooting in India, for example, I would sit with the local people in the street and eat their food without any worries about what was being transferred to me. Knowing what I know now, this makes me believe that I probably collected those parasites and their infections over my lifetime. Being raised on a farm, I had no fear of dirt or anything like that. Even a healthy human being apparently has parasites and good bacteria living inside of them without any symptoms. But in my case, they've taken over and are running the show in my body. It seems that the stress of my father's death when I was seven, the Epstein-Barr, the appendicitis, and the hepatitis B all by the time I was barely twenty most likely weakened my immune system and therefore I'm not able to fight the microbes.

The more research I do, the more I realize that the giant parasite that came out on Friday the 13th probably was born, raised, and had set up camp in my body for twenty to thirty years. Looking back I remember a few times in my life when I had strange and intense pains under my belly button. About ten or fifteen years ago, when I was in my Santa Barbara home, I'd occasionally have a horrible pain in my stomach that would take my breath away. It was like something was turning inside me; the pain was so bad that I actually got down on the floor. Back then, I thought it must have been something I ate or a spasm from the laxatives I took.

As if uncovering decades-old aliens in my body isn't enough, I can feel David distancing himself from me more and more. If I was in a healthy state, this would really upset me, because I am a very intimate person, but at this point very little moves or shakes me. I notice it though and it's confusing. *Isn't marriage and partnership supposed to be all about the good times and the bad? In sickness and in health? I know, I am the one who changed, but it's out of my hands.* One day, David mentions to Bella that things are different between the two of us since we got married.

"Do you think this illness is her choice?" Bella responds kindly but to the point.

That afternoon, Daisy helps me through a bad reaction to the Biltricide. I vomit uncontrollably but the next morning, she finds me in the bedroom packing for David. My hands are trembling and shaking while I try to lay

out his clothes. I put outfits into different Ziploc bags, label them and photograph them for every day he'll be away.

"What are you doing?" she asks, looking worried.

"I'm trying to be a wife," I say. I feel like I've lost so much so I am com-
promising and trying to hang on to the littlest things I used to do for my
husband that I know he loves and hopefully appreciates.

Chapter Twelve

....

IF GOD BRINGS YOU TO IT,
HE WILL BRING YOU THROUGH IT.

On April 10, Daisy and I take our second trip together. This time it is to Tijuana for an appointment with Dr. Louie Yu, who has a lot of experience with ozone. Although I've done a lot of treatments with ozone over the years, I never tried RHP, which is not approved in California, and stands for recirculatory hemoperfusion. Through an IV catheter, your blood is extracted from one arm; goes through a tube into a dialysis machine, where it is infused with ozone and filtered; and then is returned into the other arm through an IV. I feel confident about this because Daisy has done this treatment about twelve times herself with great results. Dr. Klinghardt thinks it may help me as well.

April 10, 2015
RISE UP AND ATTACK each day with courage.
Thank you, Mexico, for being open to ancient medicine . . .
#OzoneRHP #TijuanaMexico
#SearchingForACure #ChroniclymeDisease

When we arrive at the clinic, and I use the word "clinic" very, *very* loosely, I feel as if I am in a movie, a bad movie. It's no longer in the same location Daisy had gone to before. Instead, it looks like an abandoned apartment building which is almost finished being remodeled but isn't decorated yet. We are brought into a room with two chairs and a machine in the center of it. Daisy looks at me, surprised and upset.

"Do you want to leave?" she asks.

"Mmm, I don't know," I say. We did our due diligence and carefully planned this trip; it's just a different scenario than what we thought. Yes, I'm nervous and afraid. This is another unusual situation but then again it's similar to some of the other times I've come to Tijuana for treatment. Plus we've traveled such a long way that I try to stay calm and collected. *I can't let my emotions take over.*

"You must think I'm crazy," Daisy says with a smile. But it's the whole situation that's insane. *How did I end up here?* I pace around the room a couple of times, trying to force myself to relax and ease into the situation. *God, I pray that you've placed us in the right hands.*

"I'm a little worried that this place isn't sterile enough," I say.

"I brought new disposable tubing just for you," Daisy says. *This is why I call her my Nurse Nightingale.* Finally, the nurse walks into the room, apologizing for being a little bit late. She looks impeccable and is very nice, which puts me at ease. My veins are beat up and weary after so many treatments. She eventually finds one and starts the RHP, which lasts about two and a half hours. It's fascinating to see how my very dark, almost black blood comes out of one arm and then, after being washed by the ozone, becomes bright red and healthy-looking before it's let back into my body through a tube in my other arm. Seeing this gives me hope that RHP is a good move.

My body is exhausted but I am excited by the possibility of better health. On our drive back to L.A. I notice an unusual sense of clarity in my brain and my eyesight, which as you know has been one of my worst symptoms. Unfortunately, only days later, this treatment hits me like a ton of bricks and the little progress I thought I made disappears quickly. I feel severely ill again, and my skin and eyes are turning yellow. Apparently, the treatment stirred up old infections in my liver like the hepatitis B and Q fever. I am down for the count but magically the universe provides what is necessary for the next step in my journey. The day after Tijuana, I get a call from Dr. Oz, who wants to visit me and get an update on my health. He comes over for coffee, and as we talk I immediately share my parasite story. In fact, I'm so obsessed with parasites that it's all I can talk about. *He must think I'm nuts.*

"I've saved so many of them, but no lab here in L.A. can tell me what they are," I say.

"Send them to my friend Dr. Omar Amin, who owns one of the best parasite labs in America, the Parasitology Center in Arizona," Dr. Oz says. "His lab has the tools to identify exactly what they are." *Hallelujah.* We contact Dr. Amin and send him some of my parasites. A couple of weeks later, I get back a proper result with real information. *Finally some answers!* This is the only lab that identified and confirmed the rope worms I already knew I had.

Weeks later Daisy and I take our second trip to Dr. Klinghardt in Seattle. His muscle testing continues to show that heavy metals are a huge part of the problem with my brain, so he injects my jaw with DMPS, which is a chelator that removes heavy metals from the blood. He also injects the scars from my back surgery. When we leave, my face blows up. I have lumps in my jaw, and the pain is excruciating. *I feel as if I'm having an out-of-body experience. Haven't I had enough of these by now?*

We're sitting on the terrace at Sophia Health Institute getting some fresh air when Blanca calls me.

"Lucky isn't feeling well," she says. "What should I do?"

"Please take him to the hospital immediately."

There, the doctor tells Blanca that Lucky has heart failure and his kidneys are shutting down.

"He's not doing well, if you want to see him before he dies, hurry up," Blanca says.

Our flight isn't until late tonight, but we head to the airport hoping to get on an earlier one. We land in L.A. I go straight to the hospital, where I meet Bella and Lucky, who gives me the saddest look. I'm devastated and start to cry because I can feel the outcome of this. *My baby Lucky. We've had him for thirteen years.* I don't want him to die in the hospital, so I bring him back to the house in Malibu. I wrap him in a blanket and together we lie on the grass in the backyard for hours. It's his favorite spot to bask in the sun. I am meditating as I envision helping him pass over to the other side. His breathing is very slow, yet it seems like he is holding on until Anwar gets back from school. I Face-Time with Gigi, who is in Miami shooting *Sports Illustrated,* so she can see Lucky one final time. I can see his little ears move when listening to her voice. When Anwar comes home, he lies with us on the grass until the sun sets. Together we hold Lucky in our arms when he takes his final breath.

Losing Lucky is absolutely devastating. He was such a big part of our family, and energetically he was my partner in crime. I raised my children with him. Back in Santa Barbara, if I left the kids outside by the pool to get something in the kitchen and one of the kids tried to go in the water, he wouldn't stop barking until I got back. It's a difficult loss to process for the children and me but someone told me that Lucky maybe gave up his life to save mine. I don't know if that's true but I do know that he will always be a little angel on our shoulders.

Through the Lyme community, I hear about the Infusio Treatment Center in Germany. David, Daisy, and I meet with the founder, an alternative medicine practitioner who happens to be in L.A. His stem cell treatment is different than the one I did in Korea which works with plasma. Here they extract stem cells, growth factors, and other important elements from your blood, which then grow for ten days before they are reintroduced through an injection in your arm. I guess anything sounds promising to me right now and we aren't always in agreement about treatments and protocols, because Daisy's approach is more integrative, David's is all conventional, and I am just going by intuition. I think this treatment sounds interesting, but neither of them feels particularly strongly about it. David says it's because he doesn't like the guy's crocodile shoes, which I feel is a weak argument when I'm discussing the next step in my very serious search for a cure. Daisy isn't sure it will help based on the fact that the founder isn't willing to collaborate enough with Dr. Klinghardt's protocol. She is skeptical when he says that he has a cure for Lyme, because even top doctors like Dr. Klinghardt never speak of a cure but rather remission. I kind of like his confidence and want to believe him. At this point, I love everybody's input, but I need to keep moving and search the globe or else I'm not sure I'm going to make it through. I feel weak, and, besides my usual symptoms, my calves have become numb, along with two fingers on my right hand. I'm at my wit's end and just need to escape from everyone while I fight on my own.

I also long to be with my mom and brother in Europe, so I go against David and Daisy and leave for Frankfurt on another one of my stubborn missions, determined to find a cure. I travel with the last bit of hope deep down inside me. By the time I arrive, I'm herxing like crazy from the antiparasitic medications and still passing what feels like endless parasites. I feel desperate, so I record a video diary on my phone.

Video Diary
April 2015
I arrived in Frankfurt yesterday and today is my first day starting a new treatment. I will be here for 14 days, away from my children, which sucks. I had a terrible flight coming from Los Angeles. The minute we took off, I had severe inflammation in my brain, and my eyes, which were already bothering me when trying to get through the airport, so I stopped to buy extra-strength reading glasses. I feel like my eyesight is getting worse by the day. I actually feel like I have worms in the back of my eyeballs, which is blocking my vision.

I always considered myself a smart person, especially with medical stuff, but I'm in a maze where every time I turn a corner there is something new and crazy that I don't understand. Since I passed that 16-inch rope worm on Friday, Feb. 13th, I've been researching all over the world. I have found this book that has given me a lot of the answers by a Russian scientist. I feel like if I could just leave my body right now, I would be okay. And it's not that I'm depressed. I don't feel depressed, just defeated because I'm losing this battle.

If anything happens to me, and in case I don't wake up, I want to make sure that there is an autopsy done by a medical team of my eyeballs, brain, gut, and sinuses because I want to prove that something is living inside of me and killing me slowly. I don't know how to fight it but I AM fighting it and I will continue to fight it. I'm blessed with resources and the ability to be in Germany and try another protocol. Most don't get that opportunity. I'm just really at the end of my rope with my rope worms. I feel so alone but too embarrassed to share this with anyone. Lyme disease is one thing, the word Lyme disease sounds fancy compared to the whole chapter of rope worms and parasites that I know are blocking the healing of my body.

At this point, it's probably not the Lyme that is keeping me down, but the worms. I feel like my body has been invaded by some crazy creatures. They just keep coming out. I have pieces of flesh coming out of me, something is eating my insides that nobody is seeing. I have no choice but to keep going. I know I'm not the only one. I know there are millions of people walking around with this problem, feeling so sick and helpless and not understanding what is going on.

For three years, it's been so hard to get diagnosed and to be treated for Lyme and now I have aliens coming out that no parasite testing has ever showed. It's so frustrating, but I try to keep finding gratitude while telling myself that I have the best circumstances in the worst situation.

I brought my parasite bible and sixty disposable enema bags, so I set up a makeshift lab in the hotel bathroom. The hotel was able to provide me the basic ingredients such as milk, salt, baking soda, et cetera—and I am pleasantly surprised that they even got the harder-to-find ingredients like nettle and eucalyptus leaves from the biological pharmacy. During the day, I am at Infusio for treatments and at night I come back to my hotel room and prepare the hideous parasite cleanses and enemas as directed by the Russian scientist. This honestly is the most insane experience I've ever had. That said, I'm rigidly committed, which means that I lie on the bathroom floor for one hour in the early morning before going to the clinic and one hour when I get back at night with whatever potion the book says I should use. Imagine holding warm milk with salt or a carefully brewed eucalyptus potion up your butt for an hour! YES it's crazy, but I am a desperate person on a mission. I'm afraid and I'm in this thing all alone.

I haven't really told David about what I am going through. That is, until what looks like pieces of intestinal tissue come out of me after one of my enemas. *These are actually pieces of my intestines!* I've been a vegetarian for the past year, eating mostly fruits, vegetables, and olives, so I know it can't actually be meat because I have not ingested any. I've tried to be optimistic and private, but after seeing this, I'm convinced that I'm losing my life to some strange internal attack that's gone undetected by my medical team. I start to send David e-mails with photographs of all the alien discoveries from the past couple of months. I didn't want to scare him—that's why I didn't share before—but at this point I honestly don't think I am going to make it through. I'm at war, and physically and emotionally exhausted.

The only bright spot in this experience is that my brother and mother drive up from Holland and stay with me at the hotel. What I love about my family is that they're low maintenance. We don't need to do anything but sit, talk, and enjoy our togetherness. My mom is a strong woman, and even though what I'm going through is all very unusual, she doesn't flinch or panic. She is a calming force in the middle of the worst storm of my life.

April 28, 2015
I've learned more from my pain than I could have ever
learned from pleasure . . .
#SearchingForACure
#ChronicLymeDisease #GermanyDay2

On the tenth day of my treatment, I'm still afraid that I'm losing the battle. Instead of sharing this with my mom, I wait for her to go back to her room before I record my second video diary. I want my family to know that I want my body used for science. I don't want to die in vain after all that I've gone through. If God isn't going to grant me healing and a cure while I'm alive, I want to make sure that I help millions of people suffering from chronic neurological Lyme disease when I am dead.

Video Diary
May 2015
Today is day ten of my fourteen-day treatment and I feel really sick. I fight every day with all that I have, and with my children in my mind, but I don't know how much longer my body can take this. I feel like there is a demon inside of me, one that is sucking the life out of me, my legs, my arms, and my brain. It's taking everything that I have. Not sure how much longer I can hold on. It has been years. Every day, seven days a week, twenty-four hours a day, and it just doesn't seem to come to an end. I have faith and know that I have to trust the process, which I've surrendered to. But some days I just don't know if I'm going to wake up the next morning because I feel so sick. I keep on fighting but I'm just not sure my body can do

this much longer. Nobody deserves to suffer like this, stuck in a maze of chronic disease.

So if I die, please make sure that my body gets used for research and an autopsy is done. Because I don't know what can keep some-body sick for so long. I'm almost going on three years. How does one stay alive? Why can't I figure this out? Who is going to help all the millions of people out there who are suffering just like me? I just don't know.

May 7, 2015
Sweet dreams to my new stem cells, may they strengthen
my immune system to destroy the silent killer inside me
and turn this mess into a message . . .
#ExhaustedButDetermined
#SearchingForACure #ChronicLymeDisease #INeedAMiracle

Even though I don't feel better, I'm hopeful and optimistic when my stem cells are injected into my body. I cover the injection site with a smiley face Band-Aid to set the right intention. There is no such thing as instant gratification, although I'm promised that I will feel something in the next three months.

On my way home, I stop in Paris for one night to see Ellie. Her ALS is advancing, and her health is deteriorating rapidly. She's so happy to see me and I jump into bed with her; we laugh and reminisce about the great times we shared before we both got sick. Of course, looking at her makes me not even want to talk about what I am going through. ALS is by far the most brutal disease that I've witnessed in my entire life. The only common thread between us is that we both want to live to see our children grow up. Ellie's body is completely paralyzed and lifeless, so she needs twenty-four-hour care to keep her head propped up so she can breathe through her breathing machine. She doesn't sleep much while I'm there; in fact, she hasn't slept much for years, so we talk most of the night about all kinds of very serious things. She tells me how she wants to end her life and makes me promise I will be there to hold her hand when that time comes. It's fascinating to see someone completely debilitated physically yet with a mind that is perfect, witty, smart, and functioning at a hundred miles per hour. Thank God her husband, David, installed a voice-activated computer, because writing is the most valuable outlet for her. Because the *Housewives* documented our friendship and the beginning stage of her journey, she has a nice platform to launch her clever and outspoken blog, "Have Some Decorum," which many Bravo fans love. What's interesting is that while I have become quiet and introverted because of my lack of brain function, she has become enough of a soaring firecracker for both of us. She is often frustrated by the cards life has dealt us and angered by the judgment of my journey. On social media, she takes on anyone who says anything bad about me and gives them a piece of her mind. Her family situation is extremely difficult, and life with ALS is complicated beyond words. But our journeys are aligned so perfectly in terms of timing that I'm always available to be her 24-7 lifeline and personal shrink. I've talked her off the cliff many times when she feels trapped in her lifeless body.

"Thank you for listening," she often says. "But tell me about *you. Your* struggles are important, too."

"Who am I to complain?" I respond. "A couple of parasites and half a brain is nothing compared to what you're living with." I wish I could bring her to Dr. Klinghardt because he told me that there is a direct correlation between Lyme and the onset of ALS. Ellie is too far along to even try to attack Lyme. Our girlfriend Diandra Douglas was just diagnosed with Lyme as well. The three of us lived in Santa Barbara at the same time and two of us have Lyme and Ellie has ALS. *What are the chances of that? Three friends?*

I leave Paris with a very heavy heart. I hate leaving Ellie behind, so far away from the home in Santa Barbara we once knew. We say our good-byes in tears. I kiss her beautiful golden locks and promise I'll be back soon. I feel helpless because I wish I could do more for this extraordinary human being. I love her so very much.

My plane ride home is sad. I can't help feeling defeated and disenchanted with my European expedition and slightly embarrassed to admit to David and Daisy that I have not made much progress. I walk in the door with my tail between my legs. At this point, I've run out of ideas. I don't think there is one more place to go or doctor to see. My whole life, I've been the leading lady in the Yolanda show with great confidence and direction, but now I have my doubts.

"I'm done," I tell David. "Here's the baton. You and Daisy are in charge, because I have no more ideas." I can tell Daisy is really worried about me and feels uneasy about the fact that she doesn't know what treatments I have done in Germany. Unlike any other doctor or clinic I've gone to, as far as I can determine Infusio didn't keep any records of what they did.

"If you do exactly what I say, I'll take the baton," David says. I agree without a moment's hesitation. The parasite pictures I e-mailed David from Germany really scared him and got his attention.

"We are not doing any more treatments until you get a full-body scan and see what's in your intestines to make sure it isn't cancer—or anything worse than Lyme," he adds. If you have cancer hiding somewhere in the body, stem cell treatments are believed to make it grow faster. This is David's fear. I don't think that's what's wrong with me but I am not going to argue because I passed the baton.

May 16, 2015
Woke up not too cute with some aches and pains, but I WOKE UP.
#MyUniform #WaitingForACure #ChronicLymeDisease

The three of us sit around the kitchen table, and David writes a list of what he thinks should be my next steps:

1. Endoscopy camera capsule to see what's going on in my intestines
2. Body scan
3. Check out stem cell treatment in Bahamas
4. Dental X-rays

The first appointment involves swallowing a camera, a procedure usually used to detect polyps, inflammatory bowel disease, ulcers, and tumors in the intestine. This will allow the doctor to examine my gastrointestinal tract because the camera capsule, which has its own light source, will travel through my intestines, snapping pictures along the way. Hopefully, this will provide us with some information about what has been living inside me. The morning of the appointment, I wake up with a severe migraine. I'm also sweating, with stomach cramps from the gallons of MoviPrep solution I've been drinking for the past forty-eight hours to clear out my system for the procedure. It feels as if there's a blockage in my body, which is strange considering that I haven't eaten for two days. My stomach is cramping and I have the urge to go to the bathroom as it feels like something big and hard is coming out of me. When I look down in the toilet, I see a six-inch-long spiral-shaped parasite. I scoop it out of the toilet. It's hard as a rock. In fact, it's so calcified that I can literally hold it straight up in the air. *What the hell is THIS? What planet did this alien come from?* Because this strange, dead beauty is too big to fit in one of my sterile lab cups, I fill a big glass jar with alcohol and water to bring it with me to UCLA.

Daisy takes me to the camera-swallowing procedure, and as we walk through the hospital, I link my arm into hers just to maintain my balance. The nurse helps me swallow the camera. *I've done hundreds of exterior photo shoots, but I am about to shoot one on the INSIDE of my body.* I hand the jar with my calcified parasite alien to the nurse, who says it will be sent to a lab for analysis.

Shockingly, days later, I get the following e-mail from Dr. Eric Esrailian, co-chief of the division of digestive diseases at the David Geffen School of Medicine at UCLA.

> *Hi Yolanda.*
> *The capsule views of the GI tract were completely unremarkable. I know that doesn't make you feel better, but it's actually good news. I just checked the parasite test and the results are still pending. If there is indeed a parasite, it will be diagnosed.*

Unremarkable? After everything that has come out of me? I don't need a TEST to determine whether I have parasites. I HAVE the actual parasites and photos too! It feels like such an injustice for a doctor to tell me it's "unremarkable" and "good news." Clearly they don't have the diagnostic testing to analyze this. But that doesn't mean that it's not real and most likely the cause of many of my symptoms.

I just don't know where to turn anymore. And quite frankly I have no hope left. I don't even want to do any more treatments. Daisy and Paige are texting me from the LymeAid event in San Francisco, where I was supposed to get an award tonight. They're trying to cheer me up, but I'm done and I'm going on strike.

Early Monday morning, Daisy and Paige come over to the apartment and are annoyingly optimistic and excited about all the Lyme doctors they met at the event and possible new treatments they heard about there. They're trying to motivate me to go to Dr. Klinghardt.

"I just don't care anymore," I tell them.

"But we do; you've done such great work for the Lyme community and have come such a long way," they say. "You're not giving up now." The next day, Daisy and I fly to Seattle to see Dr. Klinghardt. Thank God someone understands me and can validate my severe symptoms. He is giving me a lot of clarity and shines a bright light on the road ahead of me. I leave Seattle with a new protocol and a more positive perspective.

The next item on David's list is a full-body scan, which I did at the beginning of my journey without any findings except inflammation in the left frontal lobe of my brain. After the scan, Dr. Jabour comes into the waiting room with a serious look of concern on his face.

"I need to send this to a specialist because I'm not quite sure what I'm seeing, but I'd like to do a breast MRI as well so we can look at this from different angles," he says. "Let me show you what we found." He pulls my scan up on a large monitor and points to black spots all over my chest area—especially under my left armpit, right clavicle bone, around my breasts, and inside my rib cage. These weren't on the scan I did back in 2012. A strange sense of relief washes over me. *Did we finally hit the jackpot? Did David just save my life? As unsettling as this might sound, maybe this explains why I've been coughing for four years and why I sweat from the slightest bit of exertion! Whatever it is, I feel empowered by this knowledge, and nothing can be worse than the nightmare I just went through.*

After the case was reviewed by three of the country's top specialists together they conclude that the black spots on my scans are free-floating silicone from my breast implants that broke ten years ago during a water-skiing fall. I had them replaced immediately but silicone from the rupture must have been left behind. Usually implants are encapsulated in the pocket of the breast, so any leakage should stay within that area. In my case, the silicone seeped out of the capsulation and traveled throughout my body. It could also be the result of the extreme heat detoxing I did in Europe to kill my Lyme bugs, with things like infrared saunas and hyperthermia. Whatever the cause of its escape, this free-floating silicone is creating a constant immune response in my body. I turn another corner in this dark maze. I see clarity and it motivates me to fight this with all that I have, even though my gas tank is empty.

David and I return to the apartment with a lot to think about. I get back into my white robe, which has become my safe cocoon. I can't help feeling overwhelmed. I settle on the couch to digest all of this recent information and startling discovery. A million things are going through my head, but suddenly I remember something: about a year or two earlier, a visitor came to our house in Malibu with his girlfriend. I don't remember who they were or why they came, but she was really kind and handed me a book called *The Naked Truth about Breast Implants*.

"This is something you really need to read," she said. Little did she know that reading was one of the hardest things for me to do at the time because I couldn't retain much information.

"Thank you so much," I said politely. It's fascinating how the universe provides information at certain times in our lives, but we're just not ready to listen. This is a perfect example, because as soon as this woman left, I flipped through the book for a second before putting it under the coffee table. Now I immediately call Blanca at the house in Malibu to ask her to find the book and have Alberto bring it to me ASAP. Daisy and I go through it, highlighting all the important information. Simultaneously, she starts researching implant disease. *What a rude awakening this is!* It's shocking to learn that throughout the 1980s and 1990s, class-action lawsuits claimed that Dow Corning's silicone breast implants caused a range of serious health issues, leading to a multibillion-dollar class-action settlement. *Why didn't I know anything about this?* Oddly enough, just eight months earlier, something drove me to randomly call my plastic surgeon who did my implants.

"Do you think my implants have anything to do with my inability to get well?" I asked.

"Absolutely not," he said with such confidence that I trusted him. After all, he is a very well-educated man and one of the most successful plastic surgeons in Los Angeles and, most importantly, someone I consider a friend. *Doesn't he not know about the medical research and papers detailing the dangers of silicone implants? How could he not? So, if he did, why didn't he share this information with me over the years? What makes doctors turn a blind eye to these undeniable facts? Business? Aren't they supposed to have your best interest in mind? Who can you trust these days?*

Implants are handed out like cupcakes in Beverly Hills. I'm not joking when I say that parents give them to their daughters as high school graduation gifts. Breast augmentation has been the top cosmetic surgical procedure performed in this country for years, with the number going up 202 percent from 1997 to 2015. In 2015, Americans spent an estimated $1.2 *billion* on more than three hundred thousand breast augmentations, according to the American Society for Aesthetic Plastic Surgery.

My mind is racing, as fast as my half brain can, thinking about every step of my life. *Forget about me! What about my babies and the fact that I breast-fed them?* Before Gigi was born, I asked my plastic surgeon and my pediatrician if it was safe to breast-feed with silicone implants. They both said yes. But twenty years later, plenty of studies confirm the danger of silicone toxicity and its effect on the immune system. I'm so frustrated and afraid of the unknown that I want to scream. *How could I have been so stupid and uneducated that I allowed a man to make me think I even needed those stupid implants to begin with? My body was perfect exactly the way God intended it to be. Why in the world did I mess with it? I was a fucking moron to put this shit in my body.* Although none of these findings change my late-stage Lyme diagnosis, it's another profound aha moment at a time when I'm barely existing, *not* living life. The silicone leakage explains why three years of hard work has not paid off. *Is this the core of my problem? Is this why I can't get well? Is this why my body is toxic all the time without any realistic explanation?*

June 1, 2015
Being positive in a negative situation isn't naïve, it's leadership on a mission.
#DeterminedToFindACure #AffordableForAll #ChronicLymeDiseaseAwareness

After the discovery of the free-floating silicone, I go back to read the reports of my previous mammograms. Because of my mother's breast cancer in her midforties, I've always been very conscientious about getting annual mammograms. Usually, I wait for my doctor's office to call me and say all is fine, but I never take the time to read the actual written reports. They clearly state that minor drops of silicone appeared on my mammograms, but they were tiny and encapsulated, meaning they supposedly couldn't go anywhere, and their amount and location were the same every year.

I must say that I will be forever grateful to David for leading me to this discovery and making me do that scan, which I probably wouldn't have done without his fear of cancer. I think he might have just saved my life, because the silicone findings could change my whole case. I feel weak and sick but I have a heart full of hope about the next chapter of my health journey. After all these years, it suddenly feels like we found the key to the next door that is about to open. I want the silicone out of my body NOW! Daisy researches this procedure, called "explant surgery." I honestly don't know how I'm going to get through it because I feel weak and sick.

Kelly Preston tells David about the Okyanos Cell Therapy in the Bahamas, where they specialize in an adipose stem cell procedure. I'm always very interested in things that are outside the box; however, I get infuriated when we receive an e-mail with the details of the procedure and its extremely high price tag from the head of the clinic.

> Dear Sir:
>
> With all due respect for your technology and extraordinary accomplishments, I have done treatments in about 12 different clinics all over the world and have never seen prices like yours. I am looking for a cure affordable for more than 0.01% of the millions of people suffering from this debilitating disease and want to bring awareness to the medicine of the future, but not at your outrageous prices. You might want to rethink this quote with your heart rather than your brain. I am just a normal person trying to stay alive and battle through a three-year nightmare and I feel taken advantage of.—Yolanda

This just doesn't feel right anymore. After so many pricey yet unsuccessful treatments, I'm angry and emotionally bankrupt by so many people. I start to feel that everyone is trying to take advantage of my desperate need to get well. But David feels strongly about this treatment and is willing to pay for it. Daisy consults Dr. Klinghardt, who agrees that adipose stem cell treatment will strengthen my overall health and prepare my body for the explant surgery.

Daisy and I get on a red-eye to Miami, where we change planes for the Bahamas. Although the clinic and Bahamas are beautiful, the hotel is hot, musty, and filled with mold, which I'm severely allergic to. We sleep with all the windows open just to keep the fresh air coming through. The next day, we take a taxi to the hospital, where we meet with the doctor. He examines me and explains the procedure.

"Do I even have enough fat on my thighs for this?" I ask. I've lost so much weight in the last year or so.

"Don't worry. I can take it from more than one area," he says.

"Do you think the free-floating silicone is the cause of all of my problems?" I ask.

"It's probably a huge part and you need to deal with it," he replies. "I've worked with Dr. Lu-Jean Feng, one of the best explant surgeons. I'd love to introduce you." Daisy immediately starts researching Dr. Feng, who is a top surgeon in Cleveland, Ohio. She's done an impressive nine thousand explant surgeries.

That afternoon after my appointment, instead of going back to bed, I lie out on the wet sand in my white bathing suit, while my body is kissed by the Bahamian sun. Watching the waves crash on the shore is calming, especially as I try to connect with the earth and make sense of this journey. There are so many different very important chapters that seem to be unfolding at the same time. After years of a slow buildup, this feels like a volcano erupting all at once. I feel anxious about the junk floating inside my body and wish I could go straight to the explant surgery, but deep in my heart I know that being here in the Bahamas is the only way to strengthen my body after the parasites almost sucked the life out of me. *So many crazy years. Is everything finally starting to fall into place? I finally feel with every bone in my body that I have to surrender to the journey that God has planned for me.* I watch the sun set slowly on the horizon, trying to breathe in every last drop of energy it is willing to give me. I go to bed that night feeling energetically recharged and ready to take on tomorrow.

In the morning, a car is waiting to take us to the clinic. Even though I'm supposed to be fasting, I need my rebellious presurgery coffee, so I ask the driver where we can get a latte. Daisy smiles at my naughtiness but obviously doesn't approve. After a stop at an Italian deli, we make our way to the clinic. I change into a soft green surgery gown and cover my hair in a net. Before I get into the hospital bed, Daisy takes a picture for my photo diary. By now, this has become a laughable ritual. I look at that picture and for the first time I notice that my once-muscular calves have turned into skin and bones. This is a frightening look, and the moment I really realize what this disease has done to me. Funny enough, I stopped looking in the mirror a long time ago because the fight has been so internal.

As I get into the bed and the anesthesiologist places my IV, I FaceTime my children. I try to perk up my voice to pretend I am okay. I don't want them to worry and need to tell them how very much I love them. After all, they're my reason for living, and with their beautiful faces freshly in my mind, I slowly drift into a deep sleep. The fat removal takes a couple of hours. I wake up to Daisy's smile, feeling mellow and with minimal pain.

"Right now you're having an IV of mannitol, which will help the stem cells cross the blood-brain barrier," Daisy says. "The kids and David called to check on you. Everything is fine." I feel emotional and start crying. I was really scared, but now I am so happy to be alive. An hour later, the stem cells are put back into my body with an IV and injected into my compromised eyes, right ulnar nerve, facial nerve, and tibial nerve.

"Your fat had the highest number of cells that I've ever seen, 195 million of them," he says.

"What does that mean?" I ask.

"That your cell health is really good." *At least something is healthy. Thank God for those good-old Dutch genes.* This is an outpatient procedure, so we go back to the hotel. Daisy sleeps on the pullout couch in the living room to watch over me. In the middle of the night, I wake to find myself in a big puddle of blood, and the full-body compression stocking I'm wearing is drenched. It looks like a murder scene. I call for Daisy. Although they told us when I left the clinic yesterday that my incisions were left open, neither of us was prepared for this. It's a lot more blood than I could have ever imagined. "I'm speechless" is all I can say to Daisy. I feel scared. *This is barbaric! Who bleeds like this?* The sheets and towels we go through are more than the housekeeping staff bargained for, and they complain, which makes me even feel worse.

Two days later, we're on our way back to L.A. I'm happy to report that there is a distinct improvement in my overall health. It appears that it has reduced the inflammation in my body significantly, which suppresses the chronic cough that I've had for years. My plan is to rest up and build strength for the explant surgery, which is scheduled for two months from now. It dangles in front of me like a finish line that I can't wait to reach.

Chapter Thirteen

· ·

LEARN TO TRUST THE JOURNEY,
EVEN WHEN YOU DON'T UNDERSTAND IT.

I need to regenerate with a lot of quiet time and without any outside stimulation. The quieter my space, the stronger I feel my own life force and the more clearly I can think. And with a lot of time to think, I begin to reevaluate my life. I have learned to be at peace within myself. Although it has been a turbulent time, I've evolved so much as a human being and am starting to sense the higher purpose of my journey. I can't rely on my brain function, but my sixth sense and little inner voice are strong. I recognize the blessings in my life that feel like acts of grace, like a divine presence has touched me and it's going to keep me safe.

I am starting to see all the amazing opportunity life has brought us but I am also starting to feel the very toxic energy that has entered my atmosphere, mainly from being on the *Housewives* and probably my children's visibility in the world. Even though I'm living life from the sidelines, I can feel everything energetically shifting at this point. I can even feel it by the way David and I sleep together. We're not noodled up like we used to be. He has clearly lost interest in the depth of my soul where I exist at this moment in time but instead longs for his life outside our home. Though I see this very clearly, there's nothing I can do about it right now. I can't handle conflict and my energy must stay focused on my health journey. I'm not ready for the potential consequences of a marriage conversation, so I should not have it. *I will focus on my marriage 200 percent and tie up all the loose ends when my health permits and I can think straight.*

Right now, I need to get strong for my explant surgery. The recovery from the stem cell procedure is not easy, the bruising is frightening. I'm literally black and blue from my waist down to my calves. It looks as if a train ran over me. I also have severe, deep bone pain. I rest for weeks and go to the hyperbaric chamber every day as I try to heal.

It's also almost time to start my fourth season on the *Housewives.* Although I've been sick since I first appeared on the show, I'm now at my worst and in complete surrender, not to my disease but to my circumstances. During the other seasons, I could muster up a pretend smile and push for a little bit of energy here and there. I learned to rest and save my spoons one day so I could film the next. After all, I didn't want to lose my job or be a sick person. Yet, today I'm not in control of my life anymore, and, after all these years, I finally realize that there is no timetable when it comes to my healing. I'm not on my husband's timetable, my friend's timetable, or that of a TV show and its cast.

June 18, 2015
I have surrendered, but I won't stop and won't shut up.
I will keep chasing wellness until I catch it.
#WeMustFindACure #ChronicLymeDiseaseAwareness
Global epidemic growing in the shadows!

As usual in the weeks before the start of filming, the producers call to inquire about my upcoming schedule. *Schedule? What schedule?* I can barely participate in the most basic elements of daily life. My only focus is to get to a safe place and stay alive. *How can I go back to work when getting out of bed feels like running a marathon?* I've been living in the same fuzzy white robe for a long time and probably look worse than I have in years. At this point, I don't wear makeup, nail polish, or body creams, and haven't had my hair done in eight months. I'm trying to live a toxic-free life. I've been passing parasites of all shapes and sizes the past six months, I am barely eating, and the open wounds from my stem cell treatment in the Bahamas are still healing. My skin is still jaundiced from the RHP I did in Mexico.

Alex Baskin, the head of Evolution Productions and producer of the *Housewives,* visits me at my apartment. Although he's my boss, Alex has also become a great friend and confidant over the years. In the time that I've been sick, he's come to visit me every couple of weeks with a Starbucks, to check in and give me updates on the *Housewives* drama, ratings, story lines, et cetera. In addition to our work relationship, I know that he genuinely loves me and has my best interest in mind.

"As much as I don't want to lose my job," I tell him, "I don't think I can do another season. I'm worse than last year."

"We really don't want to lose you."

"Alex, I've been in my robe since last season's filming ended. I don't even think I can handle the pressure of getting dressed. Most days I can't even get out of bed and that is *my* reality. Trust me, this is not the glamorous Beverly Hills lifestyle you're trying to portray."

"Yes. You're right. But the audience is invested in your story," he reminds me.

"But I don't think I have anything to add to the show," I say.

"Viewers want to see you get better. If you allow us, we want to share your journey," he says. "You'll bring more attention to Lyme than anyone ever has. Maybe *this* is your purpose for being on the show." Apparently, Bravo has gotten feedback from many chronically ill viewers who are thankful to see their lives—or something close to it—play out on prime-time TV. Many identify with me and are genuinely interested in how I'm doing. I know that God has given me this journey for a very specific reason and that one day I'm going to be the change I wish to see in the Lyme world.

I'm very aware that hundreds of thousands of Lyme sufferers with questions are looking at me for direction, and I'm determined to find those answers. I'm just not sure how to do it at this moment. *And don't I need to heal myself before I can help others?* As much as I'm willing to share my Lyme journey in order to educate people and bring awareness to the challenges of this invisible disease, the *Housewives* doesn't seem like the right platform to do so.

"I'm just afraid I won't be able to show up for you," I say, explaining that I can't predict how I'll feel in the next five minutes, much less a day, week, or month from now. Alex doesn't say anything else, and we leave the conversation at that. A couple of days later, he calls me with what seems like a logical compromise.

"We know you can't commit to anything, but if you let us follow you to your medical appointments, we'll make the rest work," he says. "It doesn't matter how often you show up—ten times or forty times. We will work around you and the best of your ability."

I think about this and carefully weigh the pros and cons of staying on the show. Besides the responsibility that I feel to speak for those whose voices can't be heard, there is my paycheck, which is very important because it gives me the power to hold on to whatever is left of my independence. And there is always my true optimistic spirit, which makes me feel that even though things are really bad in the *moment,* finding a cure could be right around the corner. In my mind, remission isn't an option. *Maybe the explant surgery will allow everything to fall into place. The ending must be in sight soon.* I agree to give the show one more shot. I'm not sure how it's going to work out, but I'm going to give it my best effort and trust the process.

Sunday afternoon, we meet with our friends Tom and Erika Girardi. Although we talk a bit about Lyme, most of the conversation is about Erika's career as a singer, songwriter, and performer. Several of her songs have become number-one *Billboard* singles, and she and Tom are looking for David's guidance and direction in the music industry. As the three

My son, the youngest but the strongest
force in my life.

Feeling of utter desperation, searching
for a cure in Zacateca, Mexico.

My girls and the life force in every cell
of my body.

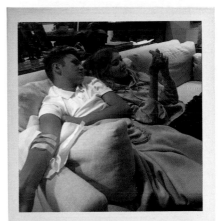

Gigi supporting Anwar during his
Lyme treatment.

Home sweet home in Holland.

Trying to push through severe
brain fog at *WWHL*.

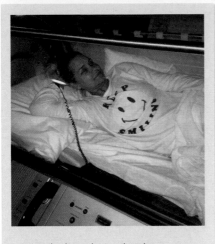

The hyperbaric chamber.

Moving my baby girl to NYC in 2014.

My sugar and spice.

The final day with our baby boy Lucky.

Neurofeedback.

Mommy duties don't stop, so out of bed
to support Anwar at his driving test.

Grateful for the family and friends
who never stopped supporting me
#HappyDutchGirl.

The power of togetherness.

The amazing staff at St. John's Medical
Center in Santa Monica, California.

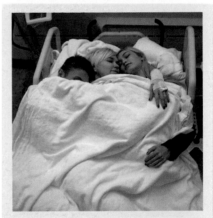

My angels and the love that never
stopped giving.

My ultimate low moment in Miami,
when drowning was actually a
thought in my mind.

The low-dose immunotherapy I made
with my own specimen.

Salute to the sunset in Korea.

Unconditional love and support
in the journey unknown.

Together we stand strong.

So much respect for nurses around the
world and their universal language
of healing.

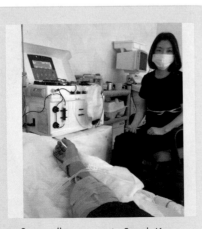

Stem cell treatment in Seoul, Korea.

Girlfriend support far away from home.

Dr. Klinghardt, a wizard who truly understands the complexity of chronic Lyme.

The storyboards that helped me uncover
the mystery of my chronic disease.

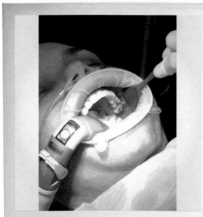

The unknown and toxic truth behind
my perfect pearly whites.

The metal-based crowns
I didn't know I had.

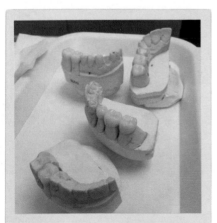

Rebuilding with toxic-free materials.

With my girlfriend Kelly after
a dental procedure.

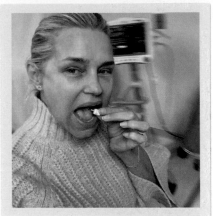

Trying to uncover my parasite mystery by capsule endoscopy.

Thanks to Dr. Gubarev's book, I was able to identify my rope worms.

The remains of a decayed intestinal parasite that came out after a two-day fast in preparation for my capsule endoscopy.

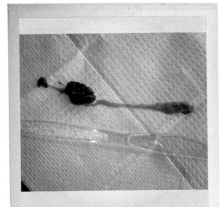

Rope worm with fecal stone attached. The toxins of these helminths weaken the immune system severely.

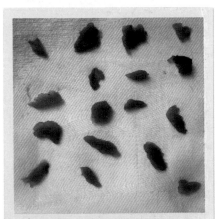

Intestinal tissue expelled after rope worm elimination protocol.

Branched jellyfish, third stage of the rope worm parasite development.

In Germany and determined to rise.

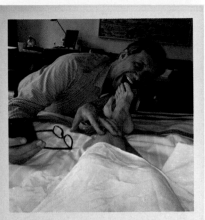

No matter what, my brother can always make me laugh.

Feeling sick and defeated in Germany, but trying to connect to the earth.

Hopeful after my stem cell injections.

Gigi, the driving force in my weakest days.

Photon laser for healing and inflammation.

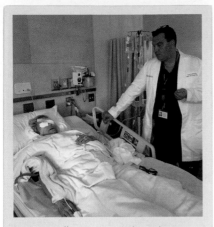

Stem cell treatment in the Bahamas.

Praying that God's plan for my life
exceeds the circumstances of this day.

Seeing this photo made me scared that
I was fighting a losing battle.

That ugly white robe that made me
feel so safe and comfy.

The master at work, injecting
my sphenoid.

In Seattle with my Lyme warriors
to see Dr. Klinghardt.

The freezing-cold water in beautiful British Columbia was actually great pain relief.

Exploring nature with my Momma.

No clock, no agenda, just hanging and enjoying this special time with family.

While completely disconnected from life, I found much strength by watching the sunset and sunrise.

Anwar for *Vogue L'Homme* and exploring the fashion industry.

Finally well enough to see my girls ride again.

Purple marking the free-floating silicone, located by MRI and ultrasound.

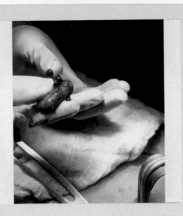

Removal of a lymph node filled with silicone during my explant surgery.

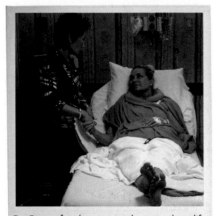

Dr. Feng after the surgery that saved my life and changed the game in my Lyme journey.

My implant encapsulated in tissue with silicone leakage attached.

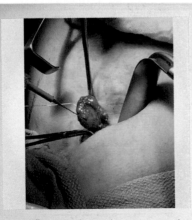

Free-floating silicone being removed during my nine-hour explant surgery.

The price you pay for vanity.

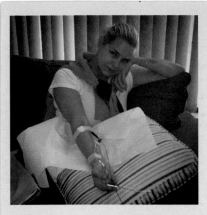

UVLRX to treat the viral overload.

Recovering in Santa Barbara with my forever love, Anwar.

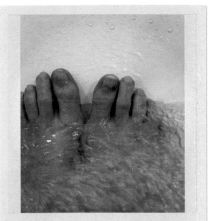

My body detoxing silicone after my explant surgery through my big toes.

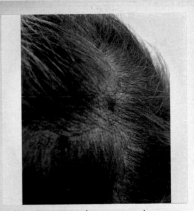

Detoxing silicone granules through my scalp.

One of the many visits in my bed.

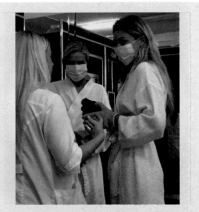

Gigi and I at cryotherapy after my surgery.

Shaky in my shoes but surrounded by love, Global Lyme Alliance 2015.

Selfie with my fellow Lyme warriors Ally Hilfiger and Thalia.

Gigi's Global Lyme Alliance speech, the gift and meaning of her words are everything.

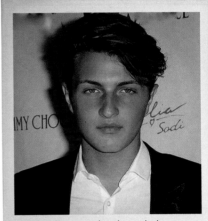

The one who shines light in darkness.

The unspoken understanding and deep compassion for our Lyme journey together.

Treating many symptoms but not the cause.

Christmas 2015 in Aspen with my angels.

One out of millions, my best friend,
Paul Marciano.

We may not have it all together, but
together we have it all.

#My Family.

My last and final *Housewives*
reunion, 2015.

My birthday, celebrating the gift
of friendship.

Tahiti, 2016, lucky and grateful to be alive.

The swim and moment I found clarity about leaving the *RHOBH*.

Slowly learning to put my thoughts in writing again, the beginning of my book.

In awe of the beauty of this life right here right now.

Healing time connected to the earth.

2016, starting to come back to life with glimpses of the finish line.

Prepping for the master cleanse.

Photo shoot with Jim Jordan, rusty but trying to get my mojo back.

So proud of my Bella for sharing her story at the GLA Gala 2016.

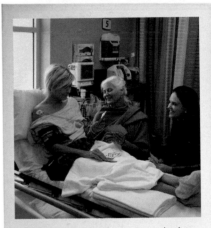

T-vam surgery, the last one on the list.

A special day to remember with my son.

My son, so much stronger and wiser than I ever dreamed he could be.

Finally on the road with my angels
at the Victoria's Secret Fashion
Show, Paris, 2016.

Gigi winning 2016 model of the year
award at the British Fashion Awards.

Christmas in Aspen, coming out on the
other side still doing what I love best.

Christmas, 2016, not skiing yet, but happy
making gingerbread houses with my tribe.

Back to life.

Happiness is in the heart not in
the circumstances of life.

of them are chatting away, I suddenly see a clear vision of Erika as a housewife.

"Have you ever considered being a Beverly Hills housewife?" I say, bluntly interrupting the conversation. "You have the house, the life, the looks, and, most important, you have the brain!"

"I never thought about it," she says. "My focus has been my music."

"That will be the platform for your music and much more," I tell her.

"Why don't you meet with my friend Alex?" I ask. It seems like a brilliant idea—if I do say so myself—for Erika, who is in her early forties, to share her music on the *Housewives,* not only to help her career but also to inspire women her age. Although I've lost my communication and writing skills, spiritually I have more clarity than ever and somehow feel that this will be a match made in heaven.

I walk away from the conversation and into my kitchen. "I found you a new housewife," I text Alex. This is one of my many witchy moments that turns out exactly as I predict. Two weeks later, Erika is hired, and after I make it out of bed to officially introduce her to the other women while being filmed, she is off to the races and cameras are rolling at the Girardi residence. Erika is a powerful and positive addition to the show. She is kind, unique, and the smartest cookie in the group. As far as *my* camera time is concerned, it is very limited. The first procedure we will film is a new chapter of my roller-coaster ride: my dental chapter. I am preparing to have my nine metal-based crowns removed as they are causing an immune response which I have known since early on in my journey but wasn't educated enough to understand. This is like peeling the endless layers of an onion in order to find the sweet spot of vibrant health.

Daisy has requested samples of my crowns from the lab that made them ten years earlier and I can see through muscle testing with Dr. Kang that it is blocking my healing just like he told me. Dr. Kang is a chiropractor I see who does nutrition-response testing, a form of muscle testing that helps strengthen my organs. I love going to see him because I connect with his humble, unpretentious energy; his little office in Koreatown feels authentic in this very unauthentic world. He is helping us investigate the dental chapter so that we can make educated decisions. This week, Daisy brings various dental materials for Dr. Kang to test and determine what my body will tolerate.

Once my beautiful pearly white crowns are removed, I will have them tested by a forensic lab to identify exactly what kind of metals are in them. It's a big deal to have what seem like perfect teeth ripped out, yet I'm willing to do *anything* to get my life back.

On the morning of June 30, Daisy and the *Housewives* film crew accompany me to my dental appointment.

"I'm really nervous and just want to make sure that whatever you put into my mouth is one hundred percent safe and metal free," I tell Dr. Hill.

"Of course," she says, touching my arm soothingly.

"How long are the temporaries going to be in?" I ask.

"A couple of weeks," she says. "But don't worry, they'll be beautiful."

"Don't worry about the beauty part," I say. I've lost *all* sense of vanity, and how things look from the outside isn't even on my mind anymore.

"Wouldn't it be great if I wake up tomorrow and have a normal brain?" I say to Daisy right before I doze off.

"Yes," she says.

"I just want my life back to take care of my babies," I say with tears in my eyes.

In addition to removing my nine metal-based crowns, Dr. Hill pulls tooth number 14, which is infected. It's fascinating to me how every tooth in the mouth is linked to organs and other parts of the body. Tooth number 14 is linked to the sinuses, jaw, spleen, stomach, breasts, and thyroid.

Obviously, this experience seems like one of the most unflattering things to film for a glamorous show about Beverly Hills, but when I set my ego aside I realize that maybe it is important to educate people about the potential dangers of dentistry and the risk of heavy metals. I'm finally learning to be my own advocate and make intelligent and prepared choices, something I had to learn the hard way. Years ago, none of the important information was ever brought to my attention, mainly because I didn't ask questions but also because I always thought that doctors and dentists had my best interest at heart. I never thought they would use or do anything that could potentially hurt me. I guess I was very innocent and ignorant.

Daisy sends the removed crowns to Avomeen Analytical Services to identify the metals that they are made of, not that the information matters to me now but I want to understand so I can write about it one day and use it to educate others. We also send my blood to Clifford Laboratories to determine what dental materials I'm allergic to and which ones will be safe to use when we install my new teeth. Looking back I should have dealt with my teeth back in Switzerland. But hindsight is twenty-twenty and at that time I was overwhelmed with all that was coming at me and, to be honest, I was still stubborn about my journey and unwilling to surrender to it.

July 10, 2015
Is it impossible to rid the body of chronic disease when
poison leaches from the mouth?
Could crowns with underlying layer of toxic metals weaken
the immune system?
#UncoveringTheMystery #MyMetalBasedCrowns #HeavyMetalToxins
#MyPersonalHealthJourney #ZirconiaCrownsExist

I feel that the stem cell treatment from the Bahamas is doing its job and in the weeks that follow, my overall health is slowly improving. I gain a little muscle mass, my hair stops falling out, my skin looks better, and I seem to have less inflammation in my body. I'm not ready to put on my dancing shoes or shake my booty, but it's enough of an improvement to Face-

Time with Dr. Feng to talk about moving forward with my explant surgery. It's booked for August 5, just one month away. I am counting the days! It feels good to be excited, and I am hopeful for a chance at a healthy future. Even though I've learned a lot about patience over the years and greatly respect my body's natural healing clock, I'm *dying* to get these implants out of my chest. Anwar calls them "roadblocks." What I once viewed as a very sexual part of my body now feels like a huge obstacle to my healing and to living my life. I'm still dealing with an array of symptoms that come, go, and spike at random times, like severe gut issues, recurring bladder infections, insomnia, intense tremors, cramping of my hands and feet, bad eyesight, migraines, and my brain dysfunction. Still, there is no weakness in my spirit and I pray for the strength to get through the days until my surgery.

Around mid-July, David and I go on a ten-day boat trip to British Columbia, our favorite place in the world, with my mom, sisters-in-law, and their husbands. We're trying to sprinkle the summer with joy and the simple things that we once loved. I hate that I still can't find the right words to have meaningful conversations with those around me, but I'm happy to sit on the couch and spend time with the people I adore. Since I got sick, traveling has been more of a challenge than a vacation. Sadly, when you don't feel well, being in the most beautiful location in the world somehow loses its value. However, this trip is exactly what the doctor ordered. I've never felt more thankful for a vacation and the ability not only to see but also to *feel* life's beauty. Because I'm still most comfortable in small spaces, the boat is the perfect space for me, where I can just be myself with my family. There's no pressure to go to fancy restaurants, do any major activities, or even leave the boat. Instead, we do simple things like play cards, watch movies, and just hang out and enjoy the views and magnificent nature that forms the backdrop to our days. Taking a break from the long-term seriousness of my life and reconnecting with nature is nourishing. It gives me newfound energy for the upcoming chapter of my health journey and it reminds David and me of the connection we have always shared in the silence of nature, away from the pressure and influences of real life. It gives me a sliver of hope that my marriage can be salvaged.

July 30, 2015
My soul is invigorated, and I am in
fighting spirit to attack one more time.
#MyHealthJourney #ChronicLymeDisease #SearchingForACure
Never felt more thankful for seeing life's beauty . . .
#BreathTaking #EaglesNest #DesolationSound

Chapter Fourteen

....

I MAY NOT "LOOK" SICK ON THE OUTSIDE, BUT ON THE INSIDE, IT'S LIKE MY BODY IS TRYING TO KILL ME.

I'm filled with excitement and fear as I count the days until my explant surgery. My mom comes back to L.A. after our trip in British Colombia and will stay with me until I leave for Cleveland, Ohio. The days leading up to my surgery are a quiet but meaningful time with my mom and children at the house in Malibu. Gigi, who loves to cook, makes our family's favorite tomato soup and grilled cheese dippers, which we're planning to eat on our peaceful and private little terrace above the lemon orchard. My mom and I make our way to the terrace before the kids join us. It's a beautiful afternoon and we snuggle up together in the warm summer air with the breathtaking ocean views in front of us. I never want to bother or worry her, but sometimes you just need your mom to tell you that everything is going to be okay. Throughout my life, my mom has been an outstanding example of strength in troubled times, something I need from her right about now.

"What do you think about the surgery?" I ask her.

"I think that everything is going to be okay, sweetheart," she says, tearing up.

"It's scary. But I just want to be healthy and alive again so that I can get out of bed, live my life, and see my babies grow up." We stop talking once the children arrive. After enjoying our lunch, I pull a large manila envelope out from underneath the table.

"You guys . . ." I pause. "I printed this out for you."

"What is it?" Gigi asks.

"It's my will." I prepared it weeks ago but never found the right moment to present it to the kids. Somehow it feels easier with my mom by my side.

"I don't like how you say that so calmly, Mommy," Gigi says.

"I'm saying it calmly because it's important. Nothing's going to happen to me, but I just want you guys to know that this will be in the safe." My life was never the same after my father died, so I've always been very conscientious about being prepared. Plus, in the past six months leading up to my surgery, I've grown afraid and worried about potentially dying: *What happens if I die? What's going to happen to my children? Who is going to take care of my mother and brother?* In my head, I was well prepared for this conversation, but in the actual moment it's difficult, and I stumble over my words.

"I just want to make sure you guys take care of Oma," I say to the children.

"Why are you talking about this right now?" Bella asks, wiping tears from her eyes.

"Yeah, I don't know why you're talking about the surgery as if something's going to happen, because if fifty-one percent of you feels like something is going to go wrong, then I don't think you should do it," Gigi says wisely.

"Gigi, nothing is going to happen, I just—"

"Then why are you showing us your will?" Bella interrupts.

"Because it's important, Bella. Very important," I say. "I'm going to be fine. Dr. Feng has done more than nine thousand surgeries like mine and nothing has ever gone wrong. I just want to make sure that my business is in order. It's my duty as your mother."

I put three children on this planet, and I take that responsibility very seriously. When my brother and I turned twenty-one, we each received money that our father left us in his will. Although it was a very small sum at a time when I was already financially established, it was the greatest gift I ever received to know that my daddy, who was only twenty-nine years old when he died, loved and cared for us so much that he figured out a way to leave us a little something. So I know from experience that this uncomfortable conversation will one day be appreciated.

The evening before I leave for Cleveland is beautiful. The kids and I snuggle up, eat popcorn, and watch a movie. I feel so content having them all in one place, just like old times, when the girls were still living at home. It helps calm me and even though I feel positive about the surgery and act strong in front of them, deep inside I'm scared. In the morning, while Alberto drives David and me to the airport, mixed emotions and nervous energy surge through me. Part of me is worried about my body being strong enough to make it through the explant procedure. On the other hand, I have a do-or-die attitude. I can't wait to get these foreign things out of my body. The protocols for Lyme, co-infections, and parasites are still a mystery at times, but having my implants removed is a black-and-white issue. I honestly don't care that my breasts are going to be flat like pancakes with raisins on top. I already let go of any emotional attachment I ever had to them and, to be completely honest, I'm kind of embarrassed and disappointed with myself, knowing that, at one time, I allowed my sexuality to be based on those fake things. *What a lack of judgment and intelligence. Who ever decided that we needed big breasts to be sexy? And how stupid was I to believe that? Why is superficial or augmented beauty revered over natural beauty?* I want my daughters to know that beauty really *is* unique and in the eye of the beholder. We're not meant to be perfect or look the same. I've always known this deep in my heart, yet I went along with what society expected of me. Like millions of other women, I was brainwashed to believe that elective procedures are safe and acceptable, yet many studies prove that they can be very dangerous to your health and slowly steal the quality of your life. I consider getting implants the number-one screw-up in my life, and I'm not proud of it. But I'm well aware and grateful for the opportunity and resources to travel all the way to Ohio for this procedure and to hopefully undo the damage I've inflicted on myself.

After a four-and-a-half-hour flight, David, Daisy, and I arrive in Cleveland. We go straight to the hotel, have a quick bite to eat, and are off to bed because we have an early appointment with Dr. Feng at her clinic. I'm excited to finally meet her in person. Her calm and kind demeanor instantly puts me at ease. I'm confident that Dr. Feng is the best doctor in the world when it comes to explant surgery. She's done many studies and testified in trials.

"Even if an implant doesn't break and is in its perfect form, does it still leak toxins?" I ask Dr. Feng

"Let me show you." She takes a brand-new silicone implant out of its original package and puts it on her desk. "Let's keep talking and we'll look at this in a little while."

About half an hour later, she lifts up the silicone implant and points to the residue on the surface of her dark-colored desk.

"That is just after half an hour," she says. "Imagine what it's like after years and years of those chemicals inside your warm body!" I'm amazed, yet not surprised. It all makes sense.

"Dr. Kahn is waiting for you, to do the ultrasound mapping," she says. "This will locate exactly where you have the free-floating silicone, which will help guide me during surgery tomorrow."

It's a beautiful August day as we drive to my appointment with Dr. Kahn, whose office is in the Cleveland Clinic. *Wow, the Cleveland Clinic is impressive. It's like its own city. It's got a coffee shop, pharmacies, a hotel.* At the appointment, Dr. Kahn runs the ultrasound over my bare chest. He points out the shadows on the screen that are the free-floating silicone. Then he takes a blue marker and marks these areas on my skin.

"Don't shower tonight," he says. "Just go back to the hotel, rest, and I'll see you right before the surgery when I'll mark these areas with needles for Dr. Feng."

As I walk out of the hospital, I need to just sit on the earth and get grounded.

"You keep walking," I tell David and Daisy. "I'll meet you in the car." I plant myself on the grass with my back against a brick wall, feeling overwhelmed. I need to marinate for a minute and digest what just happened.

Ten minutes later, I walk to the car. As I open the door, Daisy looks up from her phone.

"Yo, the lab report for your teeth has come back," she says. "They confirmed that your crowns that were supposed to be pure porcelain are actually mixed with zinc, gallium, palladium, silver, indium, tin, gold aluminum, copper, and ruthenium."

When I hear this, I actually have a little meltdown. I don't think I can handle one more thing. I don't even know why I'm crying. I'm feeling joy for answers, yet feeling sorry for myself that I've been fighting all these obstacles that people told me didn't exist. It feels like it is little me against the whole world. At the same time, I'm really proud of myself for sticking to my guns as I fought for the truth every step of the way.

We have a nice dinner and get to bed early. *I need to rest before going to the battlefield tomorrow.* At 7 A.M., we go back to Dr. Kahn at the Cleveland Clinic. He places the needles that will guide Dr. Feng to the exact locations of the floating silicone during surgery. *I look like a porcupine. What a trip. I never even knew all this existed.*

"I'm going to be a toothless, boobless, brainless wonder," I say with a smile on my face, goofing around in the car as we make our way to Dr. Feng's office. I'm trying to make light of the situation. Of course, we need to stop at Starbucks. I'm probably the only person who has coffee before surgery with needles sticking out of her body, but this rebellious ritual is comforting to me. Yes, I'm nervous, but I'm very ready to take on this devil stuck in my chest. I'm hopeful that this is the answer.

Once in bed inside the pre-op room, I FaceTime the kids to say I love them and then say good-bye to David. Daisy slips on some scrubs because she will be in the operating room with me, along with the *Housewives* film crew, who will capture this procedure on camera. Some people say, "Why would you let them film that and put it on the show?" The answer is simple: I have daughters, nieces, and girlfriends with young daughters. If I can stop even *one* teenage girl from making the stupid and potentially unhealthy decision to get breast implants, it's reason enough for me to share. It's important for all woman to know the truth about breast implants.

Education is crucial. If *I'd* had the proper information about this procedure in my midtwenties, I would have made a very different decision. So I feel very confident about sharing this part of my journey even though it is judged.

The surgery turns out to be almost eight hours long, something that no one, not even Dr. Feng, anticipated. When I wake up in the recovery room, I start crying when I see David.

"Hi, baby," he says. "It's done. It's over. You're finished. All that stuff is out." He's right, and even though I'm feeling extremely sore, I'm thrilled to be alive. *Wooooohooooo. I made it through!* Dr. Feng comes to check on me.

"Everything went really, really well, but this was one of the most difficult cases I've ever worked on," she says with tears in her eyes. *And she's done thousands!* "It was like a marathon because there was so much silicone from the previous ruptured implant. The silicone granulomas went all the way up to your clavicle bone. I removed as much as I possibly could."

After several hours in the recovery room, the nurses bandage me up and I go back to the hotel. David has an appointment with a heart specialist early the next morning, so he asks Daisy to have me sleep in her room. We are all exhausted but we don't sleep very much because my pain is unbearable—a nine on a scale of one to ten. It's like a cannon was shot into my chest. And the drains from my breasts have to be emptied every two to three hours. David did this gracefully on camera for the *Housewives*, but he left the off-camera, late-night care to Daisy. A health advocate usually doesn't nurse people around the clock, but I'm so grateful that Daisy's by my side to help me manage the unbearable pain. I've only known her for a couple of months, but we've gone through a whirlwind of experiences together already. After all, when you are naked, bleeding, and throwing up in front of someone, you can't help but get close very quickly. It's amazing that Daisy chose to sit through all eight hours of the surgery.

"What was it like?" I ask.

"Fascinating. Right at the start, the heart monitor and ventilator showed your breathing curve was off. In fact, the anesthesiologist asked me if you had chronic obstructive pulmonary disease or emphysema," Daisy says. "Yet as soon as Dr. Feng lifted the silicone implants out of your chest, the curve immediately normalized. It was startling."

The chronic cough that I've had for four years is gone. It must have been the pressure of the implants on my lungs. Two days after my surgery, David is leaving for New York and Daisy has to get home to her family and other clients, so Paige flies to Cleveland to care for me. Having raised three children with confidence, Paige takes control of the situation.

"Hello, sweetheart, here I am. There's a new sheriff in town," she jokes when she arrives. But she's no joke. She quickly gets familiar with my medication log and drain-emptying schedule. Paige is so funny and despite all my pain, she's able to make me laugh.

The next morning, I wake up shivering and very nauseous.

"You've been on pain medication too long," Paige says, even though it's only been two days. She orders me a pot of tea from room service, which I hold between my legs for warmth. She gives me two Advil. Forty-five minutes later though, I'm burning up with a 102-degree fever, and Paige's always-smiling face looks serious.

"Okay, maybe I was wrong and this isn't withdrawal. I think it's an infection," she says as she calls Dr. Feng. I'm in a lot of pain and dripping with sweat and scared. Although Paige is trying to act calm, I know her well enough to know that she's worried. "Dr. Feng said to come to her office."

The night before, Dr. Feng had kindly lent us her gorgeous black car. As we drive, I have these intense waves of nausea washing over me. When Paige stops at a four-way intersection, I can't wait one more minute. I open the door to projectile vomit, conscious about not wanting to get one drop of my disgusting vomit on the beautiful tan leather interior. Paige moves over to the right side of the road, driving with the door open. When I finish, I look up at Paige. We both start laughing hysterically. Our sisterhood has exceeded far beyond anything we could have ever imagined the day we met at the Santa Monica car wash so many years ago!

August 7, 2015
Turn a mess into a message . . . We might have hit the jackpot
by finding all this silicone through ultrasound mapping,
as shown in this selfie. Thank you, Dr. Feng, for holding my
hand and leading the way.
#UncoveringTheMystery #ChronicLymeDisease
#ExPlantSurgery@drfengclinic #MyHealthJourney #DeterminedToFindACure

Six days after the surgery, Dr. Feng removes the drains, wraps my chest in a tight bandage, and sends me on my way. Erika, who had been shooting the *Housewives* in New York and is on her way back to L.A., offered to pick us up in Cleveland on her private plane. This is a perfect little reward and I'm very grateful not to be on a commercial flight. The ride is smooth and I sleep most of the way home while Erika and Paige hang out. I'm happy to see that Gigi and Bella are waiting for me at home. This is the best medicine I can ask for. A few days later, David leaves for Asia, so the girls, Anwar, and I go to Santa Barbara for a long weekend to relax and soak in the fresh ocean air. Gigi is appointed head nurse so she changes my bandages, but all three of them take responsibility for my care. We stay at a friend's little beach house and we take very short walks, hang out, talk, and rest. It's such a great joy to watch my girls ride polo ponies on the beach and connect to nature in the beautiful place where I raised my family and that really is our home.

I feel a little better every day, and over the weeks that follow I do things to help heal, like cryotherapy where you go into a booth that is minus 140 degrees Celsius. It cools your skin and body quickly, and your body is supposed to produce its own natural anti-inflammatory molecules. This helps me reduce the swelling from my surgery immediately and should speed up healing. I also do something called Myers' cocktail IVs, a vitamin infusion to boost the immune system.

Three weeks later, I think I'm well enough to walk on the treadmill in the gym of our apartment complex. I haven't been in a gym since that day before our wedding when I practically collapsed from exhaustion in front of Dale and David. *It's time to get my ass back in gear.* I slip into my workout clothes. *My implants blocked me from healing! It's time to get on with my life. Push it, girl, it's mind over matter.* The first day, I walk for fifteen minutes. It's hard and my body feels weak. I proudly take a selfie. *I'm making real progress.* But I tend to overdo things, so in my typical fashion I push myself to walk for thirty minutes the next day. Clearly, I've overdone it, because two days in a row of walking knocks my socks off. I don't get up for weeks.

My Diary
September 5, 2015
Went to Beverly Hot Springs for body scrub to get all this dead skin off of me. Have some clear thoughts coming to me. Maybe my brain is recalibrating.

The *Housewives* is filming every day. Although my shooting time is very minimal, even when I *am* on camera, I don't do much. My body goes through the motions, but I'm not mentally involved in anything that's going on. My focus is uncovering the mystery of my chronic disease and waking up in the morning to get my son off to school. I keep track of my children, do my treatments, try to keep my husband happy, but most of all I'm just trying to stay alive.

September 12, 2015
Don't view my bad days as a sign of weakness—those are actually the days I fight my hardest. #LifeFromTheSideLines #ChronicLymeDiseaseAwareneness #1StepForward2StepsBack #DontJudgeSome1sPathUnlessUWalkedIt

Although my castmates are kind to my face and seem happy to see me when I'm able to come to work, I hear that some of them question whether I'm truly sick. Apparently, one of the women is confused by my Instagram posts and the fact that one photo shows me having a treatment and not looking well, while the next shows me smiling with my kids. How can you judge someone's health or well-being from the twenty seconds that it takes to snap a good or a bad selfie, especially someone with an invisible disease like Lyme? Over the years, I've learned that we live in a very critical world: instead of picking up the phone or stopping by to check on a friend who is obviously struggling, people prefer to stay home and judge. A Lyme patient can't just wait for the storm to pass, because the storm might last five or ten years. As a result, we must learn to dance in the rain, meaning even if you have only one good hour in each day, you must appreciate that and learn to find the smallest joys. We have good days and bad days—or, even worse, good hours and bad hours—it's just part of this heinous journey. *Does one need to have scars, suffer broken bones, or lose their hair to warrant empathy from others?* It is heartbreaking that the women talk behind my back and debate my illness publicly. How do you look at someone who is sick and say, "You're faking it"? It's hard to imagine that anyone would publicly deny or belittle another human being's disease. Who has three and a half years to fake being sick? Not me! Why would I *choose* to stay in bed for this many years when I have a wonderful life to live? What's the upside? What could I possibly gain from such a choice?

These women lack much knowledge and consciousness. Sitting on the sidelines for hundreds of days is an experience they've obviously never had, so how could I expect them to understand? I've learned to let these things roll off my Teflon back and blame it on ignorance. I see the higher purpose of my journey and exist on a very different vibration than any of these women in order to survive. If they have honest questions about my illness, they should come to my house and look at my medical files. These binders chart the course of my journey. They tell the story of a woman who is fighting her ass off against a complex and multifaceted disease.

I'm 100 percent immersed in uncovering my own murder mystery, determined to prove the crime to myself.

For one day of filming, I go to Lisa Vanderpump's birthday lunch. This is the second time I've been up and about for the show, and the moment I walk into the room I immediately feel an undertone of weird, negative energy. At this point, I'm such a raw, open wound that I can deeply feel the energy of a mosquito flying by. Getting dressed, buying flowers, and going to lunch is a great personal accomplishment for me today, but yet I can't assume people understand how this feels unless they've been in my shoes. Clearly, Kyle is angry that I haven't shown up for filming more often which really bothers me, because *she* knows me, she knows my work ethic, if I *could* be there, I would be. I kind of expected the women to have my back while filming in the same way I've protected them throughout difficult times in their personal lives on the show. I have a lot of factual information in the vault that could discredit them and their lives, but I've always chosen to work with integrity and point out their strengths instead of their weaknesses. I leave that birthday party stressed and frustrated. My brain wasn't quick enough to respond intelligently and on the spot, so I send Kyle an e-mail and cc the other women after I digest what was said.

> *Dear Kyle,*
>
> *After marinating on what went down yesterday, I wanted to bring a couple of things to your attention: I am coming out of a three-year ordeal of living in a mentally paralyzed cocoon, due to a infection in my brain called NEUROBORRELIOSIS, something you might want to research in case you would like to have an understanding of Lyme disease, the biggest global epidemic in today's world.*
>
> *I arrived with a great attitude yesterday and am proud of myself for making it out of bed and joining you girls. For you to go down on me so hard in order to create what you think is good TV is beyond my understanding and it left me quite confused. Living in my very isolated world, I am not used to being attacked in such an unkind way.*
>
> *As far as I knew, Lisa R and my incident was clearly resolved at*

Erika's house. Christopher Cullen is the producer of our show and he is doing an excellent job. I do believe that this is a collaboration of all of us, but trying to co-produce with such desperate measures felt extremely inauthentic to say the least. I am just trying to catch up and participate. I don't need your pity, but I do ask you kindly to respect my situation. Your lack of compassion is not a pretty look. I also would like to clarify that my deal with Bravo and Evolution is based on the best of my ability, whether that is three or thirty times this season, so I would appreciate it if you lower your expectations of how much I should participate in filming.

Sitting at home, staring at the ceiling, waiting for my brain to heal, is not a choice for me, but unfortunately it is the card life has dealt me. I am already feeling unaccomplished as it is so please don't make me feel like I am not holding up my part of the bargain here. If I was out living life with my family and friends, sitting front row at Fashion Week with my girls and not showing up to work I would understand your frustration, but unfortunately this is not the case. So please trust me when I say I am doing the best that I can and, like you, I only want to make the best show possible, but I can't do more than I do for reasons you will probably never understand. I think we have two strong beautiful new housewives who, given a chance, can make a great season. Let's have coffee next week and talk about this further in person.—Yo

I hear that the women use the word "Munchausen" in relation to my illness during filming. *I've never heard that word! What does that even mean?* I ask Daisy to look it up. That is such a hurtful word, it infuriates me. *Why would anyone make such a distorted and untrue statement related to my health journey? Especially in front of my friends and millions of viewers?* It's simply unconscionable that my supposed "friends" doubt and discredit my word on such a delicate and sensitive matter. But a thousand times worse and more hurtful is when they say that Anwar and Bella don't have Lyme. I like to believe that everyone has the best intentions with my children—especially those who boast about knowing them since they were babies. Only I *know* how much these children have suffered so this infuriates me. As an adult, I've learned to accept people's ignorance about invisible chronic disease, but I'm not going to accept doubt cast on my children's journey. This is where I draw the line!

By sharing my own journey, I know that I have opened up a space for debate, which is useful when it's done with the right intent and kindness. Debate and transparency is what the Lyme community needs in order to educate the public and bring awareness. Yet it is very sad to see the judgment and ignorance that come with it for all involved, including my own children.

Due to my compromised brain function and lack of energy, the slightest confrontation brings me down. I'm well aware that my tank is half full, so I'm very protective of my energy and try to use it to focus on getting well, instead of worrying about what ignorant people think of me. Sometimes easier said than done though. But here's the bigger picture: how these women behave mirrors what is actually going on in the real world. People living with long-term illnesses, especially those suffering with invisible diseases such as Lyme, depression, chronic fatigue, and many others, suffer in silence. They're judged and ridiculed and lose friends and family because their loved ones lack understanding and compassion. It's a sad part of the truth and I can only say that I'm grateful for going through this as an adult and thank God I have the ability to understand it. I often think about the teenagers with Lyme whose brains are so severely affected that they commit suicide instead of enduring the pain and judgment of their medical communities, families, and friends. *What's happened to today's world? Why are people so self-absorbed and living without compassion and empathy for others?*

Chapter Fifteen

....

YOU DON'T NEED A CERTAIN NUMBER OF FRIENDS. JUST A NUMBER OF FRIENDS YOU CAN BE CERTAIN OF.

My implants are gone, but the poison that wreaked havoc on my once perfectly imperfect body remains. Dr. Feng estimates that about five percent of the free-floating silicone was not accessible during surgery. I won't be able to move to the next chapter in my recovery until I get rid of this, so my focus right now is detoxing. This starts with a very clean diet combined with my daily IVs, shots, and detox baths. I work with a toxicologist, Dr. Hildegarde Staninger. She runs a huge panel of blood work, including some silicone blood labs, and with these results she is able to give me guidance on removing the remaining toxins in my body. She immediately makes me get rid of all the plastics in my house and use glass products only. Dr. Staninger also prescribes a lot of holistic things, including essential oils and orange-flower water. I'm fascinated with the power of the oils and how she's planning to have the toxins attach to it and evacuate my body, which feels stiff and dense so I often see Dr. Dennis Colonello. He has kept me structurally sound for many years now but he is baffled by what this disease has done to me and why he can't get certain things to move in my body. This is amazing since he's the man who keeps the entire LA Clippers basketball team running.

I continue to see Dr. Kang, who gives me direction in between my appointments with Dr. Klinghardt. I also do a lot of neural therapy during this time to clear blockages as we try to reboot my autonomic nervous system. Exercise or a small trampoline could really help detox my lymphatic system, but unfortunately my body isn't ready to do much of anything that requires a lot of energy. Still, I ask Alberto to bring my mini trampoline so I can keep it on the balcony. On a good day, I make myself jump fifty times while holding tightly to the balcony doorknob. Most of the time, I just sit on it. I smoke raw tobacco to calm my raging nervous system as I watch the happy children on the playground next door. I also do lymphatic drainage massages and I'm religious about my daily Epsom salt baths with organic baking soda or apple cider vinegar.

In the weeks that follow, I start having big sores on the top of my head and I'm shocked to see that my two big toenails are black. I learn that this is from the leftover silicone granulomas that are being pushed out, fascinating signs of the body's power and natural ability to detox. Stuff continues to come out of the strangest places, like my chest and stomach. It's really a hideous process, but I'm so fascinated by how hard my body is working and the magic healing this powerhouse is showing me.

This is why I can't be mad at my fat ass for not fitting into any of my dresses when I'm looking for something to wear to the upcoming Global Lyme Alliance gala. The thought of putting on fancy clothes and high heels and having to socialize right now is overwhelming. After all, I've spent most of the past year in my fuzzy white robe in my safe cocoon. I never weigh myself and stopped looking in the mirror a long time ago. It's been even longer since I stood naked in front of one, but it's time. I peel off my robe and nightgown and stare at my reflection. *This isn't pretty.* Even though my diet has been stellar and my implants are gone, I've gained around twenty pounds of who knows what. I've been in a healing crisis for so many years, and it shows in the scarred, sick body looking back at me. The old me would have gotten really frustrated right about now, but instead I feel a deep appreciation, compassion, and respect for my body. I've completely lost the superficial connection to the outside world and I don't care if I ever wear another dress in my life! I think I've got this and just want to stay buckled down and fight with every inch of me.

I also know that once I regain my strength and want to get back in shape, I can do it. I weighed two hundred pounds the day after I gave birth to Gigi and was shooting a bathing suit campaign ninety days later. So once my body is healed, I'll be disciplined enough to do it again. David likes me very skinny, and the old me was okay with this. But now I wonder why did I care? I have gracefully let go of trying to impress anyone. After my breast surgery, I'm in no mood to be anyone's sex object anymore. The transition to my original 1964 has been a long and arduous road but it feels good to own who I am today. This is clearly not what David had signed up for. He really hasn't changed. I am the one who changed, maybe no longer the arm candy he married just four years earlier. However, I've become a much better, more grounded, and stronger version of myself, something he isn't quite capable of seeing right now or feeling in his heart. It's becoming very clear to me that my spiritual growth in this journey is mine and mine only.

Right before leaving for New York, I get a call from Chris Cortazzo saying that we got a great offer on the Malibu house.

"The buyers have come to see it three times and are in love with it," he says. "They want to close in two weeks." *Two weeks? That's crazy. Then again, this is what I've been praying for. It's time to say good-bye to this beautiful and magical place that I once called home.*

"They want to buy it furnished," Chris says.

"Great," I reply.

"Don't you want to keep any of your pieces from Santa Barbara?" David asks. A lot of the furniture in Malibu came from my house before David and I moved in together. Strangely, I feel no connection to any material things. Zero. Right now, nothing but my health matters to me. The buyers can keep it all, even my closet and my clothes! The only thing I will miss is my beautiful, famous fridge, something I know I can rebuild again one day. At this point, I need simplicity and the thought of being free from this stress is worth everything.

The second annual Lyme gala is in October, back in New York City. I invite all the housewives because I think an evening like this will open their eyes and, hopefully, their hearts. They will finally see that I'm not the only person in the world suffering from this invisible disease; my problem is shared by millions! Hearing other people at the gala—especially children—talk about their Lyme battles will most likely change their perspective and hopefully will be a humbling experience. Unfortunately, the two women who need to hear this message the most—Lisa Rinna and Lisa Vanderpump—decline my invitation.

During this detoxing and healing time, my skin has become so sensitive, my bones hurt, and my chest is still raw inside, so the thought of flying across the country is not a happy one. Tom and Erika generously offer to fly everyone to New York on their private plane so that makes the trip a lot less stressful for my immune system. Nothing in the superficial world resonates with me anymore and the thought of getting dressed up and masking my spirit with makeup feels uncomfortable. I've been working on my speech for weeks without much success. It's such a frustrating reminder that I've lost the crucial ability to let my thoughts flow freely. The old me could easily wing a speech or memorize one, but at this point I can't do it without the teleprompter.

David and I arrive at the gala at Cipriani. I'm grateful to have my mom and children here to ground my spirit, as well as my Lyme squad: Dr. Piro, Tom, Paige, Amber, Kelly, Marc, and Daisy, who have stood by me every step of the way, never questioning my journey and always going above and beyond. I try to smile and engage with others as much as I can, but it's a rough night inside my paralyzed brain. The loud symphony of life's sounds that fills the room is hard to handle and puts me in overdrive soon after we arrive. I wiggle my way through the night the best that I can. After all, this event supports my search for a cure, and, truthfully, if only a handful of people change their perception of Lyme, it is worth being here.

At one point during the night, Dr. Piro tells me how surprised he is by the size of the event for a disease that is so little known. After talking to many people with Lyme, he comes up to me.

"I'm amazed how much this reminds me of the early years of cancer where people had this mysterious, debilitating disease but we didn't have the tools to see it and no one knew what caused it," Dr. Piro says.

Then, a frail but sweet- and kind-looking twentysomething young man walks up to me with someone who is obviously his caretaker. "This is Kevin and he's a big fan of the show and has been following your journey," his caretaker explains. "He's been struggling with Lyme for many, many years." Kevin and I start talking, and I instantly feel a connection along with a heart full of compassion. He looks exactly the way I feel: lost and disconnected from his spirit. It's almost as if I'm staring at my own reflection in the mirror.

"How are you getting better? What are you doing?" he asks.

"This isn't something that I can answer in this moment, but let me introduce you to Daisy, my health advocate so we can be in touch," I say. "I don't know how to help you in New York, but if you can move to L.A., we'll gladly make you part of our Lyme squad." Children and young people make the biggest impact on my soul. I wish I could start my own little Lyme clinic.

It's time for the speeches, so I hug Kevin good-bye and sit down at my table. After the amazing master of ceremonies, Rosanna Scotto, a New York City TV news anchor, kicks off the event, Gigi comes onstage and introduces me. It's a beautiful moment to see my twenty-year-old speak so eloquently to a big crowd with such love and understanding of my journey's higher purpose. This makes my night especially meaningful. Her heartfelt yet heartbreaking words bring tears to my eyes and wash away all the judgment I've endured these past four years. At the end of the day, my children's support is all that matters. My illness has been hard on all of us, and my kids grew up faster because of it. But I truly feel that all three of them have gained compassion and value life in a more substantial way as a result. By the time I leave Anwar and Bella at the table and make my way to Gigi onstage, the knot in my throat is thick. It takes everything I have not to just break down in Gigi's arms before my speech.

I do not deserve this award . . . This award is for Bella and Anwar. This is a token of my promise that I will not allow you to live a life of pain and suffering. I will prevail and walk to the end of the earth to find a cure so that you can live the healthy life you deserve. No child in this world should suffer the way that you do, and I commend you both on your brave and persistent effort to get well and suck up the disappointment of the endless failing protocols that you have tried.

I thank you for your extraordinary selflessness during this journey. Your unwavering love and compassion has kept me alive and fighting through the darkest days of my life. I am so sorry for all the important things I've missed in your life these past four years. I used to be a pretty cool, smart, multitasking, kickass mom, but all three of my children really got shortchanged with the dumb blonde in the white robe who mostly lives her life in bed. I did turn into a professional social media stalker, though, liking every Twitter and Instagram post you have ever made, just to let you know that I was watching you from afar and right by your side in spirit at all times. I truly feel that I would be a real coward to turn my back and walk away from this experience without sharing and giving back to the millions of people affected by this invisible disease and silent killer.

The gala is a huge success. We raise over $3 million for research, proper diagnostics, and, hopefully, a cure. It's an eye-opener for some of the housewives, too. Kyle is crying at the event, which hopefully means that she gets the message on a deeper level. When she is interviewed for the show, she says that she's taken aback by how big the gala is.

"I always felt dirty and weird when Lisa Rinna said 'Munchausen,' and being in that setting with her and not being more defensive," Kyle says. "Being here tonight and listening to what these people are saying, I feel bad about that . . . I'm tortured by it. If I had known what I know now about Lyme disease, I would never have allowed that conversation to continue."

"This closes the chapter on doubt," Erika says. "There is more than one person saying the same thing."

October 21, 2015
It does not matter how slowly you go as long as you do not stop.
#SmallVictories #ComingBack #LymeDiseaseAwareness

My thyroid continues to be a challenge as it has been ever since I had it removed seven years earlier, so we're always monitoring and adjusting my medication. My friend Dr. Paul Nassif reaches out and introduces me to Dr. Kent Holtorf, apparently an expert in thyroid disorders and Lyme who has battled Lyme and chronic fatigue himself. With great suffering comes great compassion. I like Dr. Holtorf and his review on my new extensive blood work and I start adding some of his protocols to mine. He also switches my thyroid medication to a compounded T3 and T4.

November first is David's birthday, and he wants to celebrate by seeing a Lakers game at the Staples Center. It's a loud, high-energy event with almost nineteen thousand attendees but all that matters to me is that the birthday boy is happy. We have a nice sit-down dinner at the venue and what I thought was a pretty good night.

Monday morning is my biweekly appointment with Dr. Kang. On the way home, Daisy and I always stop at Erewhon Market to pick up some healthy foods. As usual, as we are about to turn right at the corner of Third Street toward the store, I call David at his office to see what he wants for dinner.

"Good morning, my love," I say. "I'm going to the store. Do you want anything special for tonight?"

"No. I'm going out with my daughters. And we need to talk," David replies in a tone so cold that shivers run through my body.

"Are you okay?" I ask. He mumbles an answer, then quickly ends the conversation. My stomach sinks and anxiety sets in. Even though I don't know what he is referring to, my gut tells me that it's bad.

"What's going on?" Daisy asks, noticing the change in my energy.

"I don't know, but something's really wrong." I share a lot with Daisy, but not private details of life with my husband, so right before we turn into the parking garage, I get out of the car and call him back.

"What's going on?" I ask. "Why do you sound so different? So strange? Can we please talk about this?"

"I can't do this anymore," he says briskly. "But we'll discuss it tonight."

Tonight? That's ten hours from now!

"At least tell me what you're thinking," I say. He refuses. He chooses to keep me in the dark. I don't hear from him the rest of the day and by the time he comes home from dinner at 11 P.M., I'm in bed and half asleep. I try to talk to him but it immediately turns into a fight. I assume that his birthday made him realize that he has two separate lives: one with his sick wife and another with his daughters. Rightfully so, he is struggling with this scenario, although this is his fourth marriage so it's not the first time he experiences this kind of a separation between his loved ones. Unfortunately this is the same old "Foster Movie" and I am just the new leading lady. Sadly this is the truth of our reality. I learned about this family dimension soon after we got married. I feel powerless because there is nothing I can do. I can't change who people are or how they care for others. I am confident, though, that I have been a kind, giving, and fair stepmother who gave blending our families 200 percent effort in the five years *before* I got sick with nothing in return during the difficult four years that followed.

After opening up this box and this very uncomfortable subject, being in the condo is awkward. There is a huge disconnect between us and I feel like a visitor in David's environment while I am trying to fight to stay alive. In the midst of this most difficult time with my husband, Gigi gets cast for the Victoria's Secret show, which is a dream come true for her. The video of her auditioning and then being told she got the job, where she screams, sits on her heels, and starts crying, goes viral, so everyone is talking about it and texting me with excitement. Landing this job is a very special accomplishment, because Gigi and I set it as a goal when I dropped her in New York just two years earlier. She is on cloud nine while I am in the midst of a thunder storm which I don't want to share with her in this moment in time. She asks me to bring Anwar and David to the show, because she has no idea what he and I are going through. *How can I miss it? I have to pull it together and go.* But David is shooting a Disney project in Florida and then is scheduled to fly to Paris to record with Carla Bruni so he can't go. With a big knot in my stomach and feeling completely discombobulated, Anwar and I fly to New York.

When we arrive, I text David to say that we landed safely. Eight hours later, he gives a very terse response and then goes completely silent. This feeling of abandonment is the worst, most suffocating thing for me. This is on top of the many Lyme symptoms that have flared up from the stress and confusion of this life-changing experience. It's a tough pill to swallow. Still, I do what mothers do and keep it together to avoid taking away from Gigi's great joy at such an exciting time in her life. I try to focus on business and schedule a meeting for Anwar to meet with IMG. I organized a test photo shoot with Jack Guy a couple of months ago, and Gigi's agent, Louis Mattos, is interested in representing Anwar. Anwar is unsure, but I feel it's important for him to be exposed to different aspects of the fashion industry, especially because he has such talent and passion for designing. This year we decided to have him homeschooled, which has allowed Anwar, who is very creative, to spend more time sewing, cutting, and building on his own collection. Although his education is the most important thing, doing a couple of modeling jobs a year will not only give him a taste of the financial independence that he needs to acquire, it will also be a great way to start building relationships within the fashion industry.

I try to get through these couple of days the best that I can, just going through the motions, numb inside from the shock of all that has transpired over the past couple days. Though I never share details of my marriage with my children, Anwar instinctively knows something is wrong. He always stays very close to me, but he does not leave my side for a second during this trip.

Two days later, Anwar and I go to JFK to return home. A greeter takes us through security and to the lounge.

"You have about an hour before the flight," the greeter says.

"Thank you. We've got it from here," I tell him. "You can go." I get a cup of tea. While Anwar is on his phone, I sit and just stare out the window, completely paralyzed. It's the first moment I actually allow myself to feel. It's heavy and I have no clue how much time is passing by.

"Mom, when are we leaving?" Anwar asks.

"Eight P.M., my love. What time is it?" I say.

"It *is* eight!"

We jump up and rush to the lounge's front desk. "We're supposed to be on the eight o'clock flight, but we didn't hear any announcements," I tell the man behind the desk.

"We don't do announcements in this lounge," he says, as he looks up our flight. "I'm sorry, but it just left the gate." *What? We missed our flight?*

Anwar is upset and so am I. I go to the bathroom and have a complete meltdown. *I feel so overwhelmed and dumb for letting this happen. I just want to get home.* Before I leave the bathroom I dry my tears. Anwar is waiting for me right outside the door and puts his arms around me.

"It's okay, Mommy."

"No. It's not, Anwar. I can't even catch my own flight," I say.

"It doesn't matter. There's another one later," he says. And he's right. In the big scheme of things, it's just an extra two hours out of our day.

We get home really late, but at least we are home.

November 11 is our fourth wedding anniversary. Although I'm seeing another side to David, I still love him and don't want this once very special day to go unnoticed, so I send him flowers in Florida. Late that night, I receive a bouquet in return with a note that says, "11/11 *was* a very special day. Xo David." This is the final rose and it is clear that everything good is gone.

David is supposed to go from Florida to Paris, but since major suicide bombings and mass shootings are taking place in Paris right now, he cancels his trip and flies back to L.A. Yet instead of coming home to me and working on our problems, he blatantly checks into the Peninsula Beverly Hills—a hotel just two and a half miles down the road from the condo! I have already learned that David deals with emotions by cutting off all communication and performing a well-oiled disappearing act, yet not hearing from him is devastating. Not even a text saying, "I need space so I'm at a hotel." Instead, it is complete and utter silence. I guess this allows him to escape from having to deal with the facts of his life, my heart, and the sadness he is causing me. *How did we go from that beautiful boat trip in July to David living at the Peninsula in November? Yes. I get that David married a lemon! But isn't this what marriage is all about? In sickness and in health?* I'm pissed and, most of all, disappointed with his failure to keep his word and lack of loyalty. But I also feel sorry for him because he is unable to communicate with kindness and understanding. I sadly see the stuck little boy who has been running his whole life because he doesn't have the tools to fix the things he has broken on purpose.

Although I stay in treatment and on my detox protocol, I am really stressed and spend my days in bed trying to find my strength. After about ten days, David comes by the apartment to get some clothes. With my half of a brain, I try to start a discussion, but he isn't interested. His demeanor is cold and aggressive, a side of David that I've never seen before.

"Let's talk about this," I say, trying to stay calm and not engage with his negativity. *We can work things out.*

"Your sick card is up," he says. I am totally stunned Actually I am enraged. *MY SICK CARD IS UP? After having a front-row seat to my journey, he's actually saying that I used a SICK CARD? Who is he talking to? Who is influencing him? How did he come up with such an unkind statement? I don't deserve this!* David has *watched* me fight for my life over the years. He has seen me at my lowest possible point. *And yet he thinks I'm playing the SICK CARD? What happened to the sweet husband who ran my port and hooked up my daily IV antibiotics when this first started?* During one of his interviews for the show, he even says, "When you get married, it's for better or for worse, and Lyme disease is something that Yolanda and I are going to have to deal with for life . . . Lyme disease showed me that I could be a good husband because I have failed at that a few times in the past." I guess people are allowed to change their mind and maybe promises are made to be broken. I don't know how else to make sense out of this. The caregiver role isn't meant for everyone. Not everyone has the strength or the ability to battle through years of uncertainty with a chronically ill partner, and I'm the first one to admit that it's not easy. It is very hard on the caretakers in the family but like my little Bella said, I am not choosing to be sick. I readily acknowledge my own shortcomings in our marriage. Although I'm a very good sick person, I'm definitely not the wife I used to be and will probably never be that wife again. My health challenges have changed my ability to do for others the way I used to. That said, it has not changed my moral compass, integrity, or compassion for others, and if roles were reversed and *David* was sick, I would stick by him.

I thought that our relationship was a lifelong one. Of course, in any marriage, even the best, there are ebbs and flows, but I was willing to ride the waves with David because I was in our marriage for the long haul. However, once he tells me that my "sick card is up," I know that something has pushed him over the edge. He also says something else that I won't repeat but will never forget. These two statements are so below the belt that this makes it a very sad but very clear moment for me. Even though I am unsure and have no idea how much longer my health journey is going to be, I'm not afraid to continue on to the finish line by myself. Nothing and nobody is going to stop me from figuring this out. The loss of my marriage is abrupt, and not having the opportunity to communicate with David makes things ten times worse. I lost my husband and my best friend all in one day. I cry myself to sleep many nights.

The day before Thanksgiving, I get a letter from David's lawyer saying that we're officially separated. This is obviously not something he *needs* to do but something he *wants* to do. We aren't talking and David posts a picture on Instagram that says "Foster-ized Thanksgiving," showing his family without me. I get the message loud and clear.

I'm devastated and just want to stay home and hide under the covers, but my kids beg me to come with them to Mohamed's house for dinner. I go because it's important to my children, but I'm paralyzed and unable to talk or eat because the knot in my stomach is so big. Divorce, regardless of how it happens, feels like a death, especially when you don't have children together.

I'm not sure how I will do it but I have to pull up the bootstraps. My kids are watching my every move and I must lead by example just like my mom always did. I want to show them that we can get through difficult times like this with grace and great self-respect. First I've got to get out of David's condo and find a space that is mine and that my children can call home. I don't want the press to find out that I'm looking at apartments, so my friend Rebecca uses her broker and we make an appointment for Thursday morning. The day before, I see my osteopath, Dr. Trafeli, and fall asleep during my treatment, probably because of pure exhaustion and too much crying. I have a clear vision of a white bed that faces a huge window with sunlight streaming through it. It's such a strong image.

"Daisy, I think I just saw my next healing place," I say when I open my eyes. "I saw the bed and the window. I think this is a sign from the universe."

The next morning, I meet the broker and we make our way to see ten apartments on Wilshire within my price range. The second building is beautiful and it feels welcoming because the people are very friendly. In the elevator, the broker tells me that we're about to see apartment 1604. *1604?*

"1-64 is my birthday." *I guess there's no such thing as a coincidence.* We step into a very calm, open space. The broker shows me the living room and the kitchen.

"Can I see the master bedroom, please?" I ask.

The second we walk into the master, I see the bed and giant window from the vision I had the day before.

"Can you give me a couple of minutes alone?" I ask. The broker nods and leaves as I sit on the bed. I try to feel the room and process what is happening. *It's as if God is watching over me and is leading the way. This must be where I'm meant to live.* The space is really bright and feels strangely safe. Plus, there's an extra room off the master that could be the perfect treatment room, which I need to heal physically as well as emotionally. *This marriage has taken a toll on me in more ways than one. Energetically this feels like the right place for me, as if I am meant to be here.*

We leave the apartment and look at eight others. I go home exhausted and overwhelmed with the decision that has to be made. The thought of moving and starting a new life on my own is frightening. But I need to stand up for what's right and find myself a space where I can heal peacefully and where my children and I can anchor and build from. I take a hot Epsom salt bath, get back into my comfy white robe, and hide under the covers, praying for clarity. I wake up the next morning knowing that 1604 is the right place for me and make an offer on the apartment. It's accepted, so I e-mail David and tell him that I've found a place to live. "Please give me two more weeks to move out," I write. I sound strong and confident, but truthfully I'm a wreck. Many nights, I wake up in the middle of the night, cold and shaking and overcome with such a deep sense of loss.

David's manager and my dear friend Marc calls to tell me that the tabloids plan to leak the story of our separation, and it's only a matter of time before TMZ picks up on it. I wonder why David, who I thought wanted to be private, is choosing to stay at a high-profile hotel in the center of Beverly Hills rather than a friend's guesthouse. *Does he want the story to get out?* I try to stay ahead of any rumors, speculation, and incorrect tabloid stories by writing a polite and kind statement, which Marc releases to the press on December 1. It says, "We are grateful for the years we've spent together and believe wholeheartedly that we did our best. I hope that we can pave the road ahead of us with all we've learned and with the love and respect we will always have for one another." The press goes crazy, and the story is spun in many different ways. It's heartbreaking to see our marriage fall apart and be judged by so many who don't even know us personally. David is criticized for leaving his sick wife, and, even though he's being held accountable for his actions by the world, it's painful for me to watch because that's not what he deserves.

The next two weeks are an emotional roller coaster. I don't know whom to talk to or what to do. Paige comes to the rescue and with Daisy, she takes on the task of helping me move. *What was I thinking when I sold my house and sold all the furniture, too? Furniture that I've had most of my adult life? I don't even have a bed to sleep on. The thought of starting over again is overwhelming.*

Finally, on December 11, I move into my new apartment. It's chaos, but as usual my loyal friends come to the rescue. I'm a zombie, but Paige puts me in the car and drives me to buy beds and furniture. Paul, my guardian angel, sends unpackers, closet organizers, and his fiancée, Mareva, to help me get somewhat settled. Kelly, Angie, Cio, Bui, Rebecca, and Josefa also show up. Just as my mom always said, "A lot of hands make light work." My angels definitely unite. When we first move in, Anwar and I camp out on mattresses on the floor, and I make night tables from my storage boxes. The moving process is exhausting, and my inner strength is put to the test. Strangely, I have accumulated high sensitivities to electromagnetic fields and allergies to synthetic ingredients in things like creams, paints, stains, and candles, so moving into a home that is freshly painted, stained, and cleaned flares up my entire system. Daisy finds IQAir filters and fans to keep the air flowing, and we environmentally rig the apartment.

With every week that goes by, it feels more and more like home. Many of the items I unpack bring back memories. Some of them are painful so I put them right back in the box and into storage to be dealt with at a later date. I realize how much stuff I've accumulated over time and how little of it means anything to me. I truly have no attachment to material things other than the photo albums of my children's lives. Maybe at one point I wanted or needed all those things, but in this moment they seem more insignificant than ever. All I want is my health and the strength to get out of bed in the morning and go about my day in a peaceful way. To take a break from unpacking, my girlfriends push me to see the comedy *Sisters,* with Tina Fey and Amy Poehler, at the iPic theater next door to my apartment. The best line in the movie is "A house is a building; a home is a feeling." This is the exact inspiration that I need to keep in mind. I've moved in and out of many houses, but I have never lost my ability to create a home for my family, and that is a gift that nobody can ever take away from me. I can only look forward and take life one day at a time.

At the beginning of December, my fourth season on the *Housewives* airs. I try to watch the weekly episodes in order to write the mandatory Bravo blog. This is when I realize that, although my actual screen time isn't much, the story line of my illness is front and center as my castmates say some astonishing things behind my back. In one episode, I show up for Lisa Rinna's birthday party at a small Italian restaurant on Burton Way with my girlfriend Angie Simpson. At that point, I'd been living in the condo for six months and hadn't even brought my makeup bag from my house in Malibu. Truthfully, makeup isn't on my radar and at the time that was filmed it took every ounce of strength I had to throw on a T-shirt and pair of pants to go to the party. I showed up to my job and stayed as long as I could— maybe an hour at most—and everyone seemed so pleasant to my face. Yet the way I looked and my disease became the topic of conversation as soon as I left, something I see for the first time while watching the show.

"In Beverly Hills, a woman going to a birthday dinner without putting one drop of makeup on is borderline shocking," Kyle says. The only thing I find shocking is her comment! But Kyle isn't the only critic.

"She doesn't look good at all. She's got nothing on her face. Not even a little bit of under-eye cover-up or anything. Maybe you could take ten seconds to do that," Lisa Vanderpump says. She has no idea that those ten seconds take more energy than I can muster up.

And then there is Lisa Rinna's comment: "We all have this armor—hair, makeup, but Yolanda showed up vulnerable without any of her protection. That's a brave thing to do." If she thinks brave is going without makeup, she should think again. *Brave* is battling an invisible illness that has no cure and doing so for four years, 365 days around the clock. *Brave* are the families who have sold their belongings to care for their chronically ill loved ones. *Brave* is many things, but it is *not* going without mascara to her Beverly Hills birthday party! Even though I'd prefer to rise above it and not respond, I'm contractually expected to blog about the show, so I attempt to write an intelligent response.

Hello Bravo lovers,

I'd be lying if I said it's not hard to be judged by the way I look. It's almost like you have to show scars and broken bones in order to warrant understanding. Does it count that even though we don't "look" great, that we show up? It's tempting to be distracted by this negativity, but I choose to stay focused on the light at the end of the tunnel and not let anything interrupt my healing process. Being mentally and neurologically compromised for so long has presented me with life's biggest challenge, and I need all of me to fight it.

Bless the hearts of my fellow housewives! May neither they, nor their families, ever have to face such illness, because it is at that time when we learn and realize what really matters.

Ken Todd is right, I don't look good. I definitely look ill . . . but that's because I AM! I miss the days of what now feels like my old life: the hair, the makeup, a sexy dress, but most of all being in a healthy body. At the end of the day, I now want to be "real," not to be "perfect." I still like to believe though that no beauty shines brighter than that of a good heart.

If Lyme wasn't such a controversial disease, I'd probably choose to deal with my journey in a more private manner, but the amount of suffering that goes on behind closed doors all over the world is unconscionable, and I feel it is now my duty to be a voice for those who can't be heard. I want to shine a light on a disease that so many know so little about.

I could react and look at tonight's episode with mixed emotions,

*but I've grown apart from looking at what's not . . . I am blessed to
have a voice and a platform that can bring awareness to not only
my disease but to the most profound lesson of it all, which is to lead
a life with compassion, kindness, and without judgment, for everyone you meet is fighting a battle you know nothing about.*

*One day soon I hope to have the ability to write a book about
uncovering the mystery of this chronic disease and share with you
the true depth of my story, but until then I am just a housewife on a
mission with laser beam focus on one thing and one thing only . . .
my health! I have faith that God often uses our deepest pain as the
launching pad of our greatest calling. Cheers to that . . .*

Much love and a big hug, Yo

December 20, 2015
*Sometimes what you are most afraid of doing is the very thing that will set
you free. #WindowsToMyWorld #Home #NewBeginnings*

Luckily, I have become pretty resilient through the years and learned not
to waste my energy on this toxicity. Instead, I focus on my children. Gigi
and Bella are coming home from New York a couple of days before Christmas, and along with Anwar, we leave for Aspen. We celebrate Christmas
with Paige and her three kids, Alexa, Ashley, and my goddaughter Amber.
Bella is struggling and battling severe exhaustion. The altitude is hard on
both of us. Yet we have fun cooking dinners, baking, playing games, and
drinking hot chocolate by the fire. I try to accept my new normal as I focus
on applying the spoon theory to my life. I manage to take a couple of
walks and even ride the gondola to the mountaintop. I can't believe how
much has changed in the past years. *I used to speed down this mountain
like an angel with wings.* Although my marriage took a major turn that I
didn't see coming, my health has made slow and steady progress. Last

Christmas I was fighting for my life, hospitalized two days before the holiday and headed for the worst six months of this four-year journey. So today I am here and I feel much gratitude as I try to enjoy life the best that I can and with the greatest gift of all: a houseful of kids and quality time with my children and close friends. I'm not there yet, but I'm a lot closer than I was last Christmas.

December 31, 2015
I could have never imagined how much life can change in only one year.
I wonder what next December will look like.
#Reflections #MotherNature

Chapter Sixteen

....

TODAY I CAN SEE THAT THE HARD TIMES IN MY LIFE WERE ALL BLESSINGS IN DISGUISE.

I gladly say good-bye to 2015, by far the most difficult year of my journey of which I spent 90 percent of my time in bed. My little spirit somehow feels inspired for the start of 2016 and excited about 365 new days and fresh chances for a full recovery. On the one hand, I've made progress; on the other, I still have to complete the list of procedures and protocols before there's the possibility of a full recovery with a healthy body and brain. Dr. Klinghardt is the main guiding light who has been constant in helping me solve one layer of my complex, multilayered illness at a time. Sometimes I don't fully comprehend what he's telling me but I trust him with every part of my being. Knowing that I'm extremely goal oriented, he gives me a specific list of the next big steps to focus on this year:

1. Have five root-canal-treated teeth removed and replaced with zirconia implants.
2. Have two cavitations fixed. These are where my wisdom teeth had been.
3. Get tonsils removed. This is because the Cunningham Panel shows a severe PANDAS infection.

4. Get transvascular autonomic modulation (TVAM) surgery. To
   reset the autonomic nervous system.

As you can imagine, it takes courage to work through this unusual to-do list, but I follow Dr. Klinghardt's light in the midst of my storm. Together we peel away layer after layer of this giant onion. He always reminds me that the only way out is through, and I think of these words all the time while battling through my days. I'm still on my strict Lyme protocol, which includes taking quintessence, liposomal artesunate, Brazilian green propolis, liposomal stevia, cistus tea, and Sporanox; getting IVs of vitamin C, IVIG (intravenous immunoglobulin), ozone, silver, and neurotherapy into my abdominal and lower back scars; and doing ion-cleanse footbaths with cilantro drops three times a week. I'm still working closely with my toxicologist, Dr. Staninger, to detox the remaining silicone in my body.

Although the road map is clearly laid out in front of me, I have absolutely no power to speed up the healing clock and am still in bed twenty hours most days because of joint pain, severe fatigue, and Herxheimer reactions to my treatments. It's probably hard to imagine how anyone can spend that much time in bed, but unfortunately it's not an option. My body needs complete rest in order to heal. Most people start the day with an unlimited amount of energy and endless possibilities to do whatever they desire. If you're healthy, you don't realize that this is a blessing, *not* a given. Every pain-free moment is a *gift*, and I make the best of each one that comes my way, feeling grateful and determined to find my way back to life. It feels as if I'm living in a cocoon state, but connected to God, receptive, and trying to help others.

Daisy has found an apartment for my fellow Lyme warrior Kevin, whom I met in October at the Global Lyme Alliance. She's been treating him long distance, but his parents have decided to move him out to L.A., where he can be in a daily program with Daisy and see Dr. Klinghardt in Seattle. The more I struggle myself, the better I feel when I reach out to others and shift my energy to them. It kind of makes me forget about my own misery and realize that there are many others who suffer far worse than I do.

January 5, 2016
I am not afraid for you to see who I really am and what my days
are really like. I have learned to love every part of me without apology!
Happy selfie–sad selfie, good days–bad days, makeup–no makeup,
boobs–no boobs. I hope that by sharing this not so glamorous journey,
the millions of doubted and neglected Lyme sufferers will gain medical
recognition of their illness and the appropriate treatment affordable for all.
This is not a pity party, just reality with good intent.
#InvisibleDisease #ExplantSurgery #RHOBH #NotAVictimButAWarrior

I find joy and strength in guiding other Lyme patients, and even though I don't hold the answers to a cure, engaging with them is important. Helping Ellie deal with her obstacles also keeps things in perspective for me. The life of an ALS patient is Lyme on steroids. The emotional and financial burden it puts on her husband is astronomical, and although this affects their marriage, their love is strong and they stay committed. It's a heartwarming and heartbreaking journey to watch up close. Through the years, I've encouraged Ellie to write a book about her heroic battle with ALS because her brain is so sharp and her voice so witty. I'm confident that one day I'll find a publisher for her story, which is one that must be told. Below is just a tiny snippet of her book, which she calls *And So It Is*. I share it with you because I love her writing and how she describes our friendship, a true friendship, not a Hollywood one.

Who is Yolanda?
Now, in life, you have the friends who accept your invitation to a
dinner party and the friends who accept your invitation to meet you
in the recovery room after surgery—elective or non-elective. My
friend is both. She is the girl who shows up during the sunshine AND

the thunderstorms. I am talking about my friend Yolanda. But we never really call her Yolanda. No, we mostly call her Yo, Yo-yo or Yogi Bear. You might know her as one of The Real Housewives of Beverly Hills. Now, you know my obsession with reality TV. The Housewives in particular. When Yogi told me she was going to be on The Real Housewives of Beverly Hills, I shamefully was so fucking stoked. Shameful because it's rude to be a voyeur into the lives of others. Interestingly, since Yolanda has been on the show, I think we've discussed it maybe two times. We have other stuff to talk about . . .

What other stuff do we have to talk about? It turns out that we are both sick. Very, very, very sick. I have ALS and Yogi has Lyme disease. The first friend I called when I was diagnosed with ALS was Yolanda. I called my other best friend Jenny after because I was too scared to call her. I knew that my news would kill her. But I knew that Yolanda would be strong for me. That's who Yolanda is. Strong. Dutch strong. Of all the experiences Yolanda and I have had in thirteen years, they were just training wheels for what was to come. People close to Yolanda have a saying, "What would Yolanda do?" Yolanda always has the answers whether it's about boyfriends, husbands, health, decorating, children . . . Everything. She just always does everything right.

I was like a spaz, running around Santa Barbara, and Yolanda was the rock. Yolanda and I had coffee Monday through Friday for four years straight at Starbucks in Santa Barbara after we dropped our children off at elementary school. Then we would have our favorite lunch together (goat cheese salad). Then sometimes we would have dinner together at her house with all the children (chicken and pesto pasta). We spent hours every day solving the world's problems. Well, mostly Yolanda solving the world's problems. I was busy smoking cigarettes. We have been thick as thieves ever since.

Yolanda is like the big sister. She's more mature. You want all of her clothes. She makes better decisions; you don't always agree with her. She's there for every holiday, she will defend your honor, she knows what's best for you and in a crisis . . . she is there. Just like a sister. When I had my diaphragm-pacing surgery, I was in the recovery room near dead with a collapsed lung and Yolanda comes running through the door to be by my side. The next thing she did was open her purse, take out her makeup bag, and do my makeup. She wasn't going to let me die ugly.

After I got sick, Yolanda and I would talk all the time and I would tell her everything: I'm sad, I'm scared, I'm frustrated, I'm getting weaker, I can't move my legs, I just took four oxycodone, I just fell on the bathroom floor and smashed my face, etc. I told her the truth. When I would ask her how she was, she would always say, "I'm great." But as the months rolled by, I could sense a change in her voice. I would still ask her how she was and she would still say that she was great. She never complained about anything in her life because she knew that nothing compared to what I was going through. Until she got sick. I didn't even know that Yolanda was sick because she never told me. She sat in bed month after month staring at the ceiling while Lyme was ravishing her brain, but she didn't tell me because she didn't want to burden me.

But now that I know she is sick and I am okay with it, it's all we ever talk about. We decided we are going to get through this together. We talk about juicing, the value of turmeric, how hard it is to find kale in Paris, stem cells, brain barriers, mitochondrial supplements, flax seeds, hyperbaric chambers, oxygen therapy, and anything else regarding our diseases. After that we talk about our children. After that we talk about our Davids. After that, we laugh. We always laugh and say, "WTF. How did we go from two healthy Santa Barbara girls raising our children, loving our Davids, excited about our futures to two Santa Barbara girls sick as dogs and unable to get out of bed? As usual, Yolanda has all the answers. She knows that it is her mission and responsibility to find a cure for Lyme disease. All you Lyme sufferers are lucky to have her on your team *because she will not stop until she finds a cure. It never once crossed my mind to find a cure for ALS. I am only now realizing from all of you that maybe, just maybe, I could help other people with or without ALS through my blog and my book by inspiring you all to live the day with eyes wide open and to the fullest. Yolanda knew the purpose of her disease from the get-go.*

You know in your worst nightmares the thought crosses your mind about who will take care of your child if you passed away? For me, it's a reality. I actually really had to think: Who will take care of Gracie like their own child? Who will nurture Gracie? Who will guide Gracie? Who will steer Gracie straight if she gets out of line? Who will make sure she has a successful life and makes the right choices? Who will hug her and be the shoulder that Gracie cries on? Who will raise Gracie with ethics and morals? Who will tell Gracie how much I loved her? Who will tell Gracie how wonderful her mother was? Who will replace me? That person is Yogi (and my sister, of course). This is not an easy question to ask of a friend. But Yolanda didn't hesitate and said of course she would take care of my Gracie as her own. She will just put Gracie in her line of ducks. Gigi, Bella, Anwar, and Gracie. I believe her and trust her. So knowing how much I love Gracie and knowing how judgmental I am, now you can see the kind of respect I have for Yolanda. This is the person I choose to take care of my daughter with all of the love that I would. So you see, even though I have ALS, I am lucky because I have Yogi.

January 11 is my birthday. I just want the day to go by quietly, without any fanfare. In the past four years, I have not really wanted to celebrate anything having to do with myself. Birthdays just don't matter anymore. All I want is my health and the ability to get out of bed in the morning pain free and with energy to make it through my day. Celebrations feel like a waste of my precious energy. But I want to express my love and gratitude to my best girlfriends, so I have a small lunch at Spago. Despite my initial hesitation, it makes me incredibly happy to look around the table and see my die-hard inner circle, the people who are by my side through the good and bad times, especially these past four years. Some of these women have been in my life for decades; some are new friends. One of the many lessons I've learned on this journey is that friendship isn't about whom you've known the longest, it's about who comes and never leaves your side. I used to think that I needed a lot of friends to feel loved. Now I know that if you have one or two, you are good; any more than that, and you are great. I'm a very blessed and lucky girl to have my table of eight.

January 11, 2016
Celebrating endings, for they precede new beginnings.
All I wish for today is a chance at a healthy life
without counting spoons so that I can continue my
quest in finding a CURE for #LymeDisease affordable for ALL.
#MyBirthdayWish #InvisibleDisease #ChronicLymeDiseaseAwareness

I still can barely make it out of the house. I can't last long in any social setting before my body starts to sweat, my hands start to tremble, and my limited brain function completely shuts down. Going out isn't worth the stress it puts on me, so by trial and error I learn to conserve my energy. I am patiently resigned to and tapped into survival mode. I resolve to live as I am and have grown used to a life on the sidelines. I'm proud of all the extreme obstacles my body has lived through and find a new appreciation for the rest and isolation it needs to continue to heal.

It's toward the end of the season when we tape the reunion show. I feel better than I did at last year's reunion but I am still isolated and choose to stay away from the everyday drama of life outside in the world. I don't really want to talk about the divorce or my illness. But of course, both these issues come up. Some of the women have the nerve to say "Maybe it's depression" or "Maybe it's menopause." *Are you kidding? This is a full-time job. Depression and menopause are obviously the first things we looked at! They clearly don't get it.*

When one of the women says that I use my illness "as a shield and a pass to not be accountable," my dear friend Erika sets her straight with exactly how I feel. "Why wouldn't she want to see her two daughters absolutely dominate Fashion Week in Paris right now and sit front row?" Erika asks. "Who wants to stay in a bathrobe?" Exactly! What I also still don't understand is why these women choose to talk about this on national TV. They could have chosen to come to *me* and ask questions. But of course that would not make for good TV or help their story line along. Clearly, the actions of some are based on being the center of attention, the more drama they make, the more camera time they get. One of the women claimed that another one said "There goes our story line" when someone suggested that they support me rather than tear me down.

In order to protect myself, I have to rise above it all and I am able to because I am living in truth. Nevertheless, it is a painful experience to see a bunch of desperate adult women run over dead bodies to get what they think is a great show. Money, greed, and fame are ugly things and this is a very good example of when integrity and compassion for others should come first. *Anyway, I must stay focused on what is in front of me.*

When I see Dr. Klinghardt at this time, he explains that working on one's emotional health is 50 percent of the healing pie.

"Fifty percent? That's amazing. I better get to work," I joke with him. I guess that traumatic and stressful events from the past or present and strong emotional feelings are held in the body. He says that over time, this can slowly damage the gut and immune system and trigger inflammatory conditions like autoimmune diseases and various types of arthritis. To facilitate my emotional healing, Dr. Klinghardt offers to organize a family-constellation session for me. Although I've never been a big fan of therapy, I struggled these past few years with the ability to articulate problems that have occurred during this journey. I also trust Dr. Klinghardt's opinion and have no reservations about revealing anything from my past or the present. At this point, I'm down to the bare bones of myself and am ready to attack and deal with anything that can potentially block my healing. Anwar, who is here for his checkup as well, encourages me to do the family constellation, so I say yes.

In this alternative form of therapy, you look at family members and dynamics in order to uncover stressors and/or heal trauma from your past. In this session, I'm with a group of people who are not related to me—in fact, I don't even know most of them. But each one represents a family member from my life who has caused difficulties or issues. There is also one person who represents me. It's interesting for the different people from my life to be placed in front of me. Seeing myself played by strangers and having them express the tremendous life-changing loss I suffered as a young girl when my father died is fascinating and resonates deep within me. The sense of abandonment I felt then is very similar to the feeling I have now around David. This is clearly a stressor that I need to pay attention to when choosing the next man in my life. Overall, it is a great and bonding experience for me and Anwar. It's beautiful to see my son get a deeper understanding of the family dynamics of my childhood. His love and compassion for me as a human being is heartwarming, and I'm grateful that the universe provided this opportunity at this moment in time.

January 17, 2016
Just because some people are done with your journey
doesn't mean your journey is done.
#AnotherWastedSaturday #LifeFromTheSideLines #Spoonie
#LymeDiseaseAwareness #DeterminedToFindACure #AffordableForAll
PS: Bad selfie day.

Back in L.A. and back on my Klinghardt protocol. Although this is part of the life I've grown accustomed to, it's probably hard for anyone to imagine what it is like to get shots and IV's five days of the week. Friends often ask how I stay motivated but the truth is that even on a bad day the little voice inside me never gives up on wanting to live for my kids, and my determination to find a cure is driven by my fear of a debilitated life for my children, their children, and all the children in the world.

Nobody deserves to suffer this way. So even though I'm following specific protocols now, I never stop contemplating my next move. Even though I was raised in a country where marijuana was legal, I never cared to smoke it. But today I've become educated about the benefits of this powerful plant. I meet Dr. Allan Frankel, an internist who specializes in pain management using CBD oils. His insight is extremely enlightening and I start using his CBD oil in a spray formula. To treat my insomnia, I spritz a couple of sprays under my tongue before I go to sleep. CBD is a compound in marijuana that supposedly doesn't have the side effects of the better-known chemical THC, and I find its anti-inflammatory and chronic-pain-relieving benefits extremely helpful in treating many of my symptoms.

I am dead-centered on my path of knowledge and truth, and have a deep thirst to understand the purpose of my journey, but I realize that this wisdom can't be found in a book or any set way of thinking. The ultimate understanding is based on silent awareness and a connection to the higher power. So while the outside world is judging me and my journey, I'm living in the light, where I feel safe, protected, and inspired by the possible results of all my hard work. Within my bubble, I contemplate a healthy and functioning future permeated by my love for my children and a sense of responsibility and devotion to all my fellow warriors out in the world. Sharing treatments and snippets of my life with the public is the easy part, although I view the judgment without empathy in today's social media culture as a dangerous combination.

My diet is another important piece of the healing puzzle. I never used to eat organic before I got sick, because I grew up in a place and time where I thought everything *was* organic. I also never imagined that a government would allow our food to be covered in poisons that will slowly shut down our immune systems. I guess I'm really naïve when it comes to those things, because I still don't understand how the FDA won't approve something as simple as ozone therapy, which is healing, yet allow pesticides to be sprayed on our vegetables and have antibiotics plus growth hormones injected into cows, which then poison the steaks we eat and feed our children. What about the waste toxins in the sea that poison our fish and the chemtrails that poison our air? It feels like a vicious cycle that is very hard to understand for a farm girl like me, but I do know that we collectively need to take a hard look at this picture. I find it overwhelming that organic food is so expensive and not affordable for most people, so if you don't have a little piece of dirt where you can grow your own vegetables, healthy eating becomes a real challenge and almost impossible. This is an absolute crime, but that is the subject of a whole other book. Anyway to get back on track, diet is important. I've learned that some foods severely affect my energy levels and pain syndrome, so by now I am convinced that "food is definitely thy medicine" for many of the simpler ailments so many of us suffer from. This is why I'm always trying new diets. At the beginning of February, I start a two-week detox diet that includes eating anti-inflammatory, antioxidant, energizing, and immune-building foods. The first week, I consume more than thirty-five different vegetables and fourteen types of beans, nuts, and seeds. I cannot have coffee or dairy, which I miss. It may sound cliché, but you really are what you eat, especially for those of us who battle chronic disease and pain, and following the detox diet relieves some of my symptoms. It definitely takes the fatigue, joint pain, and inflammation down a notch. It almost feels like the less I eat, the better I feel.

During this time, I go to New York for a week to spend time with my girls. I also have meetings with my friend and literary agent, Jan Miller from Dupree Miller. She is taking me to see different publishing companies about writing a book. I'm not sure if I am ready yet but I know I need to start thinking about it. It's important to share my story and what I've learned along the way. Also, a very exciting moment is finally here: I am able to sit front row to see Gigi and twenty other beautiful models strut down the runway for Tommy Hilfiger. *What an incredible moment.* My girls have taken the fashion world by storm, and I haven't been able to be part of any of it.

Overall, this is a good test run out in the real world, but it's also a reminder that I still don't have the stamina I hoped for. It's an exhausting week but so good for my soul. Even though I carefully count my spoons, I have to decline most of my girls' exciting invitations in order to keep my business obligations. Besides the meetings with publishers, I have to appear on *Watch What Happens Live.* I'm physically starting to look better—especially with a pound of makeup—and although my brain function is far from perfect, I feel better than I did when I appeared on the show last year, when I couldn't talk at all. Andy's other guest is the charming and witty Craig Ferguson, who, without knowing it, helps get me through. Viewers ask questions about my castmates' ignorance, my illness, and why I changed my last name since separating from David. It's interesting that people care to ask something that seems so personal to me. The answer is: I never dropped or stopped using the name "Hadid" when I married David. Although the *Housewives* identifies me as "Yolanda Foster," my legal name on my passport is actually "Yolanda Hadid Foster." I never even changed my credit cards or my driver's license for that matter. Now that David and I are getting divorced, I wanted to drop *both* of my married names and go back to my maiden name, Yolanda van Den Herik. I like that idea but my children are against it and feel strongly that I keep "Hadid" so that the four of us maintain a unified identify. For me, it's about respecting our family unit, and if this feels right to them and makes them happy, that's really all that matters.

March 2, 2016

It's been a humbling experience to learn that most people don't understand invisible disease because they can't actually see the

sickness on one's skin. Spiritually shaming those suffering from invis-
ible chronic illnesses is something we really need to take a look at
with compassion.

Although the whole Munchausen controversy is still front and center in the public eye, I'm done with it. Why let insincere and false gossip rock my world when I need to direct my energy toward healing and staying on a path of gratitude? *I* know the truth and what I stand for, and so does anyone who truly knows me and matters to me. Back at home in Los Angeles, I focus on the next chapters in my journey: another dental surgery and my tonsillectomy.

Root canals are definitely something to pay attention to because even when the nerve from your tooth is removed and filled with latex, bacteria can still set up camp in these canals and leak toxins into the rest of your body. This might not be a problem for healthy people with robust immune systems, but for those of us with chronic conditions like Lyme, such infections can get in the way of our recovery. X-rays also confirm that I have severe cavitations just like Dr. Klinghardt told me. He wants me to go to Switzerland to have my teeth fixed because the best biological dentist lives there. Yet I don't feel strong enough to fly to Europe and be away from home again, so Daisy finds Dr. Moldovan, who is going to remove my six root canals and crowns and also debride the cavitations in my jawbone in a surgery that takes eight hours.

She uses ozone and plasma-rich growth factor (PRGF) to regenerate bone and soft tissue and help with healing. In three to six months when the posts settle, they will be attached to new crowns, also made of zirconium but in the meantime I go home from this procedure with a mouthful of temporaries. The biggest lesson here? Ask questions. Look at *everything* you put in your mouth, or any other part of your body, for that matter. Again, we can't blindly trust authority to guide us, and what works for one person doesn't necessarily work for another. Any foreign object will create some sort of autoimmune response. In a healthy person, that response usually dissipates. Yet for someone struggling on every little level in terms of health, this can be a huge problem.

Just days later, I go on a trip to Tahiti with Paul and his family. Initially, I try to decline Paul's generous invitation because I'm still in pain from the dental surgery and afraid to travel, but he is persistent.

"You need to sit in the sun, eat normal food, go ten days without needles and treatments," he says. "Give your body a break." He is right. I throw a few bathing suits in a suitcase and make my way to the airport. About an hour into the flight, my face starts to swell and my teeth begin to throb to the point that it's unbearable. I don't like taking prescription pain medication, so I haven't used any since the surgery but thank God Daisy put them in my purse before I left. After taking one of them and applying some ice packs to my face, the pain calms down and I make it through the rest of the eight-hour flight.

This trip to paradise at a charming little beach hotel with people I love turns out to be one of my best vacations ever. There is a profound shift inside of me, and I truly believe it's the beginning of a new chapter. It is crucial for me to be close to nature and connected to the earth, so I spend every day soaking in the gorgeous warm Tahitian waters with a big sun hat on my head. After a couple of days I actually feel like gently stretching my arms in the water. I haven't moved my body like this in what seems like years, so it feels incredible. The only flaw in the plan is my excruciating dental pain. But the local island people at the hotel bring me a special oil to place on the surgery sites with ice packs. My girlfriend Mareva's family is here as well, and their humble and grounded Tahitian energy is contagious. I'm so grateful for the opportunity to share their beautiful culture and the simplicity of the sun, sea, fresh fish, fruits, and fuchsia hibiscus flowers far away from the complexity of my isolated life at home. I take my daily supplements, but ten days without IVs and shots is exactly what I need. Outside the comfort zone of my cocoon, I can actually see the light at the end of the tunnel and finally experience the feeling of joy. Paul, who has always been my guardian angel, has been part of everything good and bad in my life. He's never left my side and is always there when I need him the most. I often wonder how I got so lucky, but, as I've said before, I don't believe in coincidences. He is meant to be in my life, and I treasure our friendship. The only thing missing on this perfect trip is my kids, so, as great as it is to be away, it's exciting to get home to my Anwar. Our life at our new home has settled in nicely and it feels like we are finally getting back to living in harmony. Anwar is growing and maturing into an extraordinary spiritual human being and I am proud to call him my son.

April 4, 2016
When life gives you a hundred reasons to cry, remember that
God has given you a thousand reasons to smile.
#Sunset #CountingMyBlessings #Tahiti

In the past couple of years, Paige has often talked to me about ayahuasca ceremonies in Peru. (Ayahuasca is a controlled substance in the United States.) Supposedly, they can help reset the brain to allow for deep healing, clear parasites from the body, and provide other purifying medicinal properties. The literature is fascinating and makes it sound somewhat appealing, yet the thought of traveling to Peru right now is not. I work with Micah, a healer from Hawaii a couple times a year, and at my next appointment he mentions that there is actually an ayahuasca ceremony much closer than Peru. And it's *this* weekend!

"The shaman who runs it is very well respected and really good at what he does," Micah tells me. *Is the universe placing this opportunity in my lap? Should I seize this moment?* The second I leave his office, I call Paige from the car.

"I'm in," she says before I finish telling her all the details. The next day, I call the shaman and we talk for a while, plus he asks me an array of questions about my medical history and medication use. Pharmaceutical drugs apparently do not mix with the traditional ayahuasca medicine, made from the *caapi* vine that grows only in the rain forest, which you take during the ceremony.

"This is a very serious spiritual journey that is taken without any expectations and an open heart, not a drug-induced party," he explains in a serious tone of voice.

The following Saturday, Paige and I travel together to the event. Although we're both pulled to this ceremony by some force, neither of us has done this kind of thing before, and we have no idea what we are getting into. On the way, we laugh and giggle like two young girls who are going to do something forbidden. We have a difficult time finding the place where the ceremony is to be held. The sun has set so it's starting to get dark and it's a bit unsettling to be lost.

Finally, we arrive at this big house. I'm not sure why but I had imagined the ceremony would be outside somewhere in nature, but instead we walk into what could be anyone's living room with about fifteen strangers sitting in a circle. Each one has a towel, water bottle, bucket, little mattress, and pillow. Paige and I don't have anything, not even water bottles, so we're not only late but a little embarrassed as we join this well-prepared circle. Despite the strangeness of it all, there's something warm and soothing about the energy in the room. The shaman is here with his wife, a beautiful angel dressed in white, whom I connect with instantly. She carries their young baby in a sling, so it feels like a family. Most of the people here have experience with ayahuasca ceremonies and I can clearly feel that there is some sort of bond within the group.

Finally, the ceremony starts. The shaman has three helpers, who assist us as he gives very clear instructions about how to conduct ourselves during the ceremony. Then he recites a long and very meaningful prayer. After this, he serves everyone the spiritual medicine. It is a thick and brown liquid that tastes and looks a bit like molasses. The effects of it come on slowly, but soon enough I know what the bucket is for: everyone starts throwing up. I don't vomit much, maybe because I've already gotten rid of so many toxins. Paige is next to me though, puking uncontrollably. We fasted for twenty-four hours before the ceremony, so it's interesting to see what the body expels, which looks like bile. It's yellow, but also black tarry stuff, said to be toxins.

The shaman and two women play music and sing beautiful songs, an extraordinary and integral part of this ceremony, and the lyrics about healing and the earth are mesmerizing. It's a truly profound experience that walks me through many aspects of my life with a lot of clarity about my journey. After about six or seven hours, people start to fall asleep on their little mattresses. Paige is snoozing happily beside me, yet my debilitated brain actually feels energized, awake, and open, as if the medicine activated all my brain neurons that have been asleep for years. I just lie on the hardwood floor with a great appreciation for this new experience. The shaman gave us some pillows from the couch last night but I am far from comfortable.

I can't fall asleep. It seems like a waste of time when I have so much important information to download from this experience so I walk outside and sit on the doorstep of the house. I watch the sunrise with a new excitement and understanding of my journey. Something has shifted in my energy field and I feel like I have elevated to a higher consciousness. I am exhausted and ready to go home for a hot shower and my soft bed but the shaman's wife tells me about *kambo*, a frog-venom treatment that apparently makes you purge your already empty stomach. It's said to be one of the best ways to empower your immune system and one of the strongest antibiotics and anesthetics in the world. Its pain-killing peptides are believed to be four thousand times stronger than morphine. Some say kambo can even be used as a vaccine. Not surprisingly, used traditionally by natives in Peru as part of a spiritual ceremony, kambo has not been scientifically tested or evaluated by the U.S. medical establishment or the FDA. Doing it after the ayahuasca ceremony is optional, but the shaman's wife thinks it could really benefit me. *Okay, I am sold! Can you imagine if this is the cure?* I feel courageous and I can't wait for everyone else to wake up so I can try it.

When everyone finally awakes, we sit in a circle and discuss the different experiences that each of us had during the ceremony. It's fascinating how this group of people who felt like such strangers yesterday now feel like one big family that shares a common bond with Mother Earth. Some start breaking their fast, yet as hungry as I felt yesterday, eating right now isn't appealing. I choose to do the kambo and am the first in the line of three people. I'm a little bit scared, but nonetheless drawn to it. The shaman burns five dots in the skin on the inner side of my left ankle with a wood stick. Then he applies the frog venom paste to the open holes. I instantly feel hot like fire, as if every blood vessel in my body is opening up. Instead of throwing up in the bucket, the reaction is all in my gut and I lock myself in the bathroom with severe diarrhea until it dissipates. This is definitely an intense experience but I am always enchanted by the thought of a cure.

Both exhausted and fulfilled, Paige and I head back to Los Angeles, talking and downloading the entire way. At home, after a long shower and good meal, I sleep like a baby for the rest of the day, feeling quite different and inspired. It has been an awakening experience beyond the limited perception of my mind, and I feel confident and more concrete about the higher purpose of my journey.

June 8, 2016
Choosing to make the rest of my life the best of my life.
#Sunrise #Salute #Intentions

After some great and monumental shifts in my journey, my days are back to the drill, long and in monotone. I am in treatment five days a week and praying for another healing strike. I keep thinking about the joy I felt in Tahiti just three months earlier. It's something I'm longing for again, so I invite Paige to join me on a second trip to paradise in early June, and of course she says yes. I just signed a book deal with St. Martin's Press, which is thrilling, but I don't really know how to start that process. *How does one start writing a book?* My brain is still not functioning and I am hoping that the island isolation will be a good place for me to focus and find my voice to start telling my story. Filming for my fifth season on the *Housewives* is starting soon and I feel very hesitant.

Back in October, when the previous season wrapped, I told Alex Baskin that I wasn't sure I could do another one.

"Let everything that happened this season go. Focus on your recovery, and we'll talk about it again in the spring," Alex said. "Don't make up your mind 'til then."

I love Alex and Douglas Ross. They have been loyal and honorable in our four-year relationship, and I value their opinions, so I waited to make any decisions. But it's June now and the thought of starting a new season weighs heavily on me. Of course, I want to fulfill my obligation to my contract and I can use the paycheck. On the other hand, I've clearly learned that money can't buy the health and happiness I deserve. After all the spiritual work I've done this year, the show really doesn't resonate with me anymore. It's not in line with what I stand for as a person and what I'm trying to accomplish in my health journey. I've learned to exist on a different vibration and thinking about the very unpleasant experience of last season, I know it's time to move on. Yet I don't quite know how to do that.

The weather in Tahiti this time is much cooler than it was back in March, but I don't care. Rain or shine, I'm in the water three times a day with my snorkel and flippers, slowly moving through the warm salt water, which my body loves. I also go for walks on the white sand to soak up the ions, barely ever seeing another soul. It's the perfect place to just let my thoughts run freely. Paige and I play lots of cards, read books, and have endless discussions on how we're going to find a cure for Lyme and how we are going to continue to educate the world. One afternoon, while we're playing blackjack, my phone beeps and I see a text from my producer, Chris Cullen, asking about Gigi's and Bella's schedules at the upcoming Paris Fashion

Week. They want to film it for the show. I immediately feel anxious and overwhelmed, so I don't respond. *Why this strong reaction? Why am I feeling this way?*

The next day, Chris calls again.

"Bravo wants to know how much you're going to be able to participate this season," he says.

"Ummm . . ." I am not really sure what to say. "Let me get back to you." I hang up the phone, grab my flippers and goggles, and jump into the ocean. As the beautiful turquoise water washes over my body, I look up to the heavens and pray for something to show me the way. I start to swim with slow, gentle strokes that open up my breathing, and a thousand thoughts rush through my mind. *Why would I go back on the show? I'm still not well enough. I don't have my brain. Money shouldn't be my motivation.* I also struggle with the way the show exposes my children's lives, because what started out as fun and games doesn't feel so safe anymore. Gigi's and Bella's careers have taken off with the speed of lightning and they've lost a lot of their freedom as a result. Our home should be a private, safe place to anchor and recharge their batteries. I continue to swim for a while as this internal debate runs through my head. Then out of nowhere comes a crystal-clear thought: *I'm done! I know what I need to do for me, my health, and my children.*

"Thank you," I say as I smile and look up to the sky. I swim as fast as I can back to Paige at our Tahitian hut in the water.

"I'm done," I yell out to her, as I climb up the stairs to our hut.

"What do you mean?" she asks, walking out to the deck. "Done with what?"

"The show. I'm done."

"I'm not sure that's a good idea," she says. "What about the book deal?" It's all good. The angels spoke while I was swimming, and my mind is made up. *There's no turning back now.*

"I can't worry about that," I say. "I'm writing this book because it feels like the right thing to do in my heart."

"I know you well enough to know that when you say it's over, it's *over*," Paige says. "So congratulations!" I dry off, find my phone, and call Alex.

"But the audience loves a comeback," Alex says, as one last-ditch effort to change my mind. "It will be great for them to see you get healthy, get back in the gym, write your book, and just round out your story. Finish it. Create your own final chapter." Yes, of course that all *sounds* great and would be a more glamorous ending to my *Housewives* TV career. But I feel confident that people who are truly interested in knowing how this part of my story ends will somehow get to see it. Quitting the show doesn't feel like a choice anymore. During the previous season, I demanded so much of myself, and, even though I had approval from my boss to work only when I could, I still felt as if I wasn't living up to my part. At this point, I feel like there is someone better than me for the job, someone vibrant, healthy, and living her big fancy reality, a reality that certainly is no longer mine. I made a well-deserved six figures on the show each year and am scared to give up that piece of financial independence, but for the first time in my life, I need to make a decision based on what is right for me. The old me would have made this decision based on financial gain. But this isn't a money-based decision any longer. At this point, I am so spiritually open and in tune that I trust that the universe will provide opportunities for the future.

More important, I've made great progress and am starting to feel healthier than I have in years. I can *see* the finish line. My only goal is a cure and continuing to encourage, educate, and connect people touched by illness, pain, and disability. Being laser-beam focused on my health is crucial at this point, and the stress of the show is not going to help me get healthy. In the past, giving it up would have made me feel like a quitter; now, it makes me feel strong. That door needs to close in order for the next one to open.

A lot of housewives from the various franchises play the I'm-not-coming-back-to-the-show game with the producers because they want more money or to be told how important they are. But I'm pretty sure that everyone at Bravo and Evolution knows me well enough to know that this isn't the case. I'm grateful that they are supportive of my decision, since I truly value our time together and the relationships I have built with many of them. Although some people in the world need to turn it into a negative and report that I was fired, that isn't the truth.

The first person I FaceTime is Ellie. She is happy to hear about my decision to move on. I also call my kids who are proud to see me do the right thing for myself. It has been a very powerful week here in Tahiti. I feel like I have accomplished a lot.

When I'm in solitude I can hear so much more. I figured out how I am going to write my book. I see it clearly now and my first step will be getting dates from my chronological iPhoto journal that I kept these past four years. This will create the perfect roadmap for my book.

June 15, 2016

I would have loved a more graceful exit than Season 6, but sometimes we don't get to control the ending of the chapters in our lives. I am leaving what's over without denying its past importance in my life. I believe that every exit is a new entry, and with that in mind I say good-bye to my @BravoTv family as I continue to focus on my recovery and my children, and bringing back the privacy within our home. Thank you to all the fans for your love and unwavering support these past four years. I am grateful for the housewife experience and all it has taught me. I am excited about this CHOICE and look forward to the next chapter in my life.
#RHOBH #TimeToSayGoodbye with
#Gratitude@evolutionusa
@Bravoandy @Bravotv #WWHL

Chapter Seventeen

....

CREATE A LIFE THAT FEELS GOOD ON THE INSIDE, NOT ONE THAT JUST LOOKS GOOD ON THE OUTSIDE.

My current protocol, administered at Dr. Holtorf's office, consists of doing the ten-pass ozone along with glutathione and cell peptides, which are said to strengthen different parts of the body, including the thymus, brain, liver, adrenals, uterus, and ovaries. This cocktail combined with IVIG seems to give me a nice, temporary boost in energy and calms my nervous system.

The next thing on my to-do list is a tonsillectomy. From my earliest appointments with Dr. Klinghardt, his testing revealed that there are chronic low-grade infections in my tonsils. One of these is PANDAS, which stands for pediatric autoimmune neuropsychiatric disorders associated with streptococcal infections. These kinds of infections are hard to detect, especially when you don't have symptoms, but they can spread to other parts of the body, particularly the brain, and cause inflammation as well as focal infections. This is common for Lyme patients and others with chronic illness. For me, an infection in any part of my body above the neck could contribute to my brain dysfunction and be a block to complete healing. The fascinating thing about Dr. Klinghardt is that he's not just brilliant and full of wisdom; there's also something about his testing that is genius on a whole other level. He finds things *first* and then has them fact-checked by conventional testing. He told me I had PANDAS before the Cunningham Panel confirmed it.

Since other treatments, procedures, and protocols were more of a priority, I have canceled and rescheduled the tonsillectomy three times over the past year. Every six weeks, Dr. Klinghardt injects my tonsils with procaine and ozone, and a smelly pus comes out and drains into the back of my throat and gut. So even though my tonsils never hurt or bother me, the injections are just a temporary Band-Aid rather than a permanent solution, which is why taking them out is the right thing to do. I nurtured both Bella and Anwar through the same surgery in the past year and saw that it cleared up a lot of their symptoms, like chronic throat issues, minor colds, enlarged lymph nodes in the neck, and brain fog. For myself, on the other hand, I have reservations about having a tonsillectomy at the age of fifty-two. Yet I can't put it off any longer. June 10th is booked. *No more escaping this time.*

My body and soul are rested, and the surgery goes well, but I'm not going to lie, it's a tough one. The pain kicks my ass! On the first day, I don't eat at all. The next day, Anwar makes me his amazingly delicious iced watermelon, aloe vera, and raw honey smoothie. It relieves the pain and tastes like heaven, so that's all I eat for the next week. While still healing from this, I need to have a dead tooth extracted *and* an implant placed. After all the work I had done back in March, this tooth suddenly broke, and sensitivity testing reveals that it's dead. A dead tooth can be a smoldering infection that can leach throughout the whole body. *I just can't catch a break!* Still, I truly believe that all these little obstacles that keep popping up are part of the big major cleanup that I've been doing for the past five years.

Although the tooth extraction and tonsillectomy help a lot, this double whammy so close together really knocks my socks off. I am literally in bed for three weeks and don't leave the house. A few years ago, I would've had a panic attack that I was missing three weeks of my life. Back then, I had no understanding of healing. Now I know that the body will tell you what it needs. I focus a lot on detoxing, salt baths, ionic foot baths, colonics, coffee enemas, and glutathione drips with my mobile nurse, Patrick. I start to use an injectable CBD oil in my stomach and directly into my ear to relieve the pain and inflammation in my jaw, throat, and the right side of my brain. Daisy treats me with a lot of homeopathics, and we start our own system of muscle testing my daily protocols. It seems that at this point, my body needs change, sometimes on a daily basis. I used to do this once every two weeks; now, I intuitively feel there are different needs for different things.

Daisy and I were probably scientists in our past lives, working in the same lab together—we never get tired of discussing medicine. We've talked about LDI (low-dose immunotherapy) with Dr. Klinghardt extensively over the past year because Anwar showed great improvement from this treatment. However, something occurs to me: *Why should I continue to inject myself with other people's bugs? Why not use my OWN bugs? If we're trying to desensitize my immune system, then let's be specific.* This seems like a much more precise way to attack this chapter of my journey than being injected with the typical Lyme mix, which contains more than seventy strains of various pathogens.

We ask Dr. Klinghardt how to make LDI, and he sends us an e-mail with the step-by-step directions. I am excited by the possibility of this and decide to set up a lab in my treatment room at home. Daisy is in charge of ordering all the medical supplies while I'm obsessed with the idea of creating my own cure. It's all I think about for the next couple of weeks as I carefully collect parts of me that carry the bugs I'm looking for. For example, I asked Dr. Sigari to save my tonsils after surgery because I know the PANDAS bacteria is in them. I also save my dead tooth and collect my stool, urine, blood, and saliva to make nosodes, which are homeopathic preparations created from bodily tissues. I wake up one morning realizing that I left a stone unturned by forgetting the uterus, which for every woman has a story of its own.

Daisy and I proudly look at the sterile cups with my concoctions as we patiently wait for my goods to incubate at room temperature for three to four days at a time. This project probably sounds totally disgusting to most people, but to me it is the most exciting thing I've done this year. It feels right with every cell in my body. Of course, I have no proof that this is going to work, but theoretically it should, and I am crazy inspired by the possibilities. Can you imagine if every person with Lyme could theoretically cure themselves? Daisy is my spirit twin when it comes to healing and discoveries. She is irreplaceable on my journey by now. Her tenacity, like mine, is relentless, only she has the perfect brain to execute our thoughts. It takes us about two weeks to make all the nosode preparations. Succussing each dilution *fifty times* is probably the hardest part. Daisy's hand actually develops a repetitive stress injury from this vigorous tapping. We end up with different strengths of dilutions, which we call C1 to C12, for each of the following: tonsils, tooth, stool, vag, blood, urine, and saliva, a total of eighty-four sterile vials.

I perfectly color label them and place them in organized little boxes. We curiously experiment with our own muscle testing and discover that my personal homeopathic nosodes should work beautifully as ammunition in taking back my own personal defense force. Obviously, I completely lost my belief in pharmaceuticals to cure my Lyme and co-infections, but this latest plan of attack came to me clearly. I proudly display the boxes on the shelves in my treatment room so I can look at them until it's time to carefully pack them up and bring them to Dr. Klinghardt to hopefully get his stamp of approval. What I love most about this man is that he encourages patients to learn to treat themselves. He is a team player and open to any theory and modality without ever pushing his own. Over the years, I have grown to feel like his student rather than his patient. I admire the fact that he is so willing to share all of his knowledge without attachment. He has a clear understanding that it takes a village to get patients like me back on track, and I'm so grateful to him and the rest of my medical team for getting me where I am today. My five-year journey has almost earned me a Ph.D. in Lyme—and psychology, for that matter—but nevertheless I need Dr. Klinghardt's blessing on my new nosodes. I think he always knew I was ambitious, but when Daisy pulls out our LDI boxes that we carefully carried by hand from Los Angeles, he is clearly impressed. The most impressive of all is the fact that every single one of the nosodes tests strong for me and is clearly going to be a very important piece to my healing pie, according to Dr. Klinghardt. He injects them right under the skin in both my arms and puts some under my tongue. Within twelve hours, I have pretty strong reactions that last for a good week, but they're not much different from the usual rounds of LDI that I've done in the past. This time, I feel confident and precise as I am fighting my own bugs.

I leave Seattle inspired. Energetically, all the dots start to connect. My physical body is still healing, but my body and I are finely in tune at all times. I've learned to listen carefully without any judgment and surrender to however long it is going to take.

Over the years, I found happiness within the four walls of my home. Although I live in a cocoon, I have clarity and strive for greatness every day. My bed is my office, where I am holding the anchor for my children while recuperating from my ambitious protocols. I spend more time in my bedroom than in any other place in our new home. Anwar is finishing his school year and continues to focus on designing his first collection. I start to get excited by the thought of him going to a fashion school in New York. *How amazing would it be for the four of us to live in the same city?* Our apartment has been a great landing pad and a central place where his friends can come and go. It's a full house when all three children are home, but that's the way I love it.

By now I've been single for six months. I still have no interest in dating or going out to socialize with anyone but my Lyme squad. I'm focused on becoming whole before I can share myself with someone else. My journey inside the healing cocoon isn't over yet, but I finally start to imagine my life outside its limitations, somewhere more motivating for my spirit, especially once Anwar goes off to college in the fall of 2017. There are exciting times to come if I can only get my ass out of bed already. It's time. I pray for a miracle every day, promising the universe that I get the message.

June 24, 2016
Healing a chronic disease doesn't become reality through
a magic pill; it takes sweat, determination, and persistent hard work.
@holtorfmed #LymeDiseaseAwareness.
#InvisibleDisability #WeMustFindACure #AffordableForAll

In early July, I start to spend a lot of time on this book with my cowriter, Michele Bender. We have established a nice little system of meeting and working together every morning while she is in town. My brain is better, but clear trains of thought are few and far between. At times it feels as if I'm trying to give birth to my story through a two-inch hole. Michele and I have pieced together a perfect timeline of my journey through my dated iPhone photos, calendars, lab results, Daisy's notes, and the notebooks David and I kept through the years, so the road map is there. It's been a useful training exercise for my brain. Being forced to get into the details of my story has been a difficult but healing experience.

My TVAM surgery is scheduled for July 12. During this procedure, a catheter is threaded up through the groin into the jugular vein and both sides of the carotid artery in order to stretch them. This is supposed to activate nerve fibers that are part of the autonomic nervous system and to increase blood flow to the brain. Testing shows this is still not adequate in my case. It also revitalizes the compromised nervous system and supposedly alleviates things like brain fog and other cognitive issues. I decide to postpone it for the second time. Out of desperation, I've had a do-or-die attitude throughout most of this journey, but the farther along I get in the process, the more careful and hesitant I have become about procedures that always come with a risk. TVAM is one of these, and I'm afraid of it.

It's interesting how much I value my life today compared with when I first got sick. I used to have balls of steel with no fear, but I have become highly aware of how fragile life is.

Instead, I focus on a ten-day master cleanse, which consists of organic lemons, cayenne pepper, and grade-B maple syrup but no solid food. Paige invites me to Aspen to be in nature so that I can focus on my book. Every morning and night I use the Bemer, a device Tom found that I hope will help open up my vascular system and keep my blood flow going as a way to prevent the TVAM surgery. Of the many health gadgets I've bought during these past five years, this is one I use religiously. It's hard to understand why my body still can't exercise, yet I know the importance of keeping the blood flow and lymph system going. Somehow swimming seems to be the only thing that does not set me back in my recovery, but I keep trying and looking forward to the day that I can run a 5K for Lyme disease.

July 16, 2016
Anyone can fake being sick, but it takes great talent to fake being well and smile when you feel like shit.

Regardless of this little detour, at the beginning of August I find the courage for the last surgery on my to-do list and schedule it for August 23, but not without hesitation. TVAM seems like such an invasive and unnatural procedure to me, but every time I see Dr. Klinghardt I test for it, and he kindly reminds me that it's still on the list. Even though he has never done me wrong, I have a hard time trusting this last piece of the puzzle. A couple of days before the surgery, I have a checkup with Dr. Klinghardt in Seattle.

"Why do I feel so resistant to this surgery when I've been so eager to work my way through the list?" I ask him.

"Let's muscle-test and ask the question," he says. I have not been able to differentiate between my intuition and my fear on this particular matter, so it's interesting to see that fear is the emotion blocking me from doing what most patients refer to as the "liberation surgery." So once again I pull up the bootstraps and tap into my die-hard desire for optimum health. I ask both Paige and Daisy to accompany me to the surgery in Newport Beach with Dr. Arata.

August 23, 2016
I am seeking, I am striving, and I am in it to win it with all of my heart.
#LymeDiseaseAwareness #TvamSurgery #LastChapter
#SearchingForACure #RemissionInSight

The procedure is actually a lot less eventful than I made it out to be in my head, but the aftermath and recovery bring a hard-core relapse of symptoms that puts me back in bed. The fatigue and joint pain is severe. Dr. Klinghardt warned me that sometimes the TVAM makes you worse for a couple of weeks or months, because all the bugs that live in the vascular system are forced to evacuate. This sounds right because I feel like a truck ran over me. It's a really scary feeling once a relapse hits; you never know how long it will take to get yourself out of the hole again.

For the next six weeks, I really focus on my detox protocol of colonics, juicing, a strict gluten- and sugar-free diet, salt baths, and ionic footbaths with cilantro drops. The doctors have also instructed me to be on a blood thinner, so I inject myself twice a day with 1 cc of heparin for about six weeks. I'm supposed to feel liberated, but unfortunately my brain fog and eyesight are worse. I feel closed in, that scary feeling of being locked up in my own brain, a plateau that even my positive spirit can't push through at this moment.

Chapter Eighteen

....

AND SO IT IS.

Even though it's been a long five-year journey, talking to my bestie Ellie by FaceTime always puts things in perspective. There's a lot to juggle to keep her life going in France, where she is living with her husband, David, and daughter, Gracie, who is about to start her final year of college at the American School in Paris. Six months earlier, Ellie's marriage started to crumble, not because of a lack of love or commitment but because of the financial burden of caring for her in this late stage of ALS. In March, I started to promote a GoFundMe account and raised $77,404. It is heartwarming to see how kind and helpful friends, fans, and even strangers came together to make donations for Ellie's care. Even though this bought her some joy and happiness for a couple of months, the reality is that her ALS is an unsustainable bottomless money pit for everyone involved. Emotionally and financially, this precious family of three is bankrupt, so we talk Ellie into coming home to Santa Barbara.

Doing so would be impossible if it wasn't for our friend Jeff Palmer, who brings her home on his private plane. We rent her a small cottage, a place familiar to us right off Butterfly Beach. It's next door to our favorite little church, All Saints-by-the-Sea, which is connected to the preschool Anwar used to go to. Ten years earlier, Ellie, Anwar, and I had a special routine of going to Starbucks every morning after dropping Gigi, Bella, and Gracie off at school. I could never have imagined that this is where we would end up. *It's crazy how much has happened to our happy and healthy lives. Was it the water we drank? The clove cigarettes? The horseflies? The ticks? Who knows?* All I know is that Ellie rarely cries, so when she FaceTimes me at one 1 A.M. with tears in her eyes, I know she is calling for a reason.

"I need to see you now," she says.

"I'm on my way," I tell her. Without asking questions, I throw on some sweats and make my way up the 101 North.

When I arrive, it's clear that a lot of shit has hit the fan. She pretty much tells me she is done and that these are going to be her final days. She wants everything to go on as usual. Gracie has to go back to school in Paris on the 26th, so that day the two of us sit on Ellie's bed and write her last five wishes and final will. Their banter and crazy sense of humor is heartwarming and heartbreaking at the same time. The bond between this mother and daughter is exhausted from life circumstances, but unbreakable. We cry, we laugh, and we tell stories until about 9 P.M. that night. When it's time for me to take Gracie to the airport for her flight back to Paris, it takes all I have to keep it together as I witness their final good-bye. Every time Gracie walks toward the door, Ellie begs for one more hug, as only she and I know that this will be their last one forever. *How do you say good-bye to the person you love most in your life?*

Our drive on the 101 to LAX is somber. Gracie's trying to be brave and fight the tears that roll down her cheeks. We feel defeated by a disease that only has one sentence: death. We praise Ellie for her courageous fight and discuss the past five years and all the craziness that has occurred with Ellie's family members and friends and all that has come into play in such a tragic situation. Ellie's goal was to make it to Gracie's graduation in May 2017, but we agree that it's inhumane to ask her to fight one more day.

"For five years, I've been afraid to go to sleep at night, worrying that she won't be there when I wake up. I'm tired," Gracie says. I'm not sure how to respond. I can feel the sadness and pain inside her that no words can possibly ease.

"I'll be at your graduation," I promise her. And, of course, I will.

I drop her off and drive back to Santa Barbara very early the next morning, where Ellie wants to know everything Gracie and I spoke about in the car. I assure her that Gracie was okay when she left.

"Don't worry. I'll be at her graduation and decorate her first apartment with all your stuff when she moves back to the U.S. in June," I say, holding back my tears. "I promise." Ellie's husband, David, is arriving from Paris today. I will never forget the smile on her face when she sees him walking in. It gives me goose bumps and I do everything I can not to burst into tears and have a meltdown. All the turbulence that their marriage has endured during this nightmare is forgotten in this moment, and all that is left is the pure love they've shared for so many years. David is my hero. His commitment to Ellie is that of a good, old-fashioned man, a love story that I always knew existed but haven't had the pleasure of experiencing myself yet.

Even in these final days, Ellie is still trying to boss me around, making sure we put her in the right outfit for her passing and telling me she wants to wear the latest Chanel nail polish that someone had gifted her. Most people wouldn't think about these things at this point in the game, but Ellie does because that's what makes her Ellie. Always into the finest details of everything, she is going to leave this planet in style and with grace. Sticking to my word, I polish her nails one final time, leaving out the middle finger on her right hand because it's connected to the oxygen meter. As I polish them, she opens her eyes and gazes at me with so much love. At this point, we're communicating in a higher consciousness, and I know what she is thinking without speaking.

"I promise that I won't send you off with nine painted fingers, missie," I joke with her. She responds with a tiny smile. I feel so much empathy and admiration for her beautiful little hands that have been paralyzed for so many years. They look frail and hardly recognizable from the memory

I have of her strong hands on the steering wheel of her navy blue Range Rover.

My girls are working in Europe, but Gigi contacts me by FaceTime from Paris and Bella from London. I've been talking to them, and they know the end is near. Our friend Holly takes charge of hospice, and nurses come in and out of the cottage. The moment we prepared for, for so many years, is finally here. Breathing and speaking become harder and harder for Ellie, and her voice is getting weaker as the days pass. She is slipping in and out of sleep. Sometimes, she opens her eyes when people come in and out to say their good-byes, but I can feel her spirit starting to distance from us. Amy, the priest from next door, comes in periodically, and we pray in a circle around Ellie. In the past week, we have formed a tight group of three, and our distinct, unspoken tasks run in perfect harmony. In normal circumstances, you wonder how you would let go of someone you love so much. But right now, deep in my heart, I know this is the right thing. Ellie deserves to go in peace and get out of the body that has drastically failed her. I feel a lot of clarity. I'm not afraid and find great strength in the commitment of our friendship. I always promised her I would be by her side when she takes her last breath. I don't want her to be afraid, so I keep whispering in her ear about the beautiful vision of passing we often discussed.

"Just let go. The doors to heaven are right there in front of you. You can see the light," I whisper with confidence. "I love you, my sweet angel. Please rest assured that Gracie is well and will be taken care of. Just let go."

Her breathing is starting to slow down, and finally in the late afternoon of Tuesday, August 30, Dr. Baker checks her pulse and confirms that she has passed on. It's a defining moment, but I feel much gratitude for being able to have guided and supported her through these final hours of her life. I did what I said I would and held her hand until she took her last breath and arrived at heaven's door. Even though her death means that she is finally free from suffering and her passing is peaceful, it's hard to understand in this moment, let alone imagine my life without her. This is a great loss to both me and my children, who loved her very much. They always visited her when they were working in Paris and have been part of her journey since the day she was diagnosed with ALS. But I am in survival mode. Holly calls the funeral home, then asks the family if they want to wash the body before she gets picked up. They decline.

"I guess we're the ones to do it," I say to David and Holly. It's a scary thought, but it's the right thing to do. We carefully pull out her breathing and feeding tubes and take Ellie out of her sweaty pajamas. It's not until I see her naked body that I truly understand the truth about this ravaging disease that took her life so brutally. It's a shocking vision that I will never forget. We wash and dress her in her favorite pajamas, and I paint her tenth finger and brush her beautiful golden locks. Holly, David, and I just stand there and stare at her. It's a strange relief to finally see her lie flat on a bed without being propped up with special pillows and attached to any machinery, something we haven't seen in five years. What a journey. My bestie is a true hero, and if I ever have the blessing of a healthy life myself, I would love to write a script about her life because it's a story that must be told. Watching ALS so closely destroy my best friend is the worst thing I have ever experienced.

August 30, 2016
RIP and fly with the angels, my love @ellieod. Thank you for sixteen
great years and showing me the meaning of true and loyal friendship until
your last breath. You are my hero and will live in my heart forever.
#Alswarrior #MyBestFriend

It's not until I get in the car late that night and drive down the 101 South back to L.A. that the loneliness and deep sadness hit me. *Whom am I going to talk to?* I spoke to Ellie more often than any other friend on this planet. All our history is gone except for the beautiful memories we shared.

I get home at 2 A.M., exhausted, but I can't fall asleep until I get the photo album of our trip to Canada in 2011. I slowly scroll through the pages with tears rolling down my cheeks. Selfishly, I'm sad because I'm going to miss her so much, but I know that she is in a better place and probably already decorating and organizing parties in heaven. I think about one of the last things we giggled about.

"Yogi, thank you for holding my hand and never letting go. I'll be waiting for you in heaven," she said.

"Well, you better prepare a beautiful white runway when I get there," I said.

"I will, with butterflies and white lilies," she replied.

We made a pact that when I see a special butterfly or dolphin, I will know it's her presence around me. Ellie is cremated, and we plan to wait six weeks to do a memorial at our friend Ursula's house in Santa Barbara because Gracie just started school in Paris. I am heartbroken and I feel empty inside, but I pick up the pieces and try to get on with life just the way Ellie would want me to. Anwar and Gigi are both working in Berlin. At least they're together, and I'm happy that my mom, Leo, Liseth, and the kids are traveling there from Holland to see Gigi's Tommy Hilfiger collection and Anwar's Hugo Boss show. I'm glad they have family support during this difficult time, when you just want to stay home on the couch but life forces you to go on.

Months earlier, I promised to accompany Bella on September 5 to London, where she will receive *GQ*'s Hugo Boss Model of the Year award. It's her first commitment after her summer break, which she spent mostly in treatment with daily IVs that actually made her feel worse. Bella is battling severe bouts of anxiety, insomnia, pain, night sweats, migraines, and debilitating exhaustion. It's heartbreaking to see my child battle and suffer from symptoms I know so well. We make our way to the airport but it's one of those mommy moments where you lead by example and do what you say you're going to do. I can't let my baby go to London by herself or cancel this extraordinary acknowledgment. I'm trying to pull up the bootstraps while mourning the death of my best friend.

We arrive at our London hotel late that night. I try to nurture and pamper Bella as much as I can with all the tools in my box. Unfortunately, very little of what I learned these past five years can truly ease her pain. I lie beside her and watch her finally fall asleep after I scratch her back and massage a mixture of my essential oils on the excruciating pain along her spine. I often talk to God. *Why is there no cure for this horrific disease? How much longer is this going to take? I promise I will dedicate my life to service—just please cure my children and all the children in the world who are suffering just like them. Please, please, please!*

It's hard for anyone to understand what it takes for Bella to get out of bed and get ready to step on the red carpet tonight. Once here, all I can do is gently touch her back and energetically give her strength since I can feel the anxiety she's battling. It's anxiety not about the fifty photographers who are calling out her name but about the angry Lyme bugs that we hit hard this past month in treatment. It's a long and stressful night, but she makes it to the stage. Bella's acceptance speech is short and sweet and thanks the most important people in her life. My heart breaks and tears roll down my cheeks as I watch her receive the *GQ* award, mainly because my little warrior maneuvers through a very stressful day of commitments while battling a disease and pain that nobody knows anything about.

The next day, I see the stunning photos of her in the press, and it's another one of those aha moments. How could anyone possibly understand the depth of this disease by looking at pictures like this? Or the pain that strikes her tiny frame almost every day of her life? Regardless, *we* understand the cycles and have learned to accept and live with it the best that we can for now. I remind Bella twice a day to stay on her daily protocol of pills and tinctures as she travels around the world and tries to keep all the balls in the air. She's very brave, and I admire how resilient she is. Although I enjoy my time on the road so I can nurture her, seeing my kids' struggles with the invisible disabilities of this chronic disease is heart-wrenching, and every morning I wake up thinking about what my next move will be. It's been such a humbling experience to learn that people don't understand what they can't see. "How can you feel bad when you look so good?" is a comment that Lyme patients or anyone battling an invisible disease probably hears every day.

Bella is flying to Paris to shoot her Dior campaign. I'm sad to leave her behind feeling the way that she does, but I promised Gigi that I would sit front row to see her TommyXGigi collection at Fashion Week in New York. I've missed so many special moments, and I can't tell you how much I enjoy finally being able to attend them. I'm tired, but I carefully plan and use my spoons. *Woo hoo! I am still alive!* And it's worth it because the Tommy show is amazing. I watch all the beautiful models walk down the runway at Pier 16 in Lower Manhattan, which has been totally transformed into a carnival for this show. Although I've dreamed of this moment for the past four years, I never imagined it to be this big. #ProudMommy doesn't do justice to the pride I feel. Only three years earlier, I dropped off Gigi in the Big Apple and she has accomplished so much in her life while I was home in bed. A year ago, I never could have done everything that I did this week. Even though I don't have the energy to go out much, I am able to see Bella walk for Donna Karan and both my girls for Marc Jacobs, which is more than enough. I feel blessed and grateful for the opportunity to experience these moments with all three of my kids. I can only take life one day at a time, and every day that I'm able to be out is a victory in my book.

This is my new normal, and I'm happy and satisfied with just that for most of the time. Even though I know all the rules and regulations of running this ship, it's still hard to control my ever-testing spirit, which pushes the limits that my body can't keep up with yet. When I feel just a little bit better, I want to make up for all the time I've lost, but unfortunately that's not very productive in the big picture. I move Bella and my goddaughter Olivia into their new apartment this week as well. Thankfully, it is only one floor up in the same building. With a couple of great helping hands, I'm able to pull it off, but nevertheless I push myself to my limit. I swear I will never do that again, because when I get back home to L.A., I pay the price for being reckless with my spoons and spend the next ten days in bed. Being out in the world is always a good measurement of where I am in my journey.

September 14, 2016
Mommy's job is never done.
#NYC #Moving #smallspacesolutions

I really need to focus on writing this book with Michele. My good days come inconsistently, so progress is slow. Writing is hard to do with Lyme brain, especially for someone like me. I take this whole experience very seriously, and I want my book to be the perfect soup with all the authentic ingredients, but there are so many layers to this story.

It's Paris Fashion Week, and Gigi, Bella, and Anwar are all walking for different designers. I would love to be there to watch them, but I physically can't. I need to stay on my protocol and do my treatments. I can see the light at the end of the tunnel but I can't quite touch it. There are days when I have four or five good hours when I think, "Okay, I got this," but then I crash and burn for a week at a time. *Will I ever be the same again? Can I keep elevating my new normal? Is this what remission feels like?*

Anwar has matured beyond his years and has taken a very strong position in our family. He is in Paris working and watching over his sisters right now. Homeschooling has been a great choice for his last year of high school, and it's given him more freedom to grow in other areas of his life. I'm starting to dream about moving to New York, too. My girls need me there, and I no longer have any connection to L.A. or the life I once lived here. I'm still very isolated and only see a very small group of people in my life who have stood by me through my journey. I have no desire to go out and socialize in a community that I see so clearly for what it is. I am totally satisfied in my perfectly spun cocoon, where I feel safe and am busy working on a future and all the amazing things that are important to me and my family. Being the anchor takes all my time and energy, but it's perfect for now and there is nothing I would rather do. Friends ask if I'm ready to meet their single friends, but I keep saying no because I want to wait until I move to New York. I don't want to fall in love in L.A. This is not *where* and *how* I want to grow old. Energetically, it doesn't resonate with me. Life somehow brought me back to L.A. for good reasons, but I know that journey has ended, and I'm looking forward to making my way out east in 2017. I'm so ready to experience four seasons and to live among all kinds of inspiring and creative folks in a melting pot of different cultures and the dynamic energy of normal people who seem to have normal jobs and live normal lives.

From New York, I can fly to Holland more easily and visit my family more often, which is important to me. I miss my mom and she is getting older. She has been struggling since she was diagnosed with uterine cancer two summers ago. She can't get out of bed for weeks at a time, yet every workup with her local doctor says that everything looks normal. This infuriates me. So a few weeks ago I e-mailed Dr. De Meirleir and asked him to please see my mom ASAP. After all that I have been through, I know that doctors are human. They *do* make mistakes, and, as a result, people can go undiagnosed with all kinds of diseases for years. I think my mom is one of these people.

Six weeks ago, my brother drove her to Belgium for a complete workup with Dr. De Meirleir similar to what I did four years ago. They call me with the shocking news: at the age of seventy-six, my mother is diagnosed with *Borrellia, Bartonella,* and *Chlamydia pneumoniae,* which mirrors some of my own diagnoses. Surprisingly, Dr. De Meirleir thinks she's had Lyme for more than thirty years. This news is devastating. A thousand questions go through my mind. *How am I going to fix her? What if she's had it for fifty years and gave it to me by birth? What if I gave it to MY children? Is that possible? And what are the chances that me, my best friend, sister-in-law, daughter, son, goddaughter, and now my mother have Lyme? How am I going to help her get well when I'm so far away? I already promised God that I would stay on this path. Is he trying to make sure that I don't just get on with my life, forget about this, and pretend this didn't happen? I go to sleep that night feeling shaken to the core but wake up in the morning with a lot of clarity. I must take what I've learned and apply it. I need to act, not react with my emotions. I call my mom.*

"Before we start Dr. De Meirleir's tremendous antibiotic protocol, let's first try a holistic approach," I say.

I need everybody around me to get healthy and live the healthy lives we deserve. The better I start to feel, the more I want to help others. My heart is full of compassion and empathy for those suffering and it feels good to bring clarity to them and help them find healing. I think the biggest problem we face today is that there are a lot of underlying causes that lead to disease, which has motivated me to shine light on uncovering this mystery. The amount of e-mail I get from fans from all over the world is astonishing. I read as much of them as I can because it motivates me, but it's impossible to answer every one. Still, I try to respond to those whom I feel a connection to, which are hopefully the ones who need it the most. This week I get the following e-mail from a woman named Julia:

From: Julia
Date: September 12, 2016 at 3:54:38 PM EDT
To: Yolanda Hadid
Subject: Looking for some guidance/help please xo

Good afternoon Yolanda,

I've been a huge fan and following you for some time now. I'm reaching out in hopes of getting some direction or help in any way possible for my 40 year old husband and father to our two young boys ages 4½ and almost 2 years old. We have had a year from hell to say the least. We are a normal, fun, go-getting couple and family who live on Long Island, New York.

Around the time our youngest son turned one years old (October 22, 2015), my husband, Solomon, became unable to really lift either of the kids especially our little one. Since January, he has been getting weaker and weaker in his arms to the point that now he has atrophied in both and can barely hold a cup. We have gone through numerous neurologists and doctors throughout NYC, all who have taken him on a roller coaster ride of treatments and unknown directions. He was first told by one that he had an autoimmune condition called Myasthenia Gravis, removed his thymus gland, put him through Plasmapheresis then IVIG treatments, all of which made him quickly deteriorate for these past few months. Then the doctor went on to say it was Multifocal Motor Neuropathy (MMN), a motor neuron disease. We just got back about two weeks ago from the Mayo Clinic in Minnesota, paid out of pocket $10K as our NY insurance doesn't even have great doctors in the plan who are even Board Certified believe it or not . . . even in NYC! The doctor there told my husband that he thinks it could be ALS. Talk about traumatic and tragic considering we have two little boys who aren't even in school yet. Our whole life has flipped around . . . not sure who to speak to, who to go to, who to believe or what to do at this point. My heart is in a million pieces and I am so scared each day I wake up as my boys need their daddy.

The reason for my email is because we are also talking to many people who said to look further into Lyme disease. We live in a highly populated tick-infested area and are always in the Hamptons, near beaches, playing by dunes etc. My husband was bitten by a tick six years ago in Texas, but never got treatment as he didn't see any signs or know better to look further into it. His spinal tap and blood work came back negative for Lyme, but we did however send his blood last week to the Igenix Lab in California for further evaluation.

We are seeing a few Lyme literate doctors who are recommended from ILADS [International Lyme and Associated Diseases Society] as well and hoping to get some answers. I really would prefer to have a treatment plan in place rather than just having ALS as a diagnosis and no cure or treatment behind it. Also, his arsenic levels came back 3x higher than normal in the recent tests 2 weeks ago that NO ONE ever tested him for prior.

If there is ANYTHING you can do to guide, help, mentor or provide me with, I would be forever grateful. I'm not asking for much, but for someone to help me so that I am not left alone in the dark with my two little boys and as caretaker for my husband. I've attached some photos—we are a normal family with big hearts and dreams. Not giving up this fight and really fighting to get awareness—guiding people to the right help one day! It's been a horrible few months and not sure who else to talk to.

Please feel free to email me, call me or anything at any time.

Thank you for your time and help. Sending you lots of love and healing as well.

As I read this e-mail, I feel goose bumps all over my back, and when I scroll down to a picture of Julia, Solomon, and their two little boys I feel like I've been struck by lightning. Energetically, something shakes me up and I immediately start bawling, not just for Solomon but also because I really miss my Ellie. *What if she's the one who is making this happen from heaven? Did she send them? Am I being tested?* I know a lot about ALS and I've also learned extensively about the correlation between Lyme and ALS. Sending a forty-year-old ALS patient home with one year to live is hard to accept. These boys need their father. *Make something happen, Yo!*

I immediately write Julia back and invite her to bring Solomon to Seattle the following week. Even though Dr. Klinghardt does not take new patients, I have a double appointment scheduled and feel confident that when I see him in person and explain what happened, I can convince him to get on board and try to save this young man whom I've never even met but feel strongly about. I am not sure what this all means, but I'm excited and think we might be on time to make a difference for him. My brain is going a thousand miles a minute.

"Please call Julia and get all of Solomon's medical history so you can present it to Dr. Klinghardt," I ask Daisy. "Let's also research mobile nurses in Long Island so we can figure out how we're going to implement Klinghardt's protocol when he gets back home."

At the same time, I get an interesting e-mail from a friend of a friend of a friend telling me that she is thirty days into a clinical trial for a Lyme-N supplement and having great results. She wants to introduce me to the people running the trial. So I get on the phone with Glen, the product's creator.

"Finally," he says. "I've been looking for you for three years but haven't been able to get to you. I'm happy that we're finally connecting."

"Nice to meet you. I'm excited to hear about your great results," I say. "Can you tell me what this supplement is and the philosophy behind it?"

"Well, Lyme is a man-made disease used in warfare between the Americans and Japanese, which is why no antibiotic in the world can cure late-stage Lyme," he says. I heard this theory five years ago, and my innocent spirit thought anyone who believed this was badass crazy but at this point his words make sense. *It's hard for me to imagine thinking that way about any other human beings. But I just don't know anymore whom to trust and what to believe. After all these years, maybe there is something to this theory.* I start laughing out loud.

"I'm glad the universe waited three years to put us together, because a few years ago I would've told you that you were crazy," I say. Glen and I continue our conversation and Daisy organizes all the paperwork to get the product and protocol to us. I'm not trying anything new without Dr. Klinghardt's approval. My next appointment is September 29 so we will test the product at that time.

"I survived TVAM. I'm alive," I yell out loud six days later when I walk into Dr. Klinghardt's office. He and I hug and I'm excited to see him. Over the past two years, we've grown very close. I'm convinced that this man saved my life. We sit down as we usually do, and Daisy recaps the past six weeks, presenting any testing that's been done and the progress we've made.

"I think the pellets are doing the job for you," Dr. Klinghardt says, referring to the hormone pellets from Dr. Allen that I have implanted into my butt cheek four times a year. Dr. Klinghardt had suggested this when tests showed that I had high FSH and low estrogen, because optimal hormones are the key to this final stage of my recovery.

"At first, it was hard to balance the estrogen and testosterone, but I think we finally found the perfect ratio," I say. "Although my hormones may look good, my engine is still stuck, and I don't have that get-up-and-go energy."

"So let's test and investigate," he says. "The TVAM really opened the blood flow to your brain, but we still need to detox and treat it. Let's do melatonin with Liposorb. If you can get through the sleepiness, it can really detox your brain."

"Okay."

"The bugs are improving," he says, as he continues to test. "But your back and upper spine still have them, so we need to continue doing segmental injections, and increase your Rerum to every other day."

Then I show Dr. Klinghardt the Lyme supplement that Glen sent. "I don't know what this is, but I feel like the universe is bringing this to me for a reason."

"How are you supposed to use it?" he asks.

"You nebulize with twenty drops of the supplement every morning for sixty days," I explain. Dr. Klinghardt tests it, and my body tests very strongly for the supplement.

"Interestingly, it also tests as a component that isn't part of our protocol yet," he says. But I'm not surprised because finally all the dots are starting to connect and things seem to be falling into place.

"Go ahead and let's revisit six weeks from now," he says.

My appointment is over, so we bring Solomon in. Only five minutes into the appointment, Dr. Klinghardt looks at Solomon's almost completely paralyzed arms and confirms that he has ALS. This brings dead silence to the room. However, something inside me feels that this answer isn't enough. As Dr. Klinghardt gets deeper and deeper into the layers of his testing with Solomon, he finds two things that played the biggest role in the onset of his ALS. The first is Lyme and the second is a lot of dental infections, cavitations, and two metal implants that Solomon got eight months earlier. Dealing with his dental work is the first plan of attack, but this is very costly. None of the treatments he needs are covered by his health insurance, something I already know because of my experience with Ellie. This is going to be a very expensive journey for this young family so I am not afraid to ask for discounts from the team that I sent a lot of business.

A biological dentist needs to remove all Solomon's mercury fillings, infected root canals, and implants and clean out his cavitations. Since we don't have experience with East Coast dentists, the fastest and safest way to handle this right now is to bring Solomon to L.A. immediately to see our dentist. Four days later, Solomon and Julia arrive at my apartment and stay with me and Anwar. The next morning at seven, Solomon has an eight-hour dental surgery. Daisy orders Dr. Klinghardt's Lyme and detox protocol so Solomon can start it at home. We rally around him and give him a crash course in starting his health journey. I absolutely love this couple and am determined to, hopefully, help him reverse, or at least slow down, the course of the monstrous disease. I'm looking forward to seeing Solomon at Dr. Klinghardt's at the end of November and find out how much improvement he has made. Until then, we FaceTime and I try to be a source of support. There are moments when he gets discouraged just like Ellie did but I'm hopeful that he was brought into my life for a reason. He is a fighting spirit and determined to live for his boys.

My life is still very quiet and isolated, but I am starting to feel a shift as I have grown and cultivated my cocoon of light. I've really learned to understand who it is that I am and what my purpose is on Planet Earth. I have gathered the ability to see beyond my own journey to a higher plane and from a larger perspective. Five years of deep quietness and contemplation has brought me to the depth of my soul and the true essence of who I am. It has profoundly impacted my consciousness, since I've been forced to let go of time and thoughts and feel only love. I'm receptive and ready to bring hope and guidance on a larger scale to those affected by chronic disease while continuing my search. I'm not sure yet how this is going to shape and form my future, but it will come to me more clearly as time goes by.

It has been two months since my TVAM surgery, and finally I begin to feel and see a difference. I think it has brought down my overall inflammation, and even France, my colonic lady, thinks it has really opened up the flow to my liver and pancreas. A lot of debris and disease that has been stuck in my thirty-foot-long colon is finally starting to move out. My brain function is slowly getting better, too, and though it's not consistent or reliable yet, I'm so grateful for the progress I've made, and the fact that I am writing again is the greatest gift ever. Slow and steady is the name of the game for sure. One day at a time.

One of the most kind, inspiring, and solid women in my life is Rebecca Rothstein, who has protected my interest and helped me navigate my finances for the past seven years. She is one of my guardian angels for sure. October 13 is the Global Lyme Alliance event at Cipriani 42nd Street, where Bella will receive an award for bringing awareness to Lyme disease. Besides the Lyme squad, I also invite Mohamed. I feel it's important for him to witness the true reality of his daughter's life.

The morning of the gala is rough. Bella's in severe pain, and I can't get her to wake up. It's not until three o'clock, when hair and makeup people show up, that I'm finally able to get her out of bed. Even after twelve hours of sleep, she is still exhausted. Teenagers often interpret this severe exhaustion as feeling down, and it's hard for them to understand that this is only from being overtired. Finally, Bella and I get it together and make our way to the event. When the ceremony starts, I make a short speech to introduce Bella, and I'm incredibly proud to do it.

Good evening everyone. Thank you for being here and for sharing this very important night. Most diseases you might want to battle out in the privacy of your home, but Lyme disease is so undervalued and misunderstood by the world that it is an obligation to each and every one of us to share our stories until we get the acknowledgment and respect that we deserve from the medical establishment.

With that said, though, it takes a compassionate heart to be willing to do so. It's hard for people to understand the invisible disability that ruins our life, especially behind my daughter's beautiful face that shines so bright on the covers of magazines. Every mother here today understands the hopelessness that comes with nurturing a child who battles a disease without a cure. I am so grateful and proud of my daughter Bella for speaking openly about her journey in order to bring awareness for the hundreds of thousands of teenagers and young adults who suffer just like she does but whose voices can't be heard. Thank you, Bella, for being the extraordinary person that you are and for bringing HOPE to others. I admire your courage to stand up for what's right and for joining us in the fight for a Lyme-free world. And, my love, just remember you are not the only one.

After my speech, the group Thirdstory performs "I'm Not the Only One." At the end of the song, they ask Bella to come up onstage to get her award. All I hear is a lot of noise in the room as I see my baby girl make her way to the stage. I step back. Her acceptance speech is beautiful:

I am so honored to receive this award and I am so happy that I could bring recognition to something that has profoundly changed our lives. I would really like to dedicate this award to all the teenagers in the world who are suffering from this disease without an end in sight. Like a lot of people today, my teenage years were taken from me. I was forced to start homeschooling in my second year of high school because my treatments severely interrupted my days, and eventually I had to give up my horseback riding career that I dreamt of having since I was a young child.

I know what it feels like not to be able to get out of bed from bone pains and exhaustion, days on end. Not wanting to socialize or be around people because the anxiety and brain fog is just too much. Taking naps at lunch on work days just to get through. After years of this, you begin to get used to living with a sickness instead of getting cured and moving on with life. Life isn't always what it looks like from the outside, and the hardest part of this journey is to be judged by the way you look instead of the way you feel.

We need a proper diagnostic and a cure that is affordable for all so that we can all go out in the world and build the life that we deserve to live. Thank you to my friends and family for being here tonight and every day for the past five years. Your support means the world to me. I am so grateful that I have my amazing mom to force me to take my medication, get IVs, go to our never-ending doctors' appointments, and for always understanding me when I say "I'm just not okay today." There is nobody I could have learned my strength from more than from her and our experiences together. Her compassion, patience, practice, and determination to find a cure are beyond words, and I am so lucky to have her. But I am really worried for those who are misunderstood and judged by their loved ones and left without guidance by their doctors and medical establishments. So for them and all of us here, you are not alone and thank you! Let's raise some money!!!

I'm so proud that Bella finally feels comfortable enough to share her journey with the world. Most teenagers are embarrassed and tend to isolate, but since 25 percent of Lyme patients are children, it's important for her to use her platform to bring awareness without being afraid of any judgment that might come with it. In the end, this sold-out event raises $2.7 million for proper diagnostics and, hopefully, a cure. I'm so grateful that we can be a part of this movement because, at the end of the day, maga-zine covers, success, and money don't matter if we can't get to the bottom of this and find a cure for Lyme.

October 13, 2016
Uniting for a Lyme-free world. I am so proud of my baby girl for
sharing her journey and the invisible disability of Lyme disease
in order to raise awareness. #LymeDisease #WeMustFindACure
#AffordableForAll @globallymealliance

The night after the event, we crawl into bed, snuggle up, and look at pictures from the evening. Bella looks perfectly healthy, and there is no sign of the pain she was in just hours before the event or even during it. Again, photos and social media can't possibly reveal what really is. You don't have to look sick to be sick.

Later, Paige tells me that Mohamed teared up during my speech about Bella's suffering. He also posts a video of Bella's speech on Instagram and writes the following:

> *About last night. @bellahadid was on point. And she was so beau-tiful, poised, and she killed it. Perfection. #globallymealliance I was so proud of her. And support her.*

This is all I can ask for: enlightenment and hopefully a deeper understand-ing of the truth. This is important for Bella. Daddy needs to be there and see that there are so many other people in the world who struggle with the same disease.

I now see Daisy only three mornings a week. We often brainstorm about opening a Lyme clinic one day while we continue our search for a cure. David and I finally have dinner together after nearly a year of not seeing each other. We've both been invited to Paul and Mareva's wedding in Tahiti so I want to connect before that. We meet at the Hotel Bel-Air restaurant and actually have a nice dinner with easy chitchat, just like old friends. It's pretty amazing that when you truly forgive someone for all the pain he or she has caused you in the past, it opens up a space for gratitude for all the good times you once shared.

Chapter Nineteen

....

PEOPLE OFTEN FORGET THAT
KINDNESS IS FREE.

October 16 is Ellie's memorial. Paige and I drive down to Santa Barbara. It feels like a somber day. The skies are dark and overcast.

"I don't think today is right," I say to Paige when we pull up to Miramar Beach. This is where we will have the memorial and spread Ellie's ashes with Gracie, Ellie's husband, David, Holly, and about twenty of Ellie's closest friends. "It's so gloomy."

"No. Today is perfect," Paige responds.

"It doesn't feel like it." Minutes later, a small sliver of sunlight peeks through the clouds.

"See, it *wasn't* right, but it's starting to be," Paige says, smiling at me. It takes about forty-five minutes for everyone to arrive. Although the sky is starting to clear, I'm still not feeling it. *I'm not sure why I feel so off, but this isn't how I imagined this moment. It's not the way Ellie envisioned this day that we spoke about in detail before she died.*

"Trust the process," Paige says.

"Let's just keep walking," David says. *To where? Why is everybody so annoying today?* Even though Ellie and I walked this beach a hundred times, we both know that she didn't like the water, so I'm not exactly sure where we're going to spread her ashes. *Does this even make sense?* Suddenly, we see a big construction site in the distance.

"Hey guys, what is that?" I ask my friends.

"That's the new Rosewood Miramar Beach Resort," someone says. *Now everything makes sense! THIS is where Ellie needs to be. She loved construction and loved watching things being built.* David starts to spread her ashes right in front of it, and, although it's the perfect spot, I still feel strangely uneasy. Not sure what to do with my nervous energy, I grab some seaweed that has washed up on the shore and start creating a big cross in the center of her ashes. I also draw hearts in the sand to create some happy visual. My back is to the sea when all of a sudden, I feel the energy in our group shift from heavy and sad to "Whoa!"

As I turn around, I see two beautiful, shiny, and powerful dolphins jump out of the water with two small babies right behind them. It's one of those magic moments that makes you cry with joy. What seemed like a sad day turned into the perfect moment. We all start crying and laughing. *It's all okay. She's here just like she promised she would be. It's right and it's time to let it go. Like Ellie always said: AND SO IT IS . . .*

October 16, 2016
So long, my sweet angel @ellieod. Your courageous ALS journey
kept things in perspective for all of us. I know your beautiful spirit was
there with us today as the dolphins appeared right behind us at the
shoreline. I will forever miss you.
#RIP #Elliememorial #Miramarbeach #SantaBarbara

Afterword

....

One day Paige calls to tell me about this woman, Kelly Kolodney, in Pennsylvania, who connects with the Angel Raphael, traditionally known as the Angel of Healing.

"This could be the final piece to your puzzle so I booked you a phone session," Paige says. I've never heard of this angel before, but it resonates with me. On the day of my appointment, I call Kelly who doesn't know my name or anything about my life's journey and she does a reading. I hang up the phone feeling excited about this magical experience. This message confirms everything I already know, yet I find it inspiring to hear it from a complete stranger who put it into such eloquent words. Everything that this angel said rang true and validated my own strong intuition that I'm here for a much larger purpose than just myself. I've always been a spiritual person, but this part of me has grown in so many ways as I navigated my health journey. The awareness that there is something bigger than myself has given me the strength and support to help me get to the last level of healing. I am not alone. I have my angel guides. It reminds me every day that my life can be filled with magic, love, and laughter as long as I follow my heart.

As difficult as these past five years have been, I am so grateful that this journey has led me to living in the light. In another dimension where I'm completely free from the life I *thought* I was supposed to live, a life conditioned by other people's minds and today's society. I have had it all and lost it all only to realize that less is more, money can't buy you health or happiness, and one day at a time is good enough.

My new normal is much more in tune with who I am, and I try to live life more intelligently by consuming organic foods, herbs, and water provided by Mother Earth. I am eager to continue to build on what feels like remission. Although I feel better than I have in many years, the DNA Lyme test still shows positive, so I'm not sure if complete eradication is even a possibility. However, my immune system is functioning better and better as time goes on. I feel healed within the parameters of my current life. I've learned to love the authentic me and all of my perfect imperfections. I'm grateful for every moment I get to spend on this beautiful planet with my three children, building a community that holds the same vibration as I do.

Although I am not an author, I enjoyed writing this book because it is time for us to stand up for the truth without being afraid to be judged. I speak on behalf of those who have no voice.

Lyme disease is a global epidemic that steals people's lives and slowly kills. It is unjust and unfair. *BELIEVE ME!* We must find a cure affordable for all and unite for a Lyme-free world. I hope and pray that when you heal yourself, whether it is on the physical, emotional, or spiritual level, you will then support healing your neighbor, your mother, your sister, your brother, your cousin, your friend, and someone else's child across the globe.

Acknowledgments

•••••••••••••••••••••••

It's impossible for me to thank all the amazing people who have crossed my path and positively impacted my life because that would be a book on its own! So to all of you who stood by me and never left my side during this most challenging time, thank you from the bottom of my heart. I treasure our friendship and will honor you always and forever for the rest of my life.

Special thanks to Michele Bender, Marc Johnson, Jan Miller at Dupree Miller, and everyone at St. Martin's Press.